Classics of the Foreign Film

PREVIOUS BOOKS BY PARKER TYLER

On the Film

> The Hollywood Hallucination, 1944
> Magic and Myth of the Movies, 1947
> Chaplin, 1948
> The Three Faces of the Film, 1960

Verse

> The Metaphor in the Jungle, 1940
> Yesterday's Children, 1944, with Pavel Tchelitchew
> The Granite Butterfly, 1945

Other Prose

> The Young and Evil, 1933 and 1960, with Charles
>   Henri Ford
> Conrad Marca-Relli, 1960

Classics of the foreign film

a pictorial treasury
by Parker Tyler

Spring Books · London

Originally published 1962 by The Citadel Press,
222 Park Avenue South, New York 3, N.Y.

This edition published 1966 by Spring Books,
Drury House, Russell Street, London, W.C.2.

Printed in Czechoslovakia by Svoboda, Prague
T 1582

Acknowledgments

For help in compiling the pictorial contents of this volume, the author wishes to make grateful acknowledgments to the Gideon Bachmann Collection, the Museum of Modern Art Stills Dept. (New York), the National Film Archive (London), the Cinématheque Française (Paris), Edward Harrison, Blowitz and Maskel, Bill Doll and Co., Contemporary Films, Astor Pictures, Janus Films, Donald Velde, the Memory Shop, Brandon Films, Lopert Pictures, Kingsley International Pictures, Zenith International Film Corp., King Displays, Metro-Goldwyn-Mayer International, and Movie Ad and Poster Co. For special courtesies, the author also wishes to thank Mr. Herman G. Weinberg, Mr. Jonas Mekas, Mr. Daniel Talbot, Mr. Martin Lewis, the Italian Embassy Cultural Institute, the French Film Office, Contemporary Films and Cinema 16. The publishers of the British edition of this book would also like to extend their thanks to Mr. John Gillett and his colleagues at the British Film Institute for much valuable information and advice.

Contents

Publisher's Note

As a rule, the date given to a film denotes the year in which it was made, though in certain cases it may apply to its release in the country of origin; in turn, the country of origin is determined, usually, by the locale of the actual making. Exceptions to both rules occur in the case of *Que Viva Mexico!*, which, although filmed in Mexico, was — in its original unedited form — entirely the product of the Russian team of Eisenstein, Alexandrov and Tisse, and was made during 1931 and 1932 — being divided later on by American editors into three films. A compromise on dates also has to be struck where trilogies are involved and here the estimated total duration of the making of all three films has been given.

Actors of nationality other than that of the country of origin sometimes appear in the films listed here; an outstanding case is that of *The Eternal Mask*, made with German actors in the German language, but filmed in Switzerland.

Alternative titles to films are sometimes given, primarily with a view to conventional identification. The original foreign title is given precedence when the film was generally released under that title and not a translated one. It has not been considered necessary to provide the original foreign title where it was not in general use abroad; this applies in particular to certain Scandinavian and Japanese films.

Mr. Tyler makes a number of references to American film awards and the availability or non-availability of prints of certain films in the United States. No attempt has been made to tabulate similar awards given by British organisations, although obviously many of these films have received comparable honours here. With regard to the distribution of some of the older films, it is interesting to note that the National Film Archive in London holds 35 mm prints both of *Napoléon* and *The Dybbuk*.

A Gallery of Directors

SOME MEN WHO HAVE CREATED FOREIGN FILM CLASSICS

Introduction

Sergei M. Eisenstein's genius made a Russian the world's most intellectual film director. Caught here in typical off-screen informality, he graces the Emperor's throne in the Kremlin: this photograph, peculiarly suggestive in relation to his own life and career, was taken while he filmed *October* in 1927.

Here made up as Saint-Just (known as the 'Archangel of the Revolution') in *Napoléon*, Abel Gance directed that first important epic of French patriotism on film in 1925, anticipating both the grandeur screen and modern depth-effects: one of Paris' new film houses was lately named after him in a ceremony at which he appeared.

My optimum hope for the happy reception of this treasury of films made in non-English speaking countries, presented here through picture, story and comment, is that, besides calling up fond recollections for many spectators, it will succeed in defining the bulk of the contribution by foreign nations to the art of the film from 1919 till now. An ambitious function, it might be thought, for a "picture book"! Have other picture books aimed at so high and wide a goal? Hardly . . . Yet this one does. My idea is that solid recall is fully as significant as first acquaintance, and in the nature of things probably more significant. To provoke such recall, memoranda are necessary — as many kinds and as much as the case may warrant. On this basis, the structure of each item here, each individual film, was devised. Illustration, caption and main text supplement one another, reinforce and

embellish scenes from the film with illustrative words. All this should furnish not one key, but numerous keys, to the values of each film.

Values? A leading question, even an outright problem, in almost any age. The only values that matter may be those that survive; those, that is, that can be called *classic*; hence the pivotal word in my title. It is doubtful if the concept of history could exist at all without the related concept of the classic. True, history is made every day, every hour actually. But the people of this world are a busy, perpetually preoccupied race. The individual dare not neglect his personal, family and community interests. To follow history in the large sense — the advances of science and the evolution of international affairs — one has to rely on newspapers and other such media. Yet the most thoroughgoing newspaper reader has a hundred

Monocled, picturesquely posed and professionally self-conscious, Fritz Lang looks very genuine as the director of those history-making German films: *Metropolis* (1927) and *M* (1931).

A little-known and striking view of Luis Buñuel, impassioned avant-garde film-maker, is obtained by this clip from *Chien Andalou* (1929), one of the two films he made with Salvador Dali: Buñuel's work today carries clear marks of the savage Surrealist sport of which he was fond more than thirty years ago.

paths and more to traverse; he can hardly be sure he is keeping up with that vast, rather abstract, quantity which is "history", a thing which almost never gets near his frontyard, much less his parlour. Of course, television and the newsreel, among optical media, bring a semblance of history into any odd corner; these are at least distracting: *amusing*. But history is not always amusing or just shocking. In substance, it is grave: as sad-making as it is glad-making.

In other words, history, like the daily events that help constitute it, does not necessarily or always or easily reach the depths of the individual, his soul and his heart — the feelings that matter, that cause his blood to move and his brain to register the ultimate truth of things. Like the other arts, the film (the cinema or the movies, as you like) penetrates the skin of the moment, governs the currents of time, transcends the difficulties of spatial extent like a magic carpet, and delivers us to the enduring unity of life: to all the ages of mankind and the individual man,

to humanity in its permanent condition, to things that stay and can still look true when recalled to mind. Unlike yesterday or the day before, a film classic is preserved as an entity. For several reasons it may get to look, if two or three decades (or only a year) old, somewhat different than when we first saw it. Even so, it revives the past (our past and its past) and asks for our opinion once again: our heart's attitude toward this segment of life, this gesture shaping some phase of individual and social destiny not lost to time.

Values, history — and *myth*: these are the interwoven threads of conscious life. Myth is an inalienable function of every art; myth is not what makes art difficult to understand but what makes it easy to understand. The popular misconception that a "myth" is something that was never true — or, once true, true no longer — is unworthy of the well-equipped film-goer. A myth, in *that* sense, is only a colloquial figure-of-speech. In the responsible sense, it is a permanent pattern in stories of

Victor Sjöström, a ghost from Swedish and American studios in the 20's and 30's, can remember (as Victor Seastrom) directing Lillian Gish in two of his and her finest films: above he is seen as the reminiscing hero of Ingmar Bergman's *Wild Strawberries* (1959).

Ingmar Bergman rose head and shoulders above most of his directorial colleagues as soon as the international position of the art film reached an impressive artistic level in the decade 1950-60: he's still at that height.

all kinds, making it possible for the same person to understand and relate Shakespeare's plays, Aesop's Fables, the Bible, Sergei Eisenstein's film epics and Cocteau's modernized-myth films. Basic conditions and basic relationships govern human experience within the bounds of recorded history. On these, our memories are based; by these our plans for a sensible and coherent future are made possible. Take the film, *La Femme du Boulanger*, made in 1938 as contemporary; it is as stark and simple as a story from the Bible. Many classics remind us, moreover, of Adam and Eve, the sworn domestic partners, and of Adam's temptress, Lilith. Antonioni, in his recent films, tells virtually of nothing else, and it is very clear, moreover, that his lovers in their fidelities and infidelities re-live the fate of the first human sexual partners; demonstrate whether the married pair can cleave to one another for a lifetime, and if so, with a good conscience . . . and if children can be the issue.

From the depths of a medieval forest in Japan will

come, as revived in a film of this century, news of the eternal quarrel of two men over a woman: supreme, relentlessly lethal. Or satires from France (such as Renoir's *La Règle du Jeu* and Vadim's *Les Liaisons Dangereuses*) preserve in sparkling, articulate ways the conspiracies of free-lance sexuality against the strict union of a pair of romantic lovers (whether the latter be legally or illegally joined). Every story of love has its more or less organized social will: the conventional and accepted opposing the unconventional and underground. These are old, old stories — and that is just the point! They are, but they return every day, they revive themselves and circulate before our eyes. Works of art which treat and judge them, define and celebrate them, satirically or otherwise, are the "classics" — the things of enduring values, balanced and undiminishing truths.

Not that my choice of classics derives from a private prejudice for this or that type of story-pattern, or myth; on the contrary. Glance at the contents list. Note the

One of film history's most brilliant directors, Jean Renoir, as he appears in his *La Règle du Jeu* (1939), judged by the most recent international poll of critics as one of the world's ten best films: a poll taken among 150 critics at the international film festival in Brussels, 1958, rated his *La Grande Illusion* (1937) among the world's twelve best films; both works are given extensive treatments in this book.

Russian film, *Potemkin* (1925), a work which earned phenomenal fame the world over; it tells the triumph of those oppressed by harsh masters, the bloodshed and peril attending all violent social uprisings. So does the Polish film, *Ashes and Diamonds*, made more than 30 years later. The point is not what specific political controversy each involves. Neither the flag of a nation, nor its colours, is any more decisive in *Potemkin* than in *La Grande Illusion*, which presents a view of mortal struggle on the plane of highly organized, old-fashioned, declared war between two inwardly united nations in World War I. *La Grande Illusion* is a fable of the destiny of the Chivalric Ideal, by which war was once fought according to severe forms and a code of honour. Maybe that code, those forms, were never entirely real. Yet for

many centuries men imagined they were real and behaved as if they were; they died graciously, with serenity and a sense of honour, because they believed they were.

Should the net I spread here (for the films seeming to survive time's criticism) have been limited, some just complaint might be made that I seek to evoke a world no longer viable, a world related no longer to what is contemporary, to "what is happening now". But my net has been cast under no such restrictive auspices. Things that outlast military conflict, smiles, light-heartedness and gay ironies over man's worst errors and faults, even his "sins", are far from being absent here. Inspect *The Seven Deadly Sins*, *Le Plaisir* or *Infidelity*. Does anyone suggest, because of their presence, that a certain irresponsibility is proved of the editor — that our modern

14

Jean Cocteau, astute and poetic creator of *Le Sang d'un Poète*, *La Belle et la Bête* and *Orphée*, was as familiar with the light of publicity as with that of a reading lamp: here, like an alert fox, he only *seems* to relax after doing the final scenes for his film, *Les Parents Terribles* (1948).

world is too full of urgent dangers, of absurd illusions inherited from past ages, to put confidence in the "comedy" of human frailties, human bunglings and futilities? — the comedy, for example, of René Clair's satire on the lasting peacetime struggle between the havenots and the haves, between the Tramp and the Millionaire, who Clair takes as symbols of the quarrels between capital and labour?

Conceivably it is a mistake to assume surviving value in Clair's *A Nous la Liberté* (1931). Yet if so, we must also write off the list of classics all Charlie Chaplin's films from *City Lights* through *Monsieur Verdoux*. We must call his Tramp a frivolous and foolish figure from the beginning, having deserved burial rather than perpetuation. But I doubt that, with a good heart and a good conscience, we could do this. Here I have let neither human type nor class nor nation nor political ideal go at face value or no value at all. In entries devoted to *Shoe Shine* and *Bicycle Thieves* and to the German-made *Metropolis* (preceding those Italian films by two decades) are shown the reverberations of civil and international war as the whole social scale is affected: private life and public, organized labour and organized capital; not only their *frictions*, in fact, but also their *harmonies*. I should be the last to scant, furthermore, the film's characterizations of that special social type, the artist, so vulnerable that he easily becomes clown or tragedian.

That all such human elements and their fates are still "in question", that palpably they have not ceased to engage the mind and the emotions, means that any power-

15

A nation was newly heard from in the fifties when the cream of Japan's film talent drew world attention: Akira Kurosawa, probably the best of Japanese directors, here rehearses a scene from his magnificent adaptation of Shakespeare's *Macbeth*, entitled *Throne of Blood;* he is also responsible for *Ikiru* and the superb *Rashomon*.

ful exploitation of them is potentially, or provenly, a "classic". As a film historian, thus, I have tried to make facts concerning the identity of film-makers, the times and circumstances of film-making as ample and as accurate as was feasible and possible. *A vivid evocation* of a film, not *detailed statistics* about it, however, has been my basic aim. This volume is no encyclopaedia of film facts; rather, it is a guidebook to the history of filmic vision: a picture book to be not merely an entertainment of the eye but an informant and refresher of the eye as well. It is (I trust) a treasury in the broadest sense: the culturally informed sense. Let it not go unrecorded that I have duly deferred to expert opinion in making the final draught of this roster of classics. I examined the results of recent inter-national polls and the prizewinners of the annual inter-national competitions. I pondered on these as I attended the newest films and sought films of the past in the pro-grammes of museum archives and revival theatres. Accord-ingly, numerous films represented here are multiple prizewinners; many of the leading actors, and virtually all the directors, have been heaped with honours new and old. A few *lacunae* may be discerned, and resented, by admirers of particular films and particular directors. Yet I have not consciously excluded anything or anyone unique and essential to the high level of film-making seen from the historic viewpoint. The front offered by these foregathered classics is, I daresay, global — and, I should hope, glorious.

Alain Resnais, among France's top emergent directors, appears above while tackling a scene from his best film to date, *Hiroshima, Mon Amour* (1959): this work is one of the vivid new dramas that reflect the important shift in both method and moral attitude among modern film-makers.

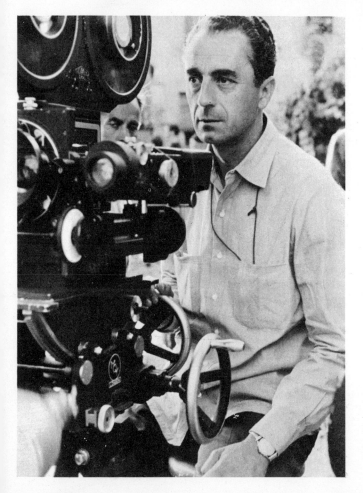

Italy's recent assumption of world leadership in film began with Vittorio de Sica's work just after World War II and was confirmed when Federico Fellini and Michelangelo Antonioni made their most important films in the decade 1950-60: Antonioni, the man behind the camera at left, represents the modern "intellectual cinema".

17

Classics of the Foreign Film

1919 · GERMANY

The Cabinet of Dr. Caligari

One of the world's most famous films (lately remade in a much modernized version) is about a beautiful, blank-faced lady who has been driven insane by an attempted rape and the murder of her lover. The villain back of it all, Dr. Caligari, here exhibits the picture of his Somnambulist who will be shown in person to those paying admission.

Like a steel spring responding to violent compression, *The Cabinet of Dr. Caligari* sprang onto the post-war scene of film-making. The style of Expressionism in painting and the theatre had served notice that society knew how to express its emotions and utilized the right

to do so. People had suffered from the universal calamity of war, and some artists among us visualized its social blight as a product of the morbid imagination secreted in the lust for power, the drive toward the destruction of man by man. The film's affecting figure of the Somnambulist, played by the famous Conrad Veidt, is victimized by a medieval-minded magician, Dr. Caligari, who uses him to commit criminal acts. The contemporary interpretation of this theme, despite the one ostensibly offered by the film, is by no means obvious or monolithic, but complex.

Of course, an art such as the film, conscious of its eternal commitment to popular culture, alternately sought (and seeks) to distract audiences with pleasant romance and to exploit the mood of violence from which the world was (and is) still shaking. Erich Pommer, producer of *Dr. Caligari*, exhibited the perennial diffidence of film producers preoccupied with business. He almost missed the knock on the door when two young authors of an original film script, Carl Meyer and Hans Janowitz, came to him insisting that he listen to a reading of their manuscript then and there. Finally

Cesare, the Somnambulist (Conrad Veidt), has almost succeeded in abducting the beautiful lady (Lil Dagover): Dr. Caligari stumbles upon the fact that the police have picked up the scent of his treasured, and usually successful, instrument of crime.

yielding, he was immediately taken by the story and started its film production under the direction of Robert Wiene.

The phenomenal result, on the other hand, had to endure the postwar taboo on German films in other countries and was shown outside Germany only obscurely and in cinema clubs. Brought to America by Samuel Goldwyn in 1921, it made a decided impression on informed critics in the United States and elsewhere. It is an historian's mistake to consider that it had no direct influence on cinematic art as a whole. True, outside Germany, it exerted a negligible technical influence, but this was only because of its patent "art" look: its mental fantasy and the artificiality of its acting and backgrounds. At the same time, even Hollywood "fairy tale" fantasies may have gained some impetus from its powerful capacity of illusion. It has remained, in any case, an illustrious museum piece, reproached by the fast set of film aesthetes and simon-pure documentarists for its militant artificiality, static manner of progressing and general archaic flavour.

But *The Cabinet of Dr. Caligari*, through its innate distinction, reveals about film a principle of unlimited importance, not necessarily obvious even to its admirers. It is very easy for the instantaneous presences of photography to create, at the photographer's will, several spheres of reality visibly coexistent in time or space or both. In what technically is a "framing story", the supposedly rational narrator of the film is telling someone about a beautiful woman just consigned to a lunatic asylum because of her attempted rape by a somnambulist, who has also murdered her lover. Yet, at the end, it appears that the whole thing has been a figment of the narrator's deranged imagination. Dr. Caligari, seen throughout as the mad magician who controls the Somnambulist, turns out to be the doctor in charge of the asylum; thus, he who was shown as mad, and to be restrained, is now the restrainer of the mad.

There are (and have been) serious opponents of the poetic imagination as a thing of romantically irresponsible vagary. In *Dr. Caligari*, as it were, the imagination wears its vagary on its sleeve for us to marvel at. The crimes of rape and murder, however implausibly dressed, have the import of the sinister. The theme of *Caligari* is much older than the Gothic romance that is its recent precursor and is implicated in two other film classics here, *M* and *The Dybbuk*, though in quite different forms. The subject is romantic genre: a magic faculty of the mind that holds love and death, crime and passion, good and evil in the same embrace. *Caligari*, however limited, is a triumph of style expression: a vision pure, open and legitimate in its specific nature as poetry, regardless of "isms" or time itself.

When his quarters are invaded by two suspicious observers (one of them the film's narrator), Dr. Caligari is able to show them that Cesare is lying passively in his cabinet; Werner Krauss, as Caligari, became celebrated.

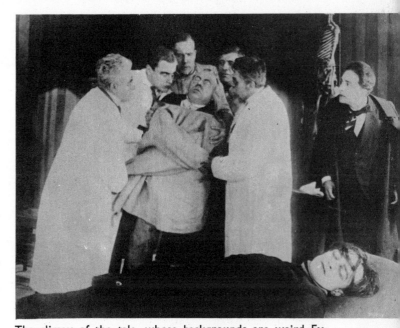

The climax of the tale, whose backgrounds are weird Expressionist sets, is Caligari's arrest as a dangerous lunatic; the narrator tells of his horror in watching the mad medievalist being put under restraint.

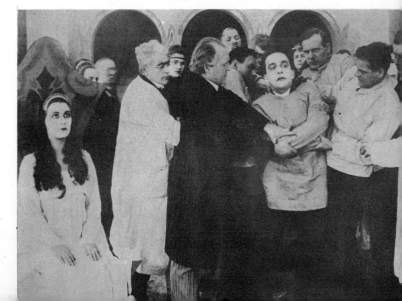

The beautiful, blank-faced lady suddenly leaves her seat in a garden to join the other lunatics; this bizarre film's anticlimax is the narrator's strait-jacketing when he accuses the asylum's director of being the Caligari of his fantasy.

The Story of
Gösta Berling

1924 · SWEDEN

The Story of Gösta Berling, made from Selma Lagerlöf's famous novel, would probably have been distinguished even without Lars Hanson and Greta Garbo; with them, it is an undeniable classic, presenting a romantic pair, each of whom quickly came into universal renown.

Mauritz Stiller's adaptation of Selma Lagerlöf's famous novel to the screen has a vivid archaeological interest in that it strikes patrons of museum showings as a very sightly relic. Its much-edited condition in our archives and its pathetic absence of sound (which, as it were, cries aloud for spoken dialogue) make it all the more persuasive; re-edited and music-scored in Sweden in 1934, it is shorter than the original, which had its own filmic ways of reconceiving the novel. What impresses most spectators, and understandably so, is the image of Greta Garbo in her first important rôle in films: a young Garbo, amazingly mature as an actress and beautiful in a way quite unlike her Hollywood image. In American films, of course, she literally learned acting and developed a new, secure authority not present here. But already, it is clear, she had phenomenal poise and was mistress of a personality hinting the most fertile possibilities. Oddly, in 1924 she was richly fleshed, with a statue-like grandeur; the angular, awkward-graceful, frigid-sultry self she became for world film audiences hides at her centre, sheltered by a glow, a straightforward femininity, that was destined to leave her forever.

As a Hollywood veteran, she fitted ideally into a modish conception of the nineteenth-century heroine of *Camille*, a woman "wasted" by passion, love becoming a cold and hollow thing, futureless. Her Marguerite Gauthier took the New York Film Critics' award for the

In this younger, more lush Garbo of her brief European acting days can be discerned her Hollywood Camille of fourteen years later. Her photogenic beauty and serious acting induced Stiller, director of this film, to bring her with him to America; the rest is history.

Hanson as Gösta Berling (left) participates in the sweet life offered him after, as a minister, he is unfrocked for alcoholism; his fortunes as a parasite in a fabulous "pension" are wild and bizarre with folklore, but he has in him the heart of a hero able to rise above his Don Juanish nature.

As Countess Elizabeth, Garbo is disillusioned with her prudish, stuffed-shirt of a husband, beside whom the reprobate Berling seems a fascinating knight in armour: pity and terror eventually purge her and Berling reveals himself as a man to be saved.

best feminine portrayal in 1938, repeating the success that her Anna Karenina (also a bereft, straitened being) had won in 1935. Mme. Lagerlöf's romance, shrouded by a "Gothic" gloom pierced with shafts of sunshine, is as whimsically, nostalgically dated as Garbo's performance in it. Its human passions are rich-blooded, opened by headlong violence, yet capable of sickening away in snowbound repression; its moods dip into deadly gloom and rise to giddy heights, glide from sinning to purity, and back again. Gösta Berling, played with genuine pathos and fine romantic swagger by Lars Hanson, is a minister whose alcoholism, a demon of bad conscience, gets him melodramatically unfrocked. In consequence, he must make a new life.

Sparked by the presence of Hanson and other actors much more experienced than Garbo, the old theatre conventions that interpret character and situation are enlivened by Stiller's sensitivity to the film as a vehicle of plastic as well as emotional drama. All the same, the work compares strangely with the new spirit as symptomatic in virtually contemporary films: the Russian *Potemkin* and the German *Metropolis*. Costume and period are disarmingly forthright presences as the former minister, of great good looks and noble heart, works his way "up" in good society but inevitably starts rattling its skeletons. As a long-unredeemed hero, he becomes, like Don Juan, a fatal bait for women, who find a touch of magic in his erotic violence and beauty. As the Countess Dohna, Garbo (then only seventeen) plays the unawakened, virtuous young wife of a cowardly, stuffy prude who cuts a very poor figure beside the tempestuous Berling, aflame under his dark star.

High-blooded passions make exotic a melodrama of worldly greed, pride of caste, lurking incest and weird

superstition. Elizabeth Dohna becomes a chivalric idol for Berling to worship and she lifts him from social disgrace and parasitism. At last, in a concluding scene much simplifying Mme. Lagerlöf's novel, Gösta and Elizabeth come together in quiet victory over all adversities. We have an excellent opportunity to study, in a film highly coloured in many ways, what the romantic conception meant to humanity before it was replaced by cold-blooded modernism and the submission to grim philosophies such as that of the absurd. We see in Gösta Berling's naïvely moral story a vanished upper class living its "national" ordeals: all too human, in a way, yet uncontaminated by the idea that human society is on the edge of utter collapse or extinction. This film knits up human history with its own history. Very few actors or actresses—among these being Anna Magnani and Katina Paxinou—have the ability to give man's "emotional history" a look of vital survival. But I hazard that Garbo, if she returned to acting, might join them.

The finely shaded plastic values of the film's photography emerge crystal-pure in this idyllic scene between the lovers: the very atmosphere is saturated with the glow of feeling quietly uniting them.

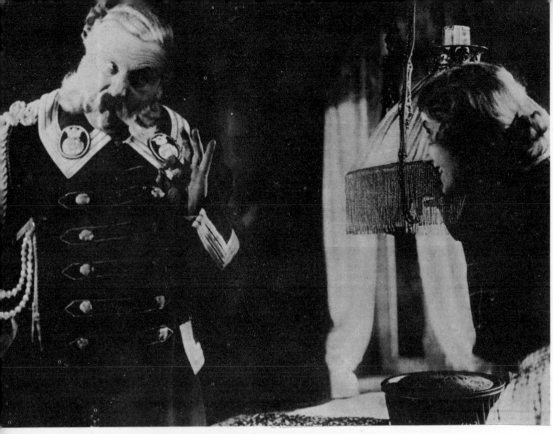

Emil Jannings' brilliant delineation of a hotel doorman who innocently preens and struts like a general: it brought him international fame.

1924 · GERMANY

The Last Laugh

Because of old age, the ornately apparelled doorman is demoted to being lavatory attendant: his "days of glory" turn into a subterranean nightmare.

Highly art-conscious in its décors, the German film during the twenties expanded the bizarre themes to which the Expressionist and Cubist schools of painting were naturally suited. *The Cabinet of Dr. Caligari*, having registered internationally, proved a source book for further exploration of its extravagant style and stark melodramatic content. One of that film's pair of authors, Carl Mayer, took up an outstanding career of film-scripting, and joined a talented director, F. W. Murnau, to create *The Last Laugh*: something much closer to life than the Caligari fantasy. Film-making was recovering from its post-war lapse and the Murnau-Mayer film found a greater audience than had Dr. Caligari, both in Germany and abroad; in the United States, it was mass-circulated. Unerasable from memory is not only one of the first experiences this country had of the fluidly omnipresent mobile camera but also Emil Jannings' powerful performance as the elderly hero, first the doorman at a very fancy hotel and then the hotel's lavatory attendant. His unexpected demotion precipitates tragedy into the deluded sphere of his life.

Like Murnau, Jannings was brought to Hollywood, where, of course, the attempt was made to duplicate the success of *The Last Laugh*; however, the American public declined to give a few overwrought, expensive tries an appreciative welcome; Garbo, possibly, remains the only foreign star whose popularity in American

24

films lasted till her voluntary retirement. Jannings, as the big, peasantish, genial, but all too humanly vulnerable, doorman makes a brilliant theatrical image. It was more vivid, perhaps, than his rôle, a year later, in *Variety*, whose pyrotechnic camera outshone even its acting. The fate of the doorman in *The Last Laugh* creates a universally sympathetic image of old age as victimized by a favourite mechanism in the German theatre: economic fate.

Because one day the hotel's manager notices its ornately uniformed doorman stagger under the load of a trunk (for he also has the duties of a porter), he considerately reappoints him to be the lavatory attendant. As a result, something nastily inhuman is brought out as a social truth, particularly a truth in Germany: the importance of the social-economic hierarchy. Once cast from his grand station near the revolving door, and in his colourless uniform belowstairs, the old man is visited with violent scorn from fellow tenants and even his own relatives. This cruel, pathetic reversal only completes the inward demoralization that has already begun its work. Formerly a "king" among his class, and accordingly admired, he is the butt of a savage spite that merely confirms his tragic sense of his status loss.

As a moral fable of modern times, *The Last Laugh* profits immensely from its simple outline and stylish clarity of presentation; the broad lines of theatrical naturalism have replaced Expressionist bizarrerie. This fact helped expedite the advanced style being introduced to the silent film by Germany and Russia. Murnau, and a few years later Fritz Lang, would influence the world's use of the film camera as itself a creator of movement and exponent of the fluent visual narrative. *The Last Laugh*'s most sparkling feat—for that era—was a scene in which the camera, variously distorting vision, shows the old doorman's drunken spree that erupts before his abject acceptance of his demotion. Apparently in concession to popular taste, the film then executes a fairy-tale turnabout for the hopeless old man's benefit. Without notice, he inherits the fortune of a gentleman whose eccentric will provides that his money shall go to that person whom he has last seen while alive: his death occurs while alone with the lavatory attendant. With this magical happening, the former doorman's life goes from bitter emptiness to the ultimate wordly fulfilment; at last he enjoys the feast of his dreams and drives away in a carriage accompanied by his one faithful friend: the old night watchman.

The film's "wild party"; this theme has fascinated many directors: Stroheim, Cecil de Mille and (in recent years) Fellini and Antonioni.

Shunned and ridiculed by neighbours and relatives, utterly crushed, the former doorman in his new domain makes a peerless image of one stunned by loss of status.

"The last laugh": the lavatory attendant (in the ending's concession to popular taste) inherits a fortune and takes pleasure in serving his only loyal friend the feast of a king.

Abel Gance had some of D. W. Griffith's sense of history as an exciting display of restlessly clotting and unclotting masses: Napoleon is seen in the midst of a crowd of celebrating well-wishers. This epic film made French history into a new, living organism.

1925 · FRANCE

Napoléon

Gance's *Napoléon* was made during 1925, although it has also been attributed to the following year. It was a miraculous precursor of later filmic achievements rather than a tangible influence on them. The huge cost of its production, for those days, the difficulty of showing it as created—it demanded a screen-width three times the normal—made it, when released, a financial failure. Abel Gance was a director in the line of Erich von

Stroheim, the type whose extravagant vision ruined their backers. His cinematic appetite was a lust. It is no surprise, then, that his pioneering cinema has kept his reputation classical. First an actor (like Vittorio de Sica) and then a script writer (like Michelangelo Antonioni), he duly became, as did both his Italian successors, a director. In 1961, a Paris cinema house was named after him, though he had done nothing of consequence until commissioned to do another epic of French history, which I have not seen and is, I believe, not yet released. He was present at the opening of the "Abel Gance", and France's Minister of Culture, André Malraux, presided over the ceremony.

Considering cinema as "spectacle", *Napoléon* easily takes priority here as a foreign classic, both for relevance of filmic means and the heroic stature of its vision. Gance has been called "learned and barbarous" by Bardèche and Brasillach in their *History of the Film* (1938). His reckless inspiration would turn brutal; he was considered, by some, capable of rank melodrama. Yet his special gift remains as native to film as an accent does to a national language. The excitement of visible movement, the dominion of its purely formal range, possessed and drove this poetic *cinéaste* as if through a physical empathy with it.

Not D. W. Griffith or anyone else has used the film medium with any truer zest than has Gance. Sergei M. Eisenstein had a calmer calculation, a more poised and precise method, than he had, but surely no purer an enthusiasm. Gance rushed in where *ciné*-angels feared to tread. He is an orchestrator of optical verve, compassing a chaos of vision as a composer does the sound of great conflict, emotional and physical. Gance's method went far beyond the convulsions of physical action and the mobility of actors' faces: he tied his camera to a runaway horse, and when the young Napoleon has a snowball fight, a snowball hits the camera lens as it would someone's eye. For Gance, the camera-eye was necessarily part of the human body; or, better, part of the physique we call the "social body". He strapped the camera to a singer's breast in order to show a theatre audience reacting to the rhythm of the *Marseillaise*, and when he made a sound version of *Napoléon*, he placed his microphones everywhere so that the sounds of the Convention Hall should come from all sides.

In the military scenes of *Napoléon*, Gance unloosed the spirit of a Tolstoi. Bardèche and Brasillach say that before 1938 it was "the only French film wherein history does not appear stiff and lifeless like a waxworks show". Gance, thus, was a sort of Delacroix in the energy he spread upon the screen, a Jacques Louis David in the scope of his pageantry. Historic social action became, for him, a magically animated mural. When the total cinematic revelation of *Napoléon* can be approximated, with the side panels making a triptych screen, the panoramic descent of the French army into Italy and the tempestuous image of Napoleon haranguing his troops must be breathtaking. Actually, and quite plausibly, this film was the climax of Gance's ambition to create an epic cinema.

In 1915, four years before *The Cabinet of Dr. Caligari* was put into production, Gance had conceived human madness as cinematic and scientific rather than psychopathological in tone: his *La Folie de Docteur Tube*, about an inventor who breaks up light waves, made extensive use of distortive lenses and out-of-focus photography: it was a complication of the primitive "trick film". His *La Roue* of 1921, likewise an advance on the "trick film", animated inanimate things. He had been arousing and manipulating with fierce abandon the *geni* of the camera: *Napoléon* was simply the *pièce de résistance* of this purposive activity. The illustrations here reveal something of his vast *mise-en-scène* as well as the maximum vigour of his movement: the way he would sweep his human material into being ideal instruments of self-propelled force. The triptych effects, with their side panels forming identical actions in reverse (left-to-right on one side, right-to-left on the other) sometimes composed one purview, as in military scenes occupying a landscape, while at other times the side panels show action peripheral to the vortex of violence whose axis is closer to us.

It was Cocteau who remarked of his own *Beauty and the Beast* (see elsewhere in this book) that a friend who deprecated it at first sight, came away from seeing it a

An early example of the influence of painting on serious film artists, this reconstruction of David's famous picture of the murdered Marat is among the best photographic emulations of a painting ever made.

second time with spontaneous praise on his lips. The atmosphere of fable and magic intended by Cocteau had at last come across to this spectator because the intervening usage of the film had blurred its definition of image, drawn together more harmoniously its light and shadow—in other words, made it more of an "hallucination". This technical factor is always to be reckoned with in any film wishing at the outset to create magical or illusory effects. History, as it appears in art, is surely more of an hallucination than as it appears in news-papers or in so-called documentary films. *Napoléon* is a work of the imagination. Today, its survival on the reel necessarily yields it to us dated and deteriorated. Is it more so, however, than those sculptural and archi-tectural fragments from the pagan world, prized today as classics? Time may cause loss to material objects and yet what aesthetes and philosophers term the pathos-of-distance is no mere idea: it is a plastic presence that carries an undying potential to us across the centuries. *Vive Gance!*

One of several uses by Gance of the triptych screen: a single broad panorama is taken in by photographing it in three sections and projecting these sections as a continuous landscape. At the left, Napoleon surveys his army's encampment; the scene has a marvellous equilibrium.

Gance's triptych is here composed of one ordinary film frame used in three ways: (1) as originally shot, it is a crowded assembly hall extending toward infinity; (2, lefthand panel) the original shot is printed in reverse and unfolded continuously to the left; (3, righthand panel) the original shot is printed in reverse and unfolded continuously to the right. A division line can be observed in the "butterfly pattern" made by a woman connecting the lefthand panel with the central panel.

Gance's invention of the triptych is shown in a third way:
A symbolic vision of France amid army banners (centre)
is the spiritual nucleus inspiring the military movement
divided into a butterfly-wing pattern on either side.

This triptych seems as if inspired by an Oriental scroll painting and has a remarkable unity despite its multiple vanishing points. Gance made his rows of soldiers swell the space with curving lines of perspective.

Sailors of the Russian battleship *Potemkin*, 1905, are seething over the fact that they are offered rotten meat at mess: the film has already established an overwhelming sense of realism.

Potemkin

1925 · U.S.S.R.

or *The Battleship Potemkin*

Potemkin, one of the most famous of all films, came as a direct antithesis to *The Cabinet of Dr. Caligari*; of course, it too was "silent". *Potemkin* was at once revolutionary Russia's notice to the world of its "populist" philosophy—that collective man, not merely an individual, may be projected as a hero—and Sergei Eisenstein's first masterful film. With 1925 the year of its release, audiences and the press in every European capital and in the United States hailed it in effusive terms, but it was largely because its political viewpoint, indigenous to Russia, seemed incidental to its "shock attraction" as concrete proof of the film medium's true potentiality. "Shock attraction" was Eisenstein's own term. Something that only thoughtful technicians, however, could suspect at the time of its début, was that the film held a whole philosophy of cinematic formalism that was to be climaxed exactly two decades later, with Eisenstein's assertion of his world supremacy as a film artist in the two parts of *Ivan the Terrible*, that remain as his farewell legacy to the evolution of the film.

Undisputed as film history is the fact that *Potemkin* was the first work to embody, in their most tangible

32

When the Captain orders those who have refused to eat the meat to be shot, the sailors stage a violent rebellion: this film narrative, on its appearance in 1925, was unparalleled in technique.

form various principles of construction peculiar to the medium: *montage* (or editing) and parallel action (the expansion of time through spatial manipulation); or, in sum, the purely formal deployment of objective action to create psychological dimensions. Eisenstein was not the first "film artist", but the first to be so pure, the first to use photography like painting-in-movement, photography like verbal imagery. As set down in his writings, his own theories inform us of this. Yet *Potemkin* must be seen to be believed. To the young, first seeing it nowadays, or to their elders, perhaps re-seeing if after decades, it is a palpable period piece. Physical facts of projection and the ageing of the film reel, arbitrary editing in this print or that, vary its grain, the rhythms of its figure action, even the quantity of its shots. One print I saw recently actually omitted the moments when the shawled woman carrying her dead child up the Odessa steps is shot down and the spectacled woman is wounded in the eye. Yet this justly

famed sequence remains a miracle of narration: the horror of an atrocious physical event grasped, as an entirety, through mass movement and marked incident of superlative invention; the separate rôle of the baby carriage is something that a Flaubert, a Tolstoi, or a Hugo would have hailed.

But casual mutilations cannot spoil the impact of so militantly positive a film. Eisenstein was a *cinéaste* in the most exclusively true sense. He cherished the genius of cinema where others wished merely to photograph natural action or invent a romance in moving pictures. His emotional viewpoint and aesthetic orientation changed with the years; his technical drive, relentless and even obsessive, never faltered except when official policy intervened from above. If this and his other films based on recent Russian history, *The Ten Days that Shook the World* and *The General Line*, diverge from his later films of distant historic subject matter, *Alexander Nevsky* and *Ivan the Terrible*, it is only that the former two seem less consciously contrived art.

The rebellion of the sailors on His Majesty's Battleship *Potemkin* in 1905; their success; the winning over of the people of Odessa at the spectacle of the laid-out

33

With the mutiny a success, the whole city of Odessa, gathered on its great flight of steps, sympathizes with the distant *Potemkin*: as history, all this is reported as more than history.

"Suddenly . . ." a film title announces, Czarist troops begin marching down the steps and firing on the sympathizers: the most famous single film-sequence ever made.

corpse of the rebellion's leader, Valukinchek; the city's aid in the form of food sent out on small boats; the massacre by Czarist troops of the townspeople gathered on Odessa's great steps to cheer the *Potemkin*, and the final sequence when the mutinied battleship expects to be attacked by the whole fleet, only to have not a single shot fired at it because the whole fleet has "come over" —this "story" is technically the reportage of the newsreel fused with the most meticulous effort to present life as something *permanently felt* no less than *fleetingly seen*. In other words, the competence of the eye that created *Caligari* as a fantasy of the mind is aimed here at everyday reality; in one stroke, the Russian Revolution as an historic landmark had reaped its full cinematic equivalent.

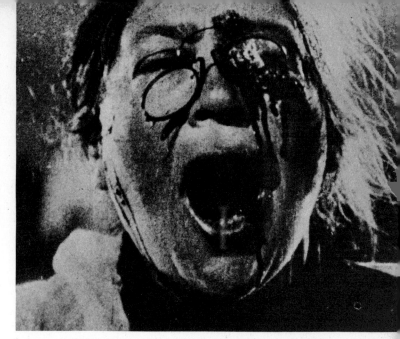

A stunned victim of the massacre on the steps. This shockingly realistic close-up has been cut from some prints of the film.

Utterly isolated with Odessa subdued, the *Potemkin* has prepared to face attack by the whole Russian fleet, which does not fire a shot; instead, the sailors of the fleet cheer them. This, wrote Lenin, was the first great act of the growing Revolution.

Frieze of fate-shrouded figures: they are trapeze artists, forming an emotional triangle, in another film that proved German film art was flying high, indeed, as the century entered its second quarter.

Variety

1925 · GERMANY

Caligari's producer, Erich Pommer, was to give impetus to Germany's rise in the film field by engaging E.A. Dupont, a director with a natural filmic gift, to make out of *Variety* a remarkable piece of counterpoint to Russia's stunning *Potemkin*. The respective stories of the two films, their messages and moods, were at opposite poles. Yet for camera wizardry, purity and compactness of style, *Variety* gained almost as much international applause as did the Russian film. As a fiction genre, Dupont's film was much more familiar than Eisenstein's: a straightforward, grimly unrelieved romance of sexual betrayal in chain-reaction, ending in crime, with the additional sensation of aerial acrobatics to keep its action in quite literal, and picturesque, suspense. Sordid in its human material, the German film possessed neither the winged fantasy of *Caligari* nor the human pathos that offsets the harsh moralities of *The Last Laugh*. One may pity the perpetrator of this crime of passion, but from the same distance that one watches his performances as an acrobat.

Behaviour-angled from ground-level instincts, the action of *Variety* is pictorially so clean, dramatically so direct, that I fancy spectators still appreciate its formal beauties, its virtually heroic centering on man, the stark animal. An American critic at the film's première in the United States perceptively greeted it as "Olympian", an epithet worthy of note. The use of the acrobats' white-costumed figures, appearing alternately in dark ordinary clothes—the former highlighted in the theatrical settings, the latter blending into the dull backgrounds of small interiors—create an unflagging, absorbing, contrasted visual rhythm for the fateful moves in the sex triangle. Its persons are "Boss" Huller, Berta, his female partner for whom he has abandoned his wife, and Artinelli, the bigtime trapeze artist who asks the pair to team with him at the glamorous Berlin Winter Garden. In one scene, the three appear like monoliths against a dark, receding background; shrouded by robes concealing their performing tights (with black death's-heads on their chests), they have the monumental presence of figures in a painted mural—one reason, undoubtedly, why the film was termed Olympian.

Murnau, who had directed *The Last Laugh,* was to have done *Variety,* but Pommer switched his choice to Dupont as the better man to exploit the film's potential sexiness. Potentially sexy it was; actually sexy it became, largely because Lysa de Puti filled the role of the female performer for whom Emil Jannings, as the burly trapeze artist, conceives an obsessive passion. Miss de Puti (unfortunately lost to American audiences afterward) was a true nymph beside the heavily theatrical image of the waning international Vamp. The role was the sort of "professional artist" for whom the history of the theatre has provided a variety of names. Censorship of sexual details, at least in the United States, was then almost as strict as *Variety*'s primitively beautiful, silent-screen story line. But the strong Continental innuendo wrapped up all the facts of the drama for those used to facing such facts.

A refined strategy rested in the suggestive device of the principals' aerial prodigies: error in timing before the audience was as crucial as error in timing behind the scenes. Inevitably, almost too inevitably, the plot crystallized upon Berta's betrayal of her lover with their new partner. Once again, eternally candid, irresistible lust assumes the shape of antique Nemesis. The sheer weight of Jannings' personal presence, the phlegmatic brute animalism of his body and face, serve to place his "Boss" Huller at the right depth. Less theatrically convincing, yet oddly plausible, is the British actor Warwick Ward's Artinelli: generally a more fetching male than Huller, but neither Italian, muscular nor insistently sensual. If sex takes charge (as it does) it is through the influences cast by the two out-of-work acrobats hired by the grand Artinelli. Here was the kind of plot-pattern that, while obvious, was universal enough to pull with the weight of a magnetic force toward its foreseen and logical climax. Discovering the betrayal, Huller kills his successful rival and goes to prison. The story is neatly unfolded through the flashback mechanism at the point when he has been pardoned for his crime. Ready to shed his convict's clothes, he is impelled to relate his past to a sympathetic warden.

A lingering pathos-of-distance is added to rapid scenes of stripped violence. Split-second contacts keep together the story line at infinitesimal points. Mere flash, in glance or flying limb, takes on a *diminuendo* when invested with suspicion. Death, the still and unalterable fact, slips in through the very gap made by the movement that is quicker than the eye.

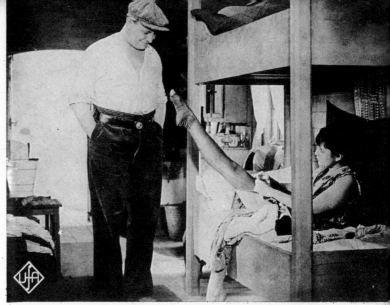

It is easy for petite, out-of-work Berta (Lysa de Puti) to ensnare, for life and death, the brawny acrobat, "Boss" Huller, played by Emil Jannings to the life.

Variety reaches from mere tumbling, as here, to very fancy work next to the ceiling – and next to scaring to death both performers and spectators. The film's naked suspense haunts the memory.

Jannings, who goes berserk with such harrowing art in *The Blue Angel,* is much more a true cock o' the walk here: his trembling, unfaithful partner does her best to pretend "it isn't so".

This rigmarole of a French farce by Labiche, a classic in the French theatre repertory, occasioned the earliest René Clair feature film to become an ornament of museums. A lady's imported straw hat is an object of fatal interest after a horse starts eating it off its wearer's head.

The eyes of high fashion never miss a trick: the fierceness of a woman's honour about her wardrobe easily gets mixed up with the pride of surviving chivalry; a bride and groom are not given a moment's peace for the duration of the prolonged rumpus.

The Italian Straw Hat

1927 · FRANCE

René Clair owes his importance in film history, I think, exactly to his temperamental flair for bringing a deep feeling for a certain theatrical tradition, slight but very distinctive, into film. His fervid allegiance to the stage farce of the latter half of the nineteenth century is well known; examples, including this one by Labiche, still appear on the stages of the world today, especially in Paris, where many of Clair's films were set. That this seminal tradition had been one immediately taken up and expanded by the very earliest films—mainly rapid movement through space producing great excitement— does not altogether account for Clair's long cherishing of a style derived from it. In 1962, his devoted temperamental emphasis was rewarded when he became a member of the Académie Française.

This event bestowed on him a unique renown. He is not the first film-maker to have been admitted to that august institution, but he is the first whose sole eligibility lay in his accomplishments as a film artist. Jean Cocteau, when admitted, had long been novelist and dramatist as well as film-maker. Marcel Pagnol (maker of four films included here) had joined the Academy's ranks when already a much esteemed novelist. Clair's film career has been long though not very steady. His

transplanting to Hollywood, after his success abroad, induced him to concentrate (at times unhappily) on the fantasy film. His habit of conceiving actors as puppets— even, as in *The Italian Straw Hat*, as stock characters: the Hussar, the Cuckold, the Fat Lady, and so on— did not work so well with the commercial formula, which must make room for the star personality and holds a soap-opera coyness that is hard to wash out. As a dedicated reviver of the past, Clair's own personality was quite enough of a "star". He felt like a puppeteer: obsessively fond of his puppets but maintaining over them the power of life and death.

He had a genius for persuading actors to help him create the illusion of a strangely unreal world—unreal, sentimental and quaint even when not involved with the supernatural—and his style works best, in my view, here in *The Italian Straw Hat*, where neither modern satire nor the supernatural engages him. Here the fragility of his artificial exteriors is not asked to bear the least burden of plausibility. The situation is preposterous and preposterously prolonged: a bridal couple's anticipated happiness is most grossly spoiled when the groom is obliged to make a strenuous search to replace a straw hat which has been literally eaten by a horse drawing a

Casualties to clothes become universal and fraught with the slapstick always dear to this film-maker's heart. If his famous "touch" at times failed to work, it was omnipresent; the Académie Française acknowledged this by making him a member in 1962.

There's a hat in that box — *the* hat; whole or in part, it is a symbol of all that is honourable on the face of the earth: it might as well be the Holy Grail. The hilarity easily translates to silent pantomime.

carriage in his wedding party; if he fails, he must fight a duel with the lover of the married lady off whose head the hat has been eaten . . .

If human passions look frivolous enough, if they must obey the most affected and obvious genteel manners under the silliest conditions, they are assured success when properly mechanized. Once set in motion, this farce seems self-propelled and more exquisitely funny than any other film Clair ever made. His satiric comedies — *A Nous la Liberté* being the most admired — were made later on. Rather too deliberately tongue-in-cheek, they have strokes of genius yet proceed in an oddly loose and makeshift rhythm. The cutting of the originals doubtless accounts, in part, for this effect; even so, the texture wears thin as the plots advance. All Clair's films are quick with delightful touches but those hardly register before flitting by or else seem becalmed, as if enamoured of the camera trained on them.

The preciousness of Clair's plastic touch is surely evident when we are instructed by modern stage revivals (at least outside Paris) of a period farce such as this. Style exists through a subtle architectonic tension: raise the voice, overstate action, press a pedal too hard and things fall apart, cease to be funny, become grotesque. Not Chaplin himself had a defter hand than Clair with sheer hilarious nonsense. Witness the final sequence of *A Nous la Liberté* when the high-hatted, swallow-tailed industrialists scramble after the paper money being blown by the wind and break up the ceremony. It is an

ineffably beautiful explosion into the absurdity of hypocritical greed. But that film needed the classic farce plot that keeps *The Italian Straw Hat* from tiring anything but the laughing muscles.

When ladies faint and gentlemen lose their tempers in a farce, the ultimate has been reached: something must break and something does; Clair gives the pre-horseless carriage era an astonishing liveliness.

The most typical image of the film's Expressionistic version of the working class: an immense, supermechanized factory as scene of the common man's robotized existence.

1927 · GERMANY

Metropolis

Industrial and progressive, mythological and ideological —that's the enduring Germany: its rôle in the modern world. Its will to create a reformed society, however practical or "good", has the quality of foresight, while neither the state nor the film world escapes the criticism of history and art, respectively. German film-makers have always had the "forward" vision of experimenting craftsmen, the vision of the machine-making mind. Let us not forget the film camera itself remains a mechanical marvel. It was Murnau who so much advanced the dolly-shot, gave the camera the wheels that suggested it was a walking man. A Czech, Karel Capek, had formulated the robot out of traditions of the homunculus in 1921. This zombie of zombies had no dependence on exhumed corpses, like Frankenstein's monster, or on animated statues such as those of ancient myth, but had his birth as a blueprint for manlike machines. In Me-

tropolis, the zombie is the trudging factory worker, formed in ranks; still flesh and blood, but reduced to the serfdom of machine operators, controlled as if by a Dr. Caligari.

Germany's economy has recovered with impressive swiftness since the end of the last World War. In Fritz Lang's Metropolis, fable of the interim between the World Wars, the industrial tycoon and his domain (circa 1927) supposedly recovers from devastation and disorder just as quickly; in fact, with miraculous suddenness of portent. The formula: a new moral harmony between the big boss and his rank-and-file minions. The tycoon, as an illustration here reveals, knows the man for the job of creating the false Maria, a female robot (capital's symbol) to counteract the true Maria (labour's symbol). The latter's chief calling is to be friend and comforter to the oppressed and poor; the fanatical artisan

The outside of Metropolis: a modern architectural illusion based on Breughel's Tower of Babel, and coming true today in terraced, tapering, mammoth apartment houses.

who produces her false version, based on a machine, is a bushy-haired blood brother of Caligari.

Where are we, to be exact, in *Metropolis*? Truly, in the fairytale land of German propaganda, where the modern world of work and poverty, luxury, leisure and play, is presented as a symbolically rigged-up city, with the Art Nouveau tradition serving Expressionistic moods and all the spaciousness of a World's Fair. Externally, with unmissable significance, *Metropolis* has the cloud-girt shape of Breughel's Tower of Babel, as spick-and-span as one of the modish, mammoth apartment houses going up right now in our large cities. Like these visionary buildings come true, to the last bit of surrounding greenery, this city conceals literally, instead of figuratively, a sad, sad condition among the working classes. Here are no "things to come", of course, as in later movie myths, but a frank fabulizing of economic unrest, the unrest even then seething below the surface in Germany.

Hitler and his propaganda minister, Goebbels, saw *Metropolis* in a small town before the Third Reich was an accomplished fact (see Kracauer: *From Caligari to Hitler* for this and other documentation reported here); as soon as Hitler was safely in the seat of power, Goebbels sent for the film's director, Lang, and informed him that the Government wished him to make Nazi films. This was not because Lang could so well portray an "iron rule"; on the contrary, it was because he had pointed out, in *Metropolis*, how such a rule could nobly and humanely transmute itself! In today's perspective,

however the film's "political lesson" be assessed, *Metropolis* remains that slandered quantity: a compelling drama. Like other, similar or dissimilar, classics included here, it is a true plastic vision of social forces, their mutation and manipulation on the style level.

No "heroic" German theatre man ever forgets Valhalla. The innovative stage producer, Max Reinhardt, had simply translated the stentorian rumble, the windy wail and eruptive temper of Wagnerian figures into fluid masses of people. This collective "voice" made the chorus a more distinct, self-propelling entity—even if it were the "silent voice" of the beggars' demonstration in *The Threepenny Opera*. The material sphere of collective human action of the ceremonial kind is the great auditorium or stadium, perhaps the factory itself: any platformed or arena'd space through which the voice may ring and gestures expand. Such a collective instrument is the Chorus in the old sense of Greek tragedy, holding the dialogue of a people with their hero-leader.

The semi-divine hero is epitomized in *Metropolis* as the industrialist's son, Freder (perpetually seen in a stylized version of Douglas Fairbanks Senior's riding outfit!), who falls in love with the friend of the poor, Maria, after defying his father and going over to the side of the workers in their rebellion. It is no accident that the same actor who plays Freder, the same director, even the same script writer as here, had collaborated to do the film version of *Die Nibelungen* (1924), which became a world success. The crafty industrialist of Lang's new film, secretly present at one of Maria's

Metropolis, indeed, holds playgrounds for the rich: here Freder, the industrial tycoon's son, plays a love game with an illusion; the woman he really loves, the true Maria, is a sacred woman of the people, their guide and comforter.

A mechanical "Maria" is created to deceive the rebellious workers, inciting them to a riot that will cause their ruthless suppression by the tycoon, Freder's father: this production-shot, showing the Robot's Caligari-like creator, chimes with the film's machine-dominated style.

appeals to the workers to let the "heart" mediate between "hand" and "brain", gets the idea of commissioning a robot, the false Maria, so she can incite the workers to riot and provide an excuse for ruthlessly crushing their uprising. But again a collective force explodes

The scheming tycoon has underestimated, however, the power of the forces unleashed from below: the great factory itself is destroyed, the water mains break and chaos takes over.

so violently that everything is wrecked in that climax of universal destruction which the Germans seem endlessly to relish.

Social chaos, conflagration and a flood from the water mains take place: we are thrust into the myth of world catastrophe. Yet Maria, saviour of little children, triumphs; the love between her and Freder helps induce the tycoon, awed by the calamity, to offer his hand in a dramatic oath of friendship to the factory's foreman when it is all over. The play, like time, goes on and ushers in totalitarianism. Hitler's régime recognized Lang's film as an exemplar of the art of propaganda. But what is it as the propaganda of art? Its theatrical virtues have unfortunately lost caste in our day. It depicts the world in the dimensions of mental fantasy; it tells the tale of style as truth, holds up man's striving as an heroic spectacle. To contemporary audiences, *Metropolis* may appear morbid and hectic, full of old-hat artifice, a posturing antique of the museums; to be taken not soberly, but hilariously. This view is not the pith of aesthetic wisdom. *Metropolis* has true vision and skill even when it creaks. It should not be scorned because it has not kept up with public relations psychology.

While the false Maria is trapped in a situation reminding one of the old-fashioned serials, the true Maria comes through to be united with her lover, Freder: a happy echo of the Romeo-and-Juliet legend.

The scope of *Metropolis*, a crest of Cubist Expressionism in the film, is vividly projected by the heroism of Maria as the poor children's only hope; idealistically, when the flood water recedes, Capital and Labour join themselves in the handshake of peace.

The Passion of Joan of Arc

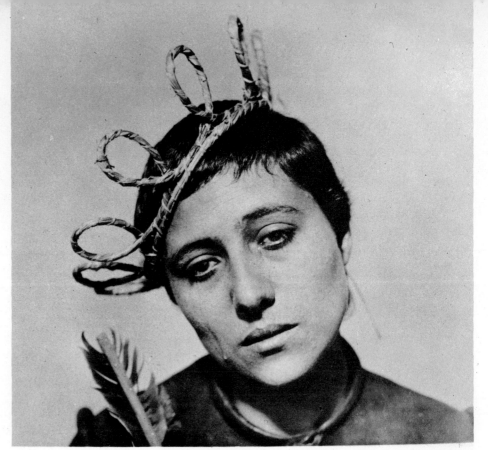

Joan of Arc, captive of the English Army, now imprisoned and on trial before Roman Catholic inquisitors, is derided with a mock crown of thorns, placed on her by soldiers. The role was played by Falconetti, who came from the same race of actors as Magnani.

Carl-Theodor Dreyer's film retains a secure, even eminent place in the repertories of film museums. The main point in the historic perspective on it is its focus on certain aesthetic questions in regard to the medium, a focus as sharp as when the film was released more than three decades ago. *The Passion of Joan of Arc* is not considered *avant-garde* although it has been recognized, since the moment of its appearance, as an art film having great and unique appeal. The fact is, its acceptance of the human reality of religious experience did not suit the revolutionary temper of the twenties, when to be *avant-garde* was to be iconoclastic in aesthetic or aesthetic-political senses. The Surrealists' fury against the Catholic Church has not yet run dry as a creative motive: see Buñuel's weird, and very recent *Viridiana*. Iconoclasm has its own peculiar motivation, belonging to group and individual on varied levels of personal action. Cocteau's Poet, destined to demolish a classic statue by 1930, would do so with maximum symbolic reference to the historic evolution of art. Pieces of anything broken up (an industrial chimney, as we shall see, collapses throughout *The Blood of a Poet*) could be magically reassembled, on a film reel, by reversing its direction; that is, the same action could be shown backwards and the broken-up regain its status as a whole. Observe that the Church, after burning Joan at the stake, was moved to revive her as St. Joan.

The imaginative Dreyer seized on the film medium's capacity to evoke the physical world not as a way of showing off, starting a great career or expressing a propaganda motive. Of course, the film medium is, and has been, subject to such uses (sometimes abuses) without extenuating aesthetic concerns. All the way from *The Passion*, as the Thirties approached, to *Ordet* as the

One of the succession of images of the priestly court interrogating Joan; the film holds an intimate dialogue of miming, no less than an intimate dialogue of words, between the woman being tried and her ecclesiastical judges.

Sixties approached, Dreyer remained a serious artist. It is not hard to decide what motive, meanwhile, prompted his distinguished, extraordinarily personal body of work: a revelation of the dangerous strategy adopted by individuals who feel all social authority opposed to them, yet are determined to assert their inmost desire and be loyal to its truth, whatever personal sacrifice and public shame be entailed. This is why the unreliably shrewd George Bernard Shaw termed Joan "the first nationalist and the first Protestant".

But a very different film could have been made about Joan as her personality is construed by Shaw's thesis. His own play about her, for example, has little in common with Dreyer's film. Dreyer's inspiration was to reconstruct, in meticulous terms of external reality, the most dramatic segment of Joan's human life: her trial and commitment to the stake. However, his plastic grasp of this segment replaced Shaw's rationalization of it. As Iris Barry very intelligently remarked, Dreyer's technique was not really so astounding except for the daring of its use in film; it owed much to the Stations of the Cross traditionally depicted in churches. At the same time, its whole spiritual reality lay in the plastic image of Joan's moral intensity and her acceptance of suffering. She is no Shavian dialectician.

The quality of this film heroine unites her with the witch theme that Dreyer treated in *Day of Wrath*, his 1943 film discussed elsewhere in these pages. Whatever *haunts* an artist is his true subject matter. With Dreyer, unmistakably, it has been the martyrdom of the witch: a "sacred" subject only insofar as it is a fatal "demonism" of the human individual, a tragic recognition of self-realization. He knew just what he was about; his scenario was arranged, his film cast, with the greatest deliberation. As produced by the Société Générale de Films and L'Alliance Cinématographique Européenne, it enters the ranks of French classics. Joseph Delteil gave final shape to Dreyer's plan from the records of the trial. The notable Rudolph Maté supplied some of the most remarkably concise and lucid camera work in film annals; his images stand out like a memorable suite of bas-reliefs or miniature paintings. The result is an historic instance of the clairvoyant camera, lacking any help from those stagey film tricks which the very early *cinéastes*, Méliès and Zecca, had employed for versions of Joan's story. If unjust criticism of Dreyer's film exists, it is the complaint that it is limited and static.

At this distance, these criticisms can be set aside with a good conscience. After all, literature had already made room for a large number of disjunct intellectual and technical methods and some such have been added since 1928. Moreover, Joan's judges must similarly have felt that *she* was static: she resolutely declined to recant. Life, truly, does not flow in Dreyer's film with the obedi-

45

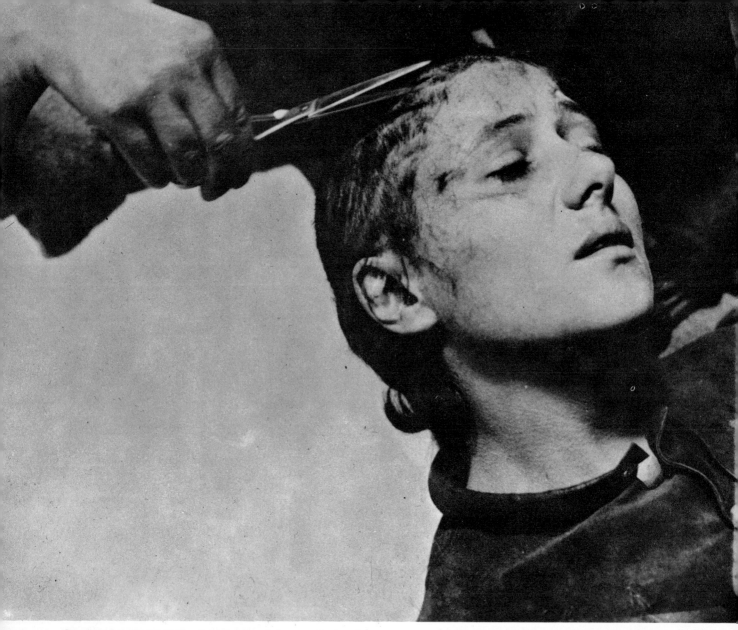

Condemned to the stake, Joan has her hair cut off: the close attention to physical details such as that illustrated here marks Dreyer's film with a conscious and unforgettable art.

ent readiness which lovers of "filmic movement" often desire so imperiously. The best reasons exist for this film's still, though never lax, attention, reasons beyond Joan's obstinate belief in herself. The interior and exterior white walls of the monastery where the trial takes place are a perfectly real "backdrop" for the sharply characterized figures of Joan and the priestly court, looking as if silhouetted against the open perspective of time. Joan contrasts with her judges as a rather masculinized peasant girl, whose only change of costume is the sackcloth gown given her before being led to the stake. The dialogue, of course, is silent, although visibly working lips invest the action with a special drama: we must wait for the next subtitle as if we heard the inquisitor's question and Joan's reply through some irksome time interval. What is immediate and fatal strug-

gles to reach us from a quantitative distance. Yet we are confronted with an eloquent physical nature. We know beforehand that Joan speaks in vain but we are freshly conscious of her as a solemnly militant, whole-souled woman refusing to abdicate the moral of her life: a holy vision and the worldly action predicated on it.

It is as if the visual medium stayed apart from either Joan or the agents of the Church determined to condemn her for their own complicated reasons. Often startled, we "read" profiles and attitudes as if by chance angles, seeming perhaps arbitrary, taken by a camera in the hands of a photographer who has unlimited licence to "take pictures" and who, seizing on picturesque aspects, renders the mere décor of the dramatic occasion: rusted armour, a worn sea shell, the textures of robes, close-ups of Joan's head as, snip by snip, she is

A remarkable, unorthodoxly composed view of Joan during the last moments in her cell while British soldiers stand outside: the grieving priest in the foreground, representing the shaken conscience of her judges, makes a forceful accent.

Another bold composition enforcing the film's stark and individual style: soldiers' helmets are treated here with striking resemblance to Eisenstein's use of them in a notable case.

The concentration of the film on Joan's head achieves one of its richest moments of compassionate vision; this is a great mask of resignation and fortitude, supremely tender.

shorn of her hair. But how remarkably like life (rather than like *Life*) are the results and the summative effect! What a lesson in candid-camera work! I feel that it would elude today's highly paid professional photographers. Just what might appear decorative in a contemporary news "coverage" by pictures, or starkly undecorative, appears here completely inner, the substance of spiritual intent.

Proof of the above contrast in values lies in the accumulated emotional effect as the film progresses. The slowness of pace becomes solemnity itself. Every moment is an anguish objectified by an image large or small, focussed as central or peripheral: Joan's gait, the forms of her questioners leaning toward her, her aloneness throughout, the martyrdom already printed on her face when in her cell. Yet at moments of concentrated fate—as we should have learned from novels if nowhere

else—the whole natural environment, every bit of testimony to physical existence, becomes a vehicle of what will leave the spirit totally naked if not destroyed. The burning witch, above all, has had to fear this; for believing in holy vision and the justice of God (if not in satanic vision and the justice of Satan) she stands in the greatest peril of retribution in the future life.

It is the building up of this special emotional crisis in Joan that makes the kindled wood stacked beneath her, the flames' increase, her visible torment and her envelopment in singeing smoke, so terrible as to produce tears. I have been present when audiences wept at Joan's death and at Marguerite Gauthier's death as portrayed by Garbo; the latter was a personal triumph, an actress's professional achievement. But Joan's . . . Mlle Falconetti simply allowed her beautiful empathy with the part to reveal itself anonymously. The peasant spectators, who

The cumulative spiritual drama of Joan's fate reaches the breaking point: a masterful realization by an actress of one judged evil and condemned to die a horrible death; the contrast provided by the other faces is consistent with the film's flow of plastic invention.

have reviled and cursed Joan, break down, weeping, and rush from the scene as though whipped by the billowing smoke: the world's judgment has been brought to its knees because a human individual, in the greatest pain, has risked all she had to risk.

Authentic atmosphere in Russians films of the post-World War I period came from Mongolia, where V. I. Pudovkin set an ingeniously melodramatic tale with V. Inkizhinov (left) brilliantly filling the hero's part: a Mongolian fur trapper. It is 1918.

1929 · U.S.S.R.

Storm Over Asia

Vsevelod I. Pudovkin, like Sergei M. Eisenstein, his colleague and sometime rival, was part of the dazzling revolutionary wave of Russian film-making that took hold in the Soviet Union after World War I and gained general fame as soon as *Potemkin* had its debut in the world's capitals. Newspaper reviews of the period remind us that partisans and nonpartisans attended showings of "Red" films in large American cities, expecting to share the melodramatic sensations which the mass audience, pro and con, finds in military combat. The same is true of sports, but regarding wars, especially international wars, there is more blood in the eye. During the Twenties, various orders of pro-Soviet Americans felt strongly about revolutionary Russia and its internal and external enemies.

Pudovkin was probably the best Soviet director to throw his talents so candidly into the arena of Our Side versus the Other Side, the Good Guys versus the Bad Guys. Ideologically, Eisenstein was just as committed to the triumph of the socialist state in Russia as Pudovkin was, yet somehow the latter, like an old-fashioned

Transformed into a member of the rebel forces after being cheated by a dealer at a great fur market, he has enough rage in his veins to make it difficult for two White soldiers to subdue him.

get-out-there-and-knock-'em-dead director, took this fact more thoroughly to heart than he took his art. *Storm Over Asia*, I think, is the most interesting product of his viewpoint and method, actually having a flair closer to that of Griffith and John Ford than to Eisenstein's. This flair, eminently cinematic, stresses serious melodrama along with a direct, simplifying approach to character and situation.

In *Storm Over Asia*, Pudovkin systematically demonstrates, as it were, how the rough-and-tumble can achieve fresh spontaneity, the eloquence of a member of a crowd who leaps up on a platform unexpectedly and bursts into fiery words. Such inspirational action, in fact, was knit with the revolutionary creed, its basic emotional posture; thus, it was logical for this same pattern to be taken over by Pudovkin's films. Set in Mongolia in 1918, when Russia was in the throes of civil war, it opens with gusto on an exotic scene full of restless, confused movement. Trappers are bringing their furs to a great market in Mongolia. The strange faces and costumes, the rush of laden carts, fierce horsemen, the antics of bargaining, the aspect of human bodies wearing, by illusion, animal pelts: all the hurlyburly of a great furry-skinned energy spreads its arabesques across the screen.

Our interest is centred in a manner common to fic-

tional modes. Out of the collective emerges a single figure, a Mongol trapper getting a price for an especially rich, whole silver-fox skin; he is very good-natured till he finds the dealer will not give him his price. The skin is so valuable, so beautiful, he hates to let it go but finally decides to sell. Seeing the unjust sum in the palm of his hand, he becomes sullen and leaves the market with ugly thoughts. Exchanging a Red uniform for his trapper's outfit, he fights the White forces, is captured (though with difficulty) and condemned to execution by the District Commander. A British soldier is to perform the duty. This sequence is Pudovkin at his best, a sharp embrace of facts, sensitive to detail: the distaste of the soldier for his job, the mute, mighty submission of the former fur-trapper, some strange power veiled by the mask of his face. Details are touched by pressing hard, but swiftly, on the pedal. The centre of the road travelled by prisoner and executioner holds a huge puddle, through which the Mongol imperviously splashes but which his companion skirts. At the fatal spot, there is hesitation, a declined cigarette, an oddly sudden shot. Coming back alone, the executioner splashes straight through the puddle as the prisoner did.

Meanwhile a certain professor has been examining the condemned man's effects and learns that he is apparently descended from the legendary Genghis Khan; this

51

Pudovkin was skilled at handling vigorous, naturalistic detail. Here a military valet tends the shell of grandeur belonging to a White Army commander, who sentences the captured trapper to be shot.

news so impresses the White commander that he is inspired (he thinks) with a stroke of genius. Mongolia will be flattered by giving it a new ruler with such distinguished native blood in his veins! All haste is made to determine if the shooting can be stopped. The countermand is too late but at least the executed man is still breathing. Brought back with the tenderest care, he is given the best possible medical attention. Then, wary and taciturn through it all, he is informed of his marvellous destiny: the reason his life has been spared. In the midst of the elaborate preparations, it is overlooked that no gratitude or pleasure appears on the Mongol's face. Give him a fine party: that's the thing to do! Everybody, including the new Genghis Khan, gets dressed up in evening clothes. It is in progress, and the Whites are busy drinking and congratulating themselves on such an important and happy occasion, when lo and behold, the supposedly obedient puppet feels the spirit

of the true Genghis Khan descend upon him, and with explosive fury, starts tearing the place apart.

Deftly led up to in mood, the event has the naïve exhilaration of the acts of fairy-tale heroes. The Whites' outmoded viewpoint, presumably, is being caricatured by a supernaturally endowed Red representing the fury of the Russian Revolution. His success (aided by a timely rejuvenation of the Red forces) has the thrilling impact of the victory reserved particularly, at ordained moments, for Our Side. Other Russian directors also utilized this popular pattern; one of the better films of this exciting type was *Chapayev*. Pudovkin was also geared to forceful tactics in the domain of his profession, for he outwitted Eisenstein in their ideological quarrels about film practice: a defeat from which the latter did not recover till *Alexander Nevsky* reinstated him in full official favour in 1938. Eisenstein seems a superior interpreter of Russian history as well as Pudovkin's superior as an artist. Yet *Storm Over Asia* has an insistent, indelible validity which Pudovkin had mastered: it is a tale drawing its lifeblood from the heart of true heroism.

This scene epitomizes the film's blend of unreal exoticism with reality-in-the-round: the Mongol, only wounded by his executioner, finds himself restored to life because the Whites have learned from his papers that he is a descendant of the legendary Genghis Khan.

A wary, dressed-up puppet, he is honoured with a party celebrating his assumption of rule as a new Genghis Khan; but to the dismay of his hosts, he suddenly goes berserk and, quite unaided, wrecks everything – revealing himself as a supernaturalized spirit of the Revolution.

The Blue Angel

The spectacle of a café performer named Lola (Marlene Dietrich) so much scandalizes a professor in search of some wayward students that he determines to denounce her: the consequences are startling enough to have made film history.

It is curious to think that sex—not nominated or rationalized sex, sex romantic or picturesque, but just sex—came into its own in the movies only when Marlene Dietrich appeared as Lola in *The Blue Angel*. Since that filmically rich year, sex has grown so sexy that frequently all the camera would need is a tilt toward the ground to become a medium of straight pornography. *The Blue Angel*, so innocently, theatrically, earnestly sexy, has come to mean, to veteran film audiences, simply Dietrich in a sardonic story of the power of bedroom lust. A blue angel, aside from its rôle in this film, would signify a supernatural being of the colour associated with Heaven. By way of this film, the term means a music hall, habitat of licentious pleasure, where Lola sings and sports her gamey legs, where a typical professor (Emil Jannings), tracking down some errant stu-

dents, sees her in action and imitates the eternal Adam falling for the eternal Lilith—not Eve.

The story, starting Dietrich on the road to world fame and rehabilitating Jannings after his mistrials in Hollywood, is a slice of level-eyed confrontation of certain embarrassing facts, facts which, sufficiently sentimentalized or exaggerated, satisfy a human craving without national boundary lines. Yet, when truth breaks through convention and the respectable becomes the unrespectable, Germans in particular feel a logical, even cold sensuality in displaying the process, messing around in it so as to sate sensationalists and, it may be, provoke

Herr Professor (Emil Jannings) doesn't find Lola such a monster, unless she could be described as a combined Venus, Circe and a few other alluring, but dangerous, mythological characters. The course of events is marked out as if on a blackboard.

moralists. Josef von Sternberg's direction also made him internationally famous and introduced a method that won commercial success abroad and founded a small cult. The physical world, von Sternberg showed, has a potent wealth of attraction that snares like an octopus devouring its victims. The backstage "labyrinth" at the Blue Angel, made of piled scenery, spilled-out trunks and shadowed crannies, offers the chiaroscuro of a sort of jungle. Like a jungle, it is balefully juicy, even as the very flesh Dietrich had to slim down in Hollywood. But *svelte* or buxom, it is the perennial domain where masculine senses—even if first they must be hypnotized—willingly lose themselves.

Von Sternberg exercises an art of *gourmandise* in whetting up the shameful details as the erstwhile professor, now Lola's slavish lover, gradually degrades himself. To yield as he does, to a passion whose object is first tolerant and amused, then half-pitying, half-contemptuous, is inevitably to go (in the eyes of German morality) from bad to worse. The professor duly goes there as a member of Lola's troupe travelling from town to town. His clown act is increasingly an explicit image of his grotesque abasement, till at last, in the midst of a performance, he is reduced to a kind of cataleptic, terrified bewilderment, and is booed off the stage. As a catastrophic end for a former professor, it is strangely convincing. But without Dietrich as the gross, wily, velvet-voiced, sibilant yet sweet, half-naked goddess of night clubs, the whole affair would be much less probable.

To be sure, Lola is a good girl in her guttural way—good enough, at least, for her impersonator to come up in classiness when her talents were processed in Hollywood. As if by natural evolution, Lola's raffish charm was refined into Dietrich's chic: Lilith suavely reclaimed herself as that unclassifiable sex quantity, the Glamour Girl, and it is doubtful if Lilith has ever been more glamorously incarnated. She was never Garbo's "competitor" precisely; she was too down-to-earth to be such a "mighty vamp". As exotic, she maintained what was inalienable from feminine elegance; also, she had gaiety—a prehistoric trait in a time when gaiety must be pumped up in actresses between sessions with their analysts. With von Sternberg faithful as her director, Dietrich became one of the big stars, but nothing she ever did supersedes the present film. Lately, *The Blue Angel* was Hollywood-reconstituted. Only Dietrich, one gathered, could make Cupid into a plausible juvenile delinquent.

The professor-turned-clown just won't crow when, according to the script, an egg is smashed on his head . . . Instead, the "crow" becomes a howl of rage as he dashes backstage to try to strangle Lola and her lover; Jannings' tragic desolation is superb.

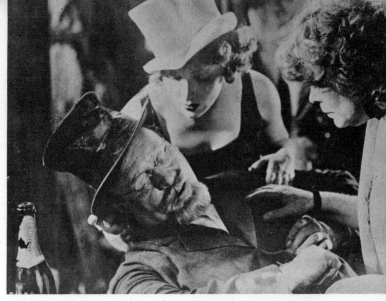

Helpless under Lola's spell and mocked by his own students, the professor bids good-bye to his career and his honour to follow Lola; his direction is plainly downward.

However, he proves equal to donning a clown's make-up and earning his keep; Lola's infidelity makes him suicidal, but he cannot leave her, he thinks, if only because his bridges are burned behind him.

1930 · U.S.S.R.

Dovzhenko's film opens with the burial of this man's ancient father, grandfather of Vassily; in heedless enthusiasm, Vassily drives his tractor over a boundary line into the field of a Kulak, a landowner fearing encroachment from the collective farmers.

Earth

Alexander Dovzhenko, an Ukrainian peasant who became both a painter and a cartoonist, started making films in 1926. After achieving the memorable *Arsenal*, attuned to the militant spirit of a Russia determined to survive, he turned to doing his masterpiece, *Earth*. This was a tribute to his heritage as a man of the Ukraine, where the soil itself had genius and the film camera seemed at home as its ideal interpreter. The Ukraine, furthermore, was where Russia's collective farm programme had its chief testing ground. The original negative of *Earth* is believed nonexistent; in any case, the prints at present circulating in English-speaking countries were made from a duplicated negative. Hence the exceptionally fine photography has suffered a loss, yet not one sufficient to prevent our giving this salute to a Russian film master who ranks at the top with Eisenstein and

Pudovkin. Despite resemblances among the three, Dovzhenko was the aesthetic antithesis of his two colleagues.

Earth, like Eisenstein's *The General Line* (or *The Old and the New*), contains a piece of popular satire smiled at by the censors in Russia: misbehaviour by the tractors which, at first, were such a great and awesome novelty to the peasants. As treated by Dovzhenko, however, the familiar tractor "accident" provokes not the heroism of a technician but of resourceful men of the soil: the tractor's water, when its radiator boils over, is replaced by the peasants' urine. This elaboration of the incident was considered too much by the Russian censors and is missing from the version we know. Though *Earth* sustained other prudish mutilations, it remains essentially unharmed as a deeply felt idyll of the land. Two dimensions of reality opened to Dovzhenko's eyes:

Meanwhile, nature and human nature, uniformly strong, lift above the horizon toward the zenith: the analogy between this girl's face and the companioning sunflower is part of the film's evocation of universal fertility.

a new order of life, collectivized and mechanized, was to be "grafted" upon the unalterably human and natural, that seasonal flowering-and-subsiding of all life that holds a sacred beauty and authority.

Vassily, grandson of an old peasant whose burial has opened the film, heedlessly drives his tractor across a boundary line into property owned by a Kulak, member of the landlord class that fears encroachment from the collective farmers. Dovzhenko's camera is like the sun's eye; the objects it perpetually registers in warm black-and-white seem as fixed as the grieving family of the old peasant beside his grave, moveless except for their hair ceaselessly tossed by a sharp breeze. Consistently, men, animals and plants are shown at the angle of the rising or the setting sun, towering above the lower margin of the film frame toward the zenith. Dovzhenko had no feverish political urge to show Russia at its task of getting things done in humming factories or nerve-ridden cities. Though he must have known, in a dynamic milieu of film-making, that his method would be criticized as static, he wished to display the unassailable

permanence of the State's agricultural base together with the pathos of its humanity: how the peasants' very enthusiasm to meet the new conditions and shoulder the collective task might incur its own peculiar penalties.

A woman is seen in birth pains: not all is light labour, mere labour, or laughter. Tears of effort and sorrowing, as always, lie in wait. Pictured lyrically, with primitive simplicity, evening has come. Now men subside happily toward the seemingly still roots of growing things, and in their happiness, dance. Three dances in *Earth* are human extensions of the soil as giddy with its generative powers. Vassily, coming home in the moonlight, "drunk" with thoughts of love's common labours, breaks ecstatically into a dance step along the white, curving road; he dances on, then crumples and falls: he has been shot dead by the Kulak whose land his tractor has invaded. His fiancée reacts by tearing off her clothes in grief. But his father, while rejecting Christan burial for Vassily, calmly organizes the funeral.

As the cortège passes the church, where the priest is praying, none of the mourners gives a sign of its ex-

An ambiguous drunkenness gleams from this modern Russian's eye: it is the puckish spirit of the dance, the expression not only of inebriated spirits but of the earth intoxicated with its sheer fecundity. When Vassily, ecstatic with love's labours, dances along a moonlit road, he is shot dead by the revengeful Kulak.

Vassily's fiancée, learning of his death, tears off her clothes in grief; this passage and two others were dropped from the original film by its censors. The funeral cortège is intercepted by the Kulak, who boasts that he has killed Vassily; ignored, he starts to burlesque Vassily's dance. ▶

istence. They are engaged in the ancient, indispensable rites. As the cortège follows the undulating landscape, it imitates the perfect quietude of its growth. Then something strangely violent and pitilessly human takes place. The Kulak who has shot Vassily appears and boasts of his crime; the mourners refuse to acknowledge his presence. In a half-mad frenzy, he then breaks into a burlesque of Vassily's dance on the moonlit road. It is sublime: the murderer's guilt and its horrid exhibition are scorned by those who are at one with the earth in its elegy, at one with it in reclaiming the growth cut down too soon.

The mourners, understanding that man is joined to nature in one implacable rhythm, proceed unconcerned; like this man and his beast, the earth thrusts itself into the sun-drenched sky even as, falling, it returns to its own solid darkness. ▶

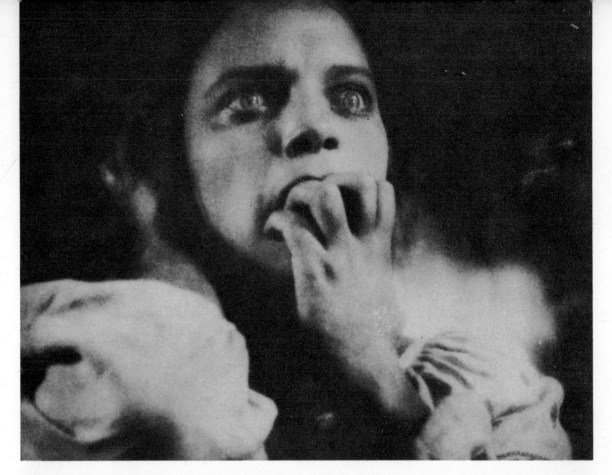

Le Sang d'un Poète

or
The Blood of a Poet

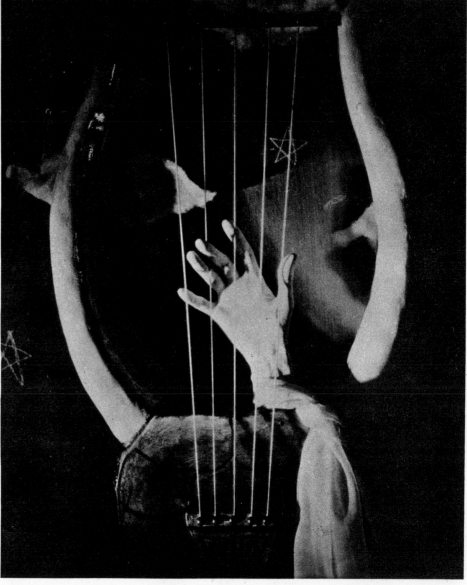

Cocteau, meaning his first film to be an animated and narrative coat-of-arms, here augments the linear star usually attached to his signature with a familiar classic emblem: cattle horns, as historically rendered into the Orphic lyre; the clouds are cotton, but the hand is Cocteau's own.

Jean Cocteau's first film started, though it came at the opening of the sound era, with a silent bang: the dynamiting of a huge, naked industrial chimney, a process it cut short to intervene with the main action, returning at the end, however, to complete the chimney's collapse with the film's farewell shot. Inserted between the two parts of this pyrotechnic bit of montage was an overtly magical narrative, dogmatically if deceptively stamping the Poet as a hero; or, more specifically, as the studio and salon fixture Cocteau had devoutly concluded the artist eternally, so to speak, is; and if not eternally, by all means *circa* 1930, the year of the film's making. *Le Sang d'un Poète* is concrete proof that Cocteau was always a politician, a fact established beyond dispute when he became a member of the Académie Française many years later.

In this maiden film, as succinctly as his film craft was able, Cocteau merely stated what any artist of his temper and articles of faith believed—or, he thought, should believe. His method was novel largely because, like the Dali-Buñuel films, *Le Sang d'un Poète* disclaimed the world of ordinary appearances, as painting

had already done, and projected symbolic action and metaphoric *tableaux vivants*. Though the aggressive authors of *Chien Andalou* explicitly denied that their film used "metaphors" or was a "symbolist work", they merely emphasized (as their next film, *L'Age d'Or*, also illustrated) the *unconsciousness* of their method. On the contrary, Cocteau was nothing if not exquisitely deliberate in both method and aim. The world of the artist, his film clearly says, is governed by laws breaking the "natural" laws that govern appearances; the strategies used to break these laws successfully are the very essence of this movie. These strategies appear, however, in a Neo-Classic uniform, as it were; for Neo-Classicism was the blood in the veins of Cocteau's Poet, who belongs to the same family as the Cid, Britannicus, the Roman lover of Berenice, Hippolytus and other heroes

The Poet, a half-naked artist in his studio, enacts an erotic abuse and finds in his hand a wound that becomes a mouth crying for air; with this as an inspiration, he plunges through a mirror and watches through keyholes a series of *tableaux vivants*, representing traditional forms of art-deaths: this one is the love-death and the figure is partly the Poet himself in a sculpture-like mask.

of Corneille and Racine who had long ornamented the French stage.

The pride of this hero is both noble and self-sacrificing. Cocteau's point was to show the typical brave agony of the Neo-Classic hero, defying death itself, as a virtual property of the eternal Poet, modern as well as ancient; this was the Artist's meaning in studio, salon and theatre, great or small. Thus, the film artist's method, Cocteau sought to demonstrate, was not only a private duty but likewise a public cause. As a contemporary virtuoso, of course, he understood, as did Dali and Buñuel as official Surrealists, that part of the strategy of the new art was to take by storm: *avant-garde* art must be a kind of "public affront". Yet Cocteau, with thoughtful shrewdness, wished to amend somewhat this savage Surrealist article of faith and exclude from the shockable (basically middle-class) public the thin upper crust of art lovers. These connoisseurs, concentrated in the nobility itself, adored the new art as an expression of high fashion; new statues were going up in the public squares of culture (*Le Sang d'un Poète* has its own way of saying this) and the aristocrats of art could appreciate the fine points of these statues.

Cocteau thus assumed and thus proceeded; he was not dismayed, apparently, when this article of his solemn creed backfired on him. He had gone so far in his didactic zeal as to place members of the nobility in theatre boxes shown in the film's final sequence; chief

among them were the Vicomte and Vicomtesse de Noailles, earning their distinguished places if only because the Vicomte had commissioned *Le Sang d'un Poète* as well as *L'Age d'Or*, both of which, indeed, exploded on the art world at the same moment and the same place: the Vieux Colombier Theatre, Paris, in 1931. But these representatives of the nobility, whose connoisseurship had supplied the funds for two *avant-garde* films, were not seen applauding Cocteau's hero as originally intended. The art-loving de Noailles had been put in an embarrassing position with certain of his relatives; he, too, was apprised of the serious risk taken by actors in films when a preliminary showing of the work's final sequence showed the nobles applauding an artist's "suicide".

Cocteau himself relates the happening in an illustrated scenario of his film that appeared, in English, in 1947. The action and the audience in the film are never shown together; hence the scenes must have been taken, in typical manner, at different times. De Noailles and the other nobles had to excuse themselves to preserve aristocratic decency. Cocteau knew it was useless to in-

At the end of a corridor, the Poet (first seen as an imitation of Rudolph Valentino in his rôle as the white-wigged Monsieur Beaucaire) symbolically kills himself to attain a new relationship to tradition. The shadow on the wall, significantly, is made by a wire sculpture of Cocteau's head.

sist that it was, in substance, a *symbolic* suicide which his evening-suited Poet enacted: a suicide anticipating his natural death, in a way, but also representing the sacrifice of his private life to the public interest: he must create works of art at any price to himself. If these works are great enough, Cocteau's message also says, his reward will be immortality. One suggestive circumstance was that the brilliant young French writer, Raymond Radiguet, a friend of Cocteau's, had died, some years before, very prematurely. The alternative was inevitable: the scene of the applauding audience had to be reshot. For this moment of *gloire* in a modern spotlight, Cocteau suavely substituted as the leader of the applause in one theatre box the well-known female impersonater, Barbette.

Cocteau's own brand of Neo-Classicism had the opportunity of a new dimension of paradox that extended the irony already lying, doubtless, in the spectacle of spectators politely gloating over the terrible ordeal of the artist's self-sacrifice. How much does an artist really "suffer"? Perhaps this has never been proved by an argument of any kind. Plato termed artistic inspiration a temporary form of "possession". Hence, in a way, the artist's ordeals, including the symbolic suicides and the mock frights that appear in *Le Sang d'un Poète*, are "simulated" rather than "real"; at the same time, our knowledge of the careers of many artists who have struggled for fame, gone hungry and cold, as well as reached insanity, or its verge, can easily fill Cocteau's symbolic *tableaux*—all of them deliberately "melodramatic"—with significant verification from social realities.

But Cocteau could not believe anything but that such realities remain the shell of the artist's object of creating a world of his own. Exterior reality is that with which he must bargain as with an audience he must please. He desired, however, to give the most intimate details of himself—what an artist always gives despite the nature of his aims—as both a generic and an individual artist. That he was orthodox enough to *seem* to bargain, to sell, to posture self-consciously, is what his radical contemporaries found repugnant. But imperturbably he went on, sure of the social centre of his art, however exquisite and exclusive; he knew the artist's isolation, his self-indulgence (illustrated, at the very start, by self-abuse), he knew his play-acting as part of his training; hence the exhibition of the Poet as keyhole witness of what goes on in the Hôtel des Folies: mimic death, drugged swoon, sexual masquerade, all that to which the artist *lends* himself without *becoming* it. The smashing of the classic statue to which he is impelled after a tragic self-appraisal as a cheat of mimicry is meticulously if allegorically worked out (see the brilliant essay by C. G. Wallis in *The Kenyon Review*, Fall, 1944).

The *danger de mort*, the "danger of death", means that in *smashing* the past, as recommended by the current *avant-garde*, one incurs the danger of *becoming* the past; that is, one day, the *avant-garde* will become the classical unless the whole notion of classicism ceases to exist. But as long as we accept the idea of history, the classic cannot perish. What Cocteau shows happening in the rest of his film is thus prophetic and carried out by his later career. The formally dressed Poet now loses a card game (destiny) to a lady who turns out to be his Muse, and again shoots himself in the head. Though poets have really shot themselves, his own suicide is symbolic, "for the public good". The dynamited chimney of the artist's career (as *Orphée* will show) can be rebuilt.

Playing a card game with a lady, both of them dressed for the evening, the Poet loses it while calling up a tragic mirage from his boyhood, and again shoots himself; at this, his opponent turns into his Muse, her long black gloves simulating a statue's absence of arms. Compare her face with that of the lady, Death, appearing in *Orphée,* Cocteau's film of twenty years later.

The apotheosis presents a real cow whose horns are the Orphic lyre and whose hide represents our terrestrial globe; the Poet's Muse passes grandiloquently from the scene, which is a theatre where an élite audience has applauded his supreme self-sacrifice to art, and leads toward the stars the symbol of the world he has conquered.

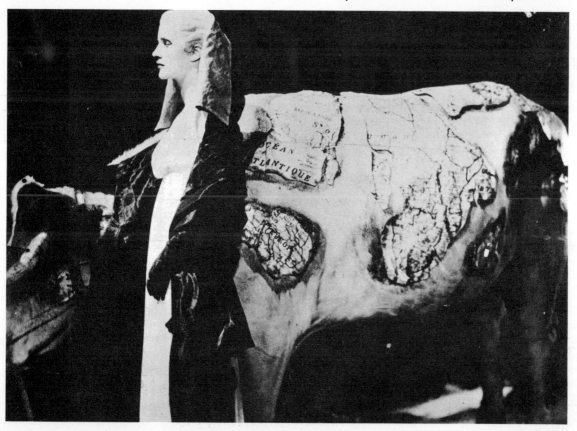

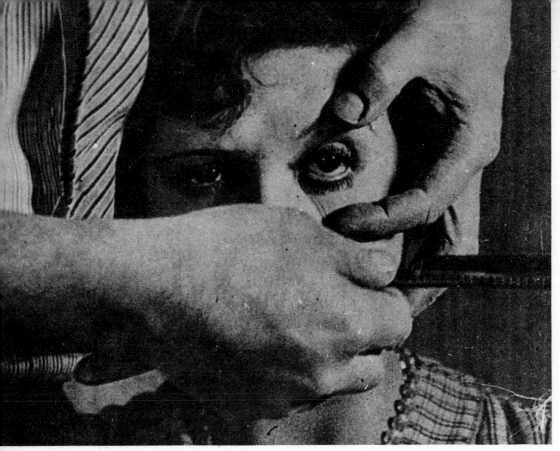

Chien Andalou & L'Age d'Or

Chien Andalou or *The Andalusian Dog* (1929) and *L'Age d'Or* (1930) had behind them the heroic passion of deliberate villainy—this villainy being nothing but the ambition, through an art work, to destroy established aesthetics; a prime hit was rung up in that no dog appeared in the former. These two unforgettable films, classics by the mandate of film history, aimed at being more shocking than the shocking, and to go the latest thing several better. "X" marking the spot, Paris, they succeeded. As Salvador Dali, their production-designer, expressed it in his *Secret Life of Salvador Dali* (1942), *Chien Andalou*, the first collaboration between him and Luis Buñuel, a Surrealist poet, was something they "would plunge right into the heart of witty, elegant, and intellectualized Paris with all the weight of an Iberian dagger". Put more sensibly, Dali claimed that this express purpose had been achieved; the film's première, as the critic Eugenio Montez wrote, was "a date in the history of cinema, a date marked with blood", and Dali commented: "Our film ruined in a single evening ten years of pseudo-intellectual post-war advance-guardism."

Chien Andalou is a perfect example of the classic *avant-garde* tenet of the invisible-made-visible: off screen, a dead donkey's eye was substituted for the organ being threatened above and duly slit in the close-up which followed.

The claim is credible. Established cinematic whimsy (largely dealing with camera tricks) had to resist the force, literally dragged onto the screen, of two dead donkeys atop grand pianos, donkeys whose putrefaction Dali had touched up as if he were Hollywood's

Chien Andalou: the minutest nerves of desire achieve the unembarrassed nakedness of ants.

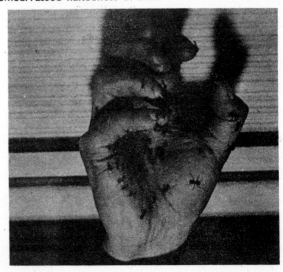

64

L'Age d'Or: this shot, reproduced in an American magazine, aroused some readers' curiosity till they learned the object being kissed is a statue's foot.

highest paid make-up man. This painter's ferocious egotism, his unbridled sensuality, sincerely but perversely cultivated, finally led him to Catholicism in the hallowed Spanish manner: that of violence and suffering as on the Cross. *Caligari* and the many fantastic films emulating it, very little known outside Europe, could be viewed "metaphysically" as pure mental aberration; inviting, in fact, clinical cure or sequestration. Not so our present intrepid soul-shockers. Film Surrealism, in *Chien Andalou* and the work with which the two film-makers followed it, *L'Age d'Or*, claimed the world as their asylum, with no improbable constellation of holds barred. Of course, the inspired pair had taken over already established Surrealist canons. Buñuel, who later would make film into his métier (though a commercially handicapped one), wrote in sober historical objectivity of *Chien Andalou*'s makers: "Both took their point of view from a dream image, which, in its turn, probed others by the same process until the whole took form as a continuity ... when an image or idea appeared the collaborators discarded it immediately if it was derived from remembrance, or from their cultural pattern, or if, simply, it had a conscious association with an earlier idea."

Doubtfully accurate, this analysis is medically solemn, even Germanic, as if the scientist gone mad, Dr. Caligari, had recovered and recalled how he and his somnambulist had put their hallucinations into artistic practice. The truth is that the two films—*L'Age d'Or* being made without Dali's active collaboration—have the angelic beauty of unself-conscious outrage on all conventions of behaviour. That everyone secretly experiences such things with the free imagination is now so much a platitude that one need not cite authorities for it. What could be more conventional, nowadays, than to formulate itching desire (whether for sex or money) with ants crawling on the inside of the hand? That *Chien Andalou* opens with a man calmly slitting an equally calm woman's eyeball with a razor (so it seems!) only serves polite notice that one has to sit back, before a rectangle echoing with earthquakes, and go with passive optical attention through the dossier of almost anyone's psychic vagaries.

That's what happens here; it happens to capitalism and clericalism in these wickedly thought-up and -out films. Yet their political and social radicalism, nowadays, seems less jolting than their timeless, direct attack on the senses, erupting like a pimple on the sun and silver-etched on darkest infinity: images speaking precisely where words would be most imprecise. Displaced sexual impulses reign supreme: the parody of the Catholic custom of kissing the toe of St. Peter's statue in faraway Rome is as distinct as photography can make it and the bepainted female kisser's state is as uncriminal as St. Peter's façade; a man's parallel act of drawing a woman's fingers into his mouth drives the ambiguous point home with Dali's sacred Iberian dagger. These films

survive with an astonishing austerity, registered by actions swept clean of nice domesticity, proper street behaviour and plausibility. Here is a common-looking world meticulously disordered so that it is through nature's divine consent, it seems, that "blood", as Dali explained, "is sweeter than honey".

Unabashed infantile connoisseurship from *L'Age d'Or*: a desirable woman's hand, thus caressed, helped to shock all the desirable women in Paris who saw it (and some others, too).

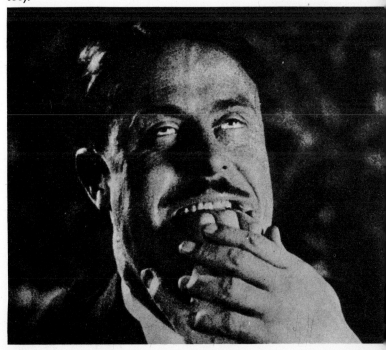

Party dresses in a feminine barracks: girls at a boarding school in Potsdam, Germany, before World War I, are trained to be the mothers of soldiers.

Maedchen in Uniform

Maedchen in Uniform, made in 1931, could not wait to become a classic. A film dealing with German militarism as an evil heritage, it had the authority of Athena leaping full-grown and armed from Zeus' brow. But here, as audiences granted, was a femininely conscious Athena, capable of realizing, as if with divinely impartial wisdom, the equal rights of Aphrodite, particularly as these swelled the breasts of female adolescents — somewhat more fragilely composed and less armoured than those of male adolescents. In point of fact, one wonders if the goddess of militant wisdom, whose bigoted parody here is headmistress of a girls' boarding school in Potsdam of the Imperial era, had not provoked an alert Aphrodite who had concluded that militarized womanhood in the person of Frau Principal was not only an offence against peace, like the German nation's ambition for world dominance, but an offence against the rights of natural passion; at least, such an assertion of "natural" rights is suggested by the argument of *Maedchen in Uniform.*

As a German criticism of the nation's own past, the film doubtless won ideological opponents as well as aesthetic admirers in contemporary Germany. The growing spirit of Nazism (the Third Reich was scarcely two years away) might well contend that the film's moral conclusion, if stood on its head, would be an object lesson on the serious matter of disciplining the young as future servitors of the State. As the daughters of poor army officers, these schoolgirls (whose uniforms suggest a prison) are "trained" to be the mothers of soldiers. Meanwhile, they suffer the normal languors of sexual efflorescence and its perverse temptations; among the pin-up boys on the walls of lockers, we learn, are some furtively pinned-up girls. The presence of Frau Principal as an incarnate Prussian militarist, her bosom decorated with insignia, and issuing stern, unwelcome exhortations, is a direct provocation to all sorts of rebellion.

We are soon acquainted with the perilous trend of one girl's rebellion. Homesick Manuela, just bereaved of her mother, and with a clinging, frightened, strangely intense nature, is fixated on a teacher, Fräulein von Bernburg, at first reluctant to respond to the girl, but finally induced by her charm and pleading to indulge her own secretly nourished feelings. Telling herself that the rule of the headmistress is too harsh and especially harmful to a highly-strung girl like Manuela, Fräulein Professor allows her pupil's emotional obsession to grow and arrogate moral rights that lead to heartrending scenes between them. The situation comes to a head when Manuela releases all her pent-up feelings in acting the male lead of a romantic costume play put on at the

66

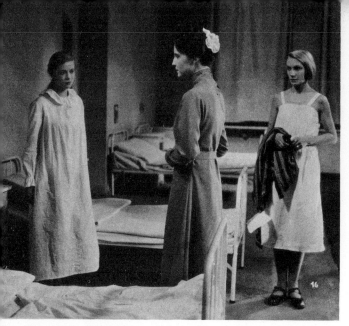

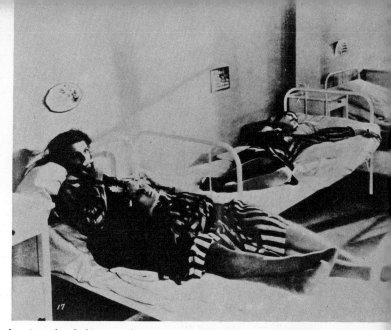

The crisis: Manuela's crush on her teacher, Fräulein von Bernburg, becomes a secret passion that tends to defy discipline.

A triumph of sheer craft in the German film: the uniforms of the *maedchen* have their stripes bent and twisted when the students relax on Sunday.

school. The contrast between the absurdly acted play and Manuela's genuineness is extremely effective. She has a personal triumph, gets tipsy on punch and praise at the ensuing celebration, and in a moment of wildness publicly announces the burden of her love.

Put so summarily, the facts must seem crude beside the uncanny tact, the virtually flawless craft, that has guided the film's embodiment. The movement is sure-footed, the plastic design in the best German tradition of formally reinforced idea. A woman director, Leontine Sagan, followed Christa Winsloe's play in accomplishing a tour-de-force of play into film. Manuela, punished by Frau Principal for the scandal she has created almost under the eyes of the visiting Princess, is isolated and threatened with expulsion. As Fräulein von Bernburg risks her own dismissal by braving her superior on the principles involved, the girl, crazed by grief and terror, seeks the abyss of the great stairwell to destroy herself and is torn from her perch in the nick of time by her schoolmates.

The near-tragedy is carried to its conclusion without faltering. Faced by the naked issue, the relentless headmistress at last quails in remorse; she has had a real setback. As Manuela, Hertha Thiele is a magic presence: a girl tinged with boyishness, whose pathos is the very depth of her natural passion. Dorothea Wieck, classic of profile, magnetic in cool remoteness, was so impressive as Fräulein von Bernburg that Hollywood sent her its fatal call. She soon met oblivion there but she is not forgotten; this film lends everything in it a dateless lustre. It is a chaste ode to sexuality.

The school play: Manuela in a male part releases her pent-up feelings with a force that brings her to near-tragedy.

Frau Principal, a domineering Prussian idealist, stages her final struggle with Manuela's Fräulein, another sort of idealist.

Mackie ("The Knife") Messer has fallen in love with Polly Peachum, whose father is King of the Beggars and strongly opposes Mackie's whimsical desire to marry Polly; nevertheless he is royally wedded to her in the warehouse where his gang stash their loot.

1931 · GERMANY

The Threepenny Opera

or *Die Dreigroschenoper*

The British, as their film classics show, can go to the utmost lengths to make fun of the human race in good faith; not so the Germans, as *their* film classics show. In converting John Gay's satire, *The Beggars' Opera* of 1728, into a piece updated to a supposed London in the 1890's, the Germans employed their native idiom to express both their consanguinity with the British and the dissidence impressed by their genius on this kinship. Kurt Weill and Berthold Brecht, who collaborated to make a new musical version of Gay's work, *The Threepenny Opera* (1931), are recent examples of German theatrical genius; that the Brecht-Weill work has a sustained vitality was proved by its revival, a few years ago in New York, with Lotte Lenya (Weill's widow) who created the original rôle of Jenny and plays it in this film. The production ran so long that Mme Lenya retired from her rôle, which was then assumed by a procession of actresses. As German-modernized, this play-with-songs is far more economically self-conscious than its British original, and proportionately more political in bearing.

Resourcefully directed by G. W. Pabst, the film version somewhat softens the stage work's gruff impact as social criticism. Yet the cinema reinforces the curious phantasmal quality of life which film so readily translates into optical terms. Society is compact of underground as of overground life; we have French versions of this sort of underground, a sort of human sewerage, in *The Hunchback of Notre Dame*, *Les Misérables* and *The Phantom of the Opera*, made over and over into popular films in France and elsewhere. It is "French" to consider "underground" life as romantic fantasy based on anachronism; "German" to consider it realistic fantasy based on society's unsolved historic problems of poverty and crime; "British" to consider it the excuse for an elaborate joke or a sociological problem which may be solved tomorrow by proper legislation. The present film, as a comic opera, huffs and puffs to be gay, achieving a sour-sweet unity of lyric pathos and gritty satire.

In Siegfried Kracauer's book, *From Caligari to Hitler*, the Brecht-Weill-Pabst film is but one specimen

Mackie's gang "case" their situation; their leader and his pal, the Police Commissioner, are in fear of Peachum's threat to stage a beggars' demonstration on Coronation Day.

offered by the prime evolution of German politics as symbolized by Caligari and practised by Hitler, who organized the political discontent of the Germans into a formidable national instrument. Hitler's counterpart in *The Threepenny Opera* is neither its "romantic" hero, Mackie Messer, head of a criminal gang, nor Tiger Brown, the corrupt Police Commissioner, but a true "underground" hero, Peachum, King of the Beggars. Peachum is the father of Polly, whom Mackie decides to marry after falling in love with her and repudiating his low-life love, Jenny. So it is the romantic passion, à la Wagner, that creates the film's intrigue and precipitates its plot. Bitterly opposing his daughter's marriage, Peachum threatens to mar the impending Coronation of the Queen by a beggars' demonstration unless Tiger Brown scuttles Polly's marriage by sending Mackie to the gallows. But Tiger is loyal to Mackie, his pal, and the pair are wedded in a majestic warehouse where the gang store all their loot.

German talent for extravagant fantasy emerges in this wedding sequence—one thinks of von Stroheim's passion for wedding parties, also derived, one suspects, from Wagner's illicit "divine marriages". All the surface amusement is threaded systematically with the sinister,

and we see the German flair for decking out crime with spectacle and fantasy as something both stifling and breath-giving. The "underground" is indeed a powerful chthonic force, quite capable of fusing heroic romance with grimy revolution. Fearing a catastrophe on Coronation Day, Tiger Brown orders Mackie's arrest and the gangster is trapped in his hangout, a brothel, by the jealous Jenny, though later, through Jenny's change of heart, he escapes from prison and rejoins his wife.

Brecht strengthened the work's social criticism by having Polly forthwith open a bank, arguing that enterprise within the law pays better than Mackie's illegal activities. While the bank prospers, Peachum sanctions and then forbids the beggars' demonstration, which then operates on its own impetus. We witness one of those alternately electric and lava-like social eruptions so graphically put forward in *Metropolis* but here suggestively realistic; like others, Peachum is ruined by the very underground power he had controlled and set in motion. The sets of the film by Andrei Andreiev are styled to carry out the authors' moral message as fashioned in bizarre, improbable, latently symbolist mould. Illusive labyrinths, seemingly commonplace, have thick shadows cast on the crystalline highlights of their walls.

Brooding jealousy in a brothel: Lotte Lenya's inimitable
characterization of Jenny, Mackie's regular girl, who first
betrays him, then effects his escape from prison; her songs
give voice to a brutal cynicism, oddly caressive.

Basically in the Expressionist manner, more extremely exploited in *Metropolis*, human individuals here appear as units against groups, and melting into groups, in a choreographic dialectic reminding us of modern abstract painting and music. Yet an odd lightness, as of the gods laughing and crying, comes through in Weill's songs, echoing *Die Meistersinger* and making the heaviness gauzy.

Mackie, now fearing arrest, takes refuge with his disreputable harem; note the hatted miss's emulation of Dietrich in *The Blue Angel*.

While Mackie and Polly, now partners in a bank, find that legal finagling pays off better than outright crime, the beggars insist on staging their demonstration: a genre image of our society's restless eruption from the depths.

Child-murderer in an agony of self-inspection: Can he be recognized? Peter Lorre's incomparable performance made his name as an actor.

M

One of the most memorable facts about this most memorable German film is not communicated by its actual surface. Yet the fact to which I refer is curiously German and quite relevant to *M*'s theme. When Fritz Lang announced its production in 1930, its proposed title was *Murderer Among Us*. At once he received threatening letters, incomprehensible to him, and was refused permission to use the film studio. Only when he glimpsed a Nazi badge under the lapel of the studio official to whom he was protesting, did Lang suddenly find the enigma solved: the Nazi Party imagined that it would be compromised by the title of this film about an actual child-murderer! When Lang agreed to change the title, he was free to use the studio without difficulty. Released in 1931, *M* is his masterpiece.

Political guilt in this century has never been so raw, so egregious, so psychologically persecuting a thing as among the Germans. There is, of course, massive testimony to this but it is not a fact by itself. It seems to correspond to a certain trait of the German soul: the will to face sin, crime and guilt, and carry the contest with them to an ultimate issue, regardless of consequences. One might call it—this quality of soul that optimistically created that hymn to Nazism, *The Triumph of the Will!*—the will to terror. Guilt and its griefs is not worked out temperamentally among German artists as it is in the works of Dostoievsky, Gogol and Gorky. In Russian films based on the writers named, we see it thrusting itself to the surface in a clamour of human confusion and dissolved quickly in shrieks and insults or in crimes that are expiated in tears or, ultimately, by suicide. The Germans intellectually, desperately, mull over crime, investigating its causes, meanwhile defending or indulging them, but always making of guilt a great psychological issue, fraught with the struggle of reason and reason. This is why that film about guilt as a submerged mental struggle, *The Eternal Mask*, made in Switzerland, is as German as the language spoken in it.

It was Germany where the Expressionist style originated; that is, where the psychic realities of crime and guilt found their ideal expressive means in art. But we must recall that the first great film incarnating this theatrical style was *The Cabinet of Dr. Caligari*, whose thesis (later evolved elaborately in other films) is that crime is primarily the product of crazed minds, a psychopathological force; this, precisely, is the theme of a whole book on the German cinema, Kracauer's *From*

72

The chase is on; the criminal underworld itself is determined to catch the monster criminal: a typical shot showing the film's melodramatic use of space.

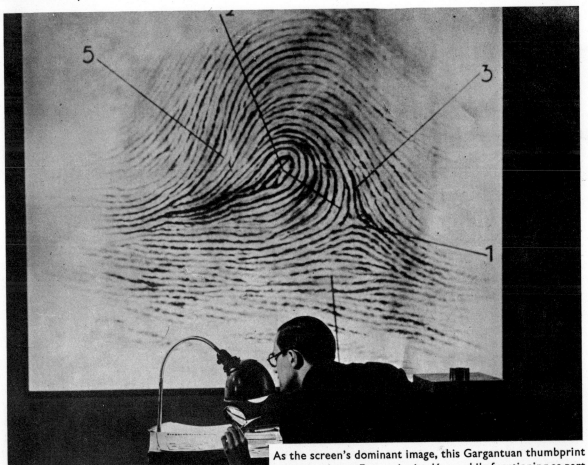

As the screen's dominant image, this Gargantuan thumbprint makes an almost Expressionist décor while functioning as part of police routine in identifying a criminal "beyond the shadow of a doubt".

The most complicated resources of crime are brought to
bear to corner the elusive quarry: not far beyond this floor
the criminal is trembling.

"M" faces his arraignment before a jury of the underworld
itself: the criminals have been better hunters than the police.

A moment of solemn pathetic horror: "M" is recognized by his voice as the man who lured away the little girl by buying her a balloon from this blind vendor.

Caligari to Hitler. Lang, however, simply wanted to make an unusually gripping movie. With the help of Peter Lorre as the child-murderer, he succeeded.

The film is stark, lucid, expeditious in its simple, if melodramatic technique. It has long been a museum piece and is surely (despite its blatant thrill-structure) the most "serious" film on this particular criminal subject, if only through Lorre's marvellous rendering of a man as incapable of not committing evil as of not suffering from committing it. The frankness of Lorre's delineation, its alert reporting by Lang's camera, and its repulsive reality constitute another unique achievement in filmic annals. Relentlessly, with a grave, tragically deliberate rhythm, the film proceeds from one of the murderer's crimes (luring a little girl to assault and death) to the growing public alarm and the all-out decision of the police to apprehend the criminal.

M would lack its peculiar force—the final sweat of its "will to terror"—if the actual hunting-down of the pitiful criminal, at last hemmed in like a terrified animal, were not the feat of the criminal world itself, disturbed by so much police activity and horrified by a crime so abnormal, so monstrous. The whole organized underworld of crime (including beggars reminiscent of those in *The Threepenny Opera*) is self-enlisted to bring the fugitive to bay. The way it succeeds, and the fantastic dénouement of M's arraignment before an underworld court, is truly a melodrama of the soul, unexampled in any other crime film. Lang filled decorative pattern, employed breathtaking pace (both fast and slow) with maximum content. As for Lorre, his career was "made".

The big day: big factory, big groups, big contrast, big gesture. It introduces the final sequence of René Clair's finest satire, a juicy, tongue-in-cheek fable about the absurdity of big money, big machines and other things "colossal" in the movies and outside.

1931 · FRANCE

A Nous la Liberté

Four years after René Clair's genre-styled *Italian Straw Hat*—that comical marriage between stage and film— this director's genial, offbeat satire turned to a contemporary theme: the buffeting of Capitalist society which, since the Russian Revolution, had been earning a very different sort of drubbing from Soviet films. As style, nothing could be further from the documentary viewpoint of the Russians than Clair's supposedly contemporary *A Nous la Liberté*. All the same, the fantastic human features of this film by Clair have a startling resemblance to what has become known internationally, in recent years, as the Beat Generation—otherwise, the Era of the Culture Bum. A stalwart, if fanciful and humorous, hoboism is the philosophy set forth by this characteristic offering of the unique French director. Two pals, imprisoned for minor crimes, plan an ingenious escape, carried out in what may be called restrained slapstick. The film remains true to this manner as the escape splits them up, and like the legendary twins, one moves along a path of life quite different from the other's. One sets out to rise to the top of the economic world, the other embraces (with traits similar to the early Charlie Chaplin's) the "sweet life" of the born tramp.

Clair's criticism of the social system never became, as did Chaplin's, grim and a little ugly beneath its comic trappings. Modern industrial society, at home or in the factory, ridiculously Baroque or streamlined, is a stage-set where everyone, worker and magnate, are the puppets which Clair took so much joy in handling. Under the spell of the fantasy all life becomes an overnourished, delusive dream capable of perishing in a flash should society ever "wake up". The humble worker and the conservative bourgeois, like the underdog tramp and the bloated capitalist of caricatured fame, are simply two poles on which Clair weaves his fluid, airy, grinning sort of farce. The fluency of which film is so eminently capable responds "like magic" to the twists of plot—conventional in the comic-opera sense—as Clair makes one escaped prisoner, the mild, happy tramp, meet and come to terms with his "twin", the posturing capitalist who now owns a thriving factory. To be worthy of the working girl he encounters and loves, the former breaks the rule of his vagrant life by taking a job in his pal's factory.

But of course the girl has a disapproving bourgeois parent, and another suitor, handsome and more eligible, so that the inevitable love chase begins and gets entangled with a crime chase—for, naturally, gangsters are an integral part of economic warfare in farce as in melo-

One of a pair of escaped convicts, to whom the image of liberty in the big world outside was so alluring as to make prison walls so much dream-stuff – accidentally separated in their break for freedom – one goes on to hear his master's voice, money, the other ... just goes on.

drama. Interesting to note is that here we have much the same theme as in Lang's *Metropolis*, prolonging a melodramatic sob at the bottom of its Wagnerian throat; yet, turned into Clair's light-opera plot, the seriousness of economic warfare assumes a debonair, even gay, stoicism. One might think from *A Nous la Liberté* that the often bloody struggles within modern industry could properly serve as a mere armature for explosive fun, to which is added (à la Clair) wily malicious strokes. If Clair sought to damage the object of his satire, it was only with his repertoire of rather innocent gibes, the best of which, by all odds, is the climax that I mentioned before in writing of *The Italian Straw Hat*.

Of course, things end happily by Clair's standard: the successful pal, ruined by chance melodrama, is reunited with the temperamental vagrant as they start out, penniless, to enjoy the Unstrenuous Life. Clair has a "nervous" style; it breathes lightly and rapidly with the tension of the guessing-game. The last phase of the game is: Cash-box, cash-box, who has the cash-box? Like a chimera, money disappears from the grasp of all who chase it. That's Clair's philosophy, and however facile and fairy-tale he makes it, it leaps up in a kind of timeless beauty and timeless laughter as all the paper money is blown into Limbo.

Of course, they meet again: the industrial tycoon whose portrait in oils appears here and he who just kept going ... Of course, gangsters and more respectable bigsticks in the world want their share of the loot; the treadmill comedy, dredged with puffs of romance, at last unites the two pals in a very, very open road.

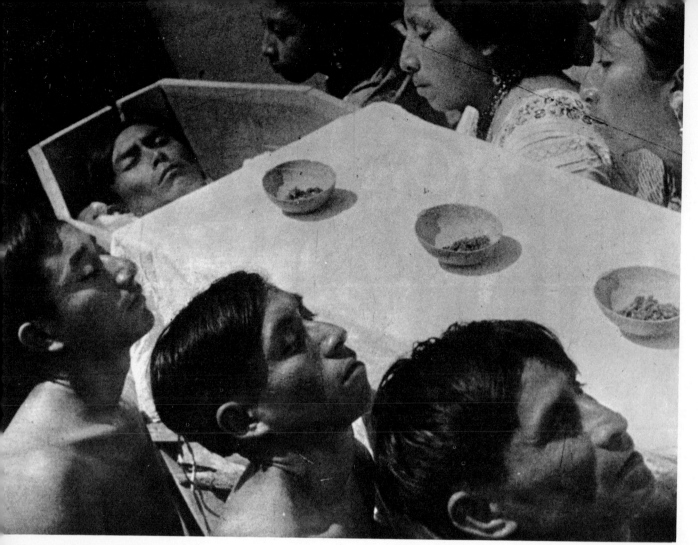

Ritual homage to the dead: Tisse's exquisite sense of photographed light and shade complements Eisenstein's unperishing grasp of beautifully balanced plastic values; the dynamic conception, as always, is Eisenstein's own.

Que Viva Mexico!

Thunder Over Mexico
Time in the Sun
Death Day   1931-1932 · U.S.S.R.

The story of this magnificent film must remain the most golden illusion ever conceived in an art medium and then shattered into pieces. It was fully realized only in the womb of Sergei Eisenstein's mind, only as symbolized by his preliminary synopsis and by the actual drawings that showed how keen-eyed a craftsman this film artist was. What remains to us (in three films respectively called *Thunder Over Mexico*, *Time in the Sun* and *Death Day*) are synthetic fragments like a disjointed dream, like a work of art as raw material; these more or less coherent "episodes" were meant to qualify one another as organic units of a single whole; the perfect realization of the original project would have been comparable to the success of Joyce's, Pound's and Eliot's metaphoric and narrative techniques in literature.

Before the project materialized, Eisenstein had been granted leave of absence from his homeland and gone to Paris. Meanwhile, the success of *Potemkin*, released first in the United States at the Biltmore Theatre, New York, in 1926, had been countrywide. Its maker, according to his biographer, Marie Seton, was someone who—it was beginning to be said in the industry—could out-de Mille de Mille if he had the chance. What "mob scenes" *Potemkin* could boast! No one was impelled to remark that "mob scenes" require as much formal order as anything else, but this omission itself went unnoticed. Film producers, for a while, hovered on the thin edge of resplendent offers to Eisenstein, who happened to have an articulate and untiring supporter in Seymour Stern, then adviser to Carl Laemmle, Sr., at Universal. Actually, it was the influence of a British script writer, Ivor Montagu, reaching the ear of Jesse Lasky at Paramount, that decided the issue of bringing Eisenstein to America to make films. Lasky went to Paris, where the Russian was revelling in his

The Feast of Corpus Christi, or modern Mexico in a traditional guise: mask and fact, present and past, come together in the same film frame; note that the eye-sockets of these skulls echo the dark heads in the preceding illustration.

holiday, and before long had Eisenstein's signature on a contract. Having meanwhile hobnobbed with sympathetic fellow craftsmen and other admirers, he had been working on a carefree "experimental" film issued as *Romance Sentimentale*. Doubtless this experimentalist piece of cinema, the offhand gesture of a devoted amateur, had become the vehicle of its director's sheer love for gay, instinctive "animal" life, which the demands of propaganda in films had somewhat stifled in the Soviet Union.

Eisenstein's prime interest never ceased being that of the true exploration of artistic possibilities. This did mean, constantly, people and stories, but not necessarily *Russian* people and stories. He was much impressed at being offered a bushel of American gold; the amount, $900.00 a week, seemed to him fabulous, even though it would have to pay, besides himself, Edmund Tisse, his superb camera man, and Grigory Alexandrov, his script assistant. Moreover, this sum was a mere retainer. When shooting began, it would rise to $3,000.00 weekly. And yet, as Miss Seton's conscientiously detailed book tells us, Eisenstein's last thought was to loll in luxury; his first was to investigate this country's people at some leisure: Negroes, gangsters, prisons — even Chicago's slaughterhouse! Once arrived, Eisenstein "poked around" in city streets.

His training in Soviet Russia had not spoiled him, for he had a true intellect, and his aesthetic drive was the least shakeable in filmdom. To the United States, however, Eisenstein brought an ingrained, radically alien and paradoxical concept: a cinema "undominated by the dollar"! It is of tragic and pointed irony that Miss Seton begins her account of the American phase of her subject's career with a chapter titled "An American Tragedy" (quotation marks in the original). Dreiser's book, alas, was never converted to the screen by Eisenstein, though to date it has been done twice on film. This Russian director was to live a wholly different "American tragedy"—one really more expressive of modern times than that conceived by Dreiser.

While insisting he had come to this country to do an "American" film, and meaning it, Eisenstein also insisted on doing it on his terms. Vain illusion! One setback was that *Romance Sentimentale*, when premièred in New York, was obviously no *Potemkin*, if only because it had passed through other hands after Eisenstein's departure from Paris; his name was on it, in fact, only because otherwise his final salary instalment would have been withheld. In New York, Eisenstein proceeded to dicker with Paramount about a suitable picture; it appeared that producer and director had most divergent ideas. During these weeks, Eisenstein lectured, once under the auspices of Columbia University and John Dewey. He had been accepted as a savant of the film, someone who not only could make films but also talk intellectual theories about them. D. W. Griffith's work had helped him form his montage theory and he

Señoritas at the bullfight: ritual drama as revived today; this is a shot from the sequence giving the progress of the torero from the dressing-room stage, and a formal farewell to his mother, through his course to the arena and the bullfight itself.

had personal talks with Griffith. Plainly, Sergei Eisenstein was a great man and accepted as such, yet it developed that he had a great man's "eccentricities". Shown around big cities, he preferred dance halls to museums or steel mills, and visiting almost anything other than local Gold Coasts. He was headstrong enough to vex Paramount by appearing, during public duties, with three days' growth of beard. People felt that he had not much of a figure, but that his head was "grand". That was true. His hair, his visionary gaze, were those of the old romantic poet's; his forehead that of a philosopher. Yet his eyes and lips, his facial expressions, could easily turn him into a super-clown, and not always a harmless one.

Why am I giving such an extensive prelude to my discussion of Eisenstein's Mexican film? Because he himself, his personality and relentless aims, the "dialectic" of his presence in America, had the "fault" of structure that brought his wonderful film project in Mexico to disaster. On the other hand, Eisenstein had not before, and never would, put a film into the works while feeling, regardless of circumstances, so much a free agent as now. Eventually he told Marie Seton: "The moment I saw Tetlapayec, I knew it was the place I had been looking for all my life." In part, his joy, and that joy's summit, had been promoted by the disastrous end

to his Hollywood prospects. Ultimately offered a book that had lain on Paramount's shelves for years, Dreiser's *An American Tragedy*, Eisenstein staunchly began the struggle between the "interior monologue" he expressly wanted to make of Clyde Griffith's story and the commercial formula upon which his employers insisted; neither party would yield. With his habitual demonic obstinacy, Eisenstein had kept giving his studio oponents "hot foots".

Quite another element, the public relations aspect, had handicapped Eisenstein in his fight to do as he pleased. Being from the Soviet Union, and a Jew besides, he was openly attacked as a Red and a Jew, and became a special target of Major Frank Pease, president of the then Hollywood Technical Directors Institute, a "patriot" of the kind with which America later became much more familiar. A pamphlet called *Eisenstein, Hollywood's Messenger from Hell*, was issued by the Institute. Marked as a "Jewish Bolshevik", Eisenstein had to do something very good, and very "American" indeed, to justify the cash expenditure on him. He and Paramount continued their wrangle. What was even

80

The peon hero of the romantic sequence: Eisenstein's eye for human and plastic beauty never missed; his aim in *Que Viva Mexico!*, though fatally frustnated, was to show the two classic strata of being, body and spirit, as simultaneous in time and interwoven in space – his technical instrument was a complex montage.

termed a "brilliant" script submitted by Eisenstein, *Sutter's Gold*, based on Blaise Cendrars' *Or*, had to be rejected on moral grounds. "Moral grounds" assumed new importance in the issue because Paramount's new "property", Eisenstein, had been branded by the Fish Committee with the epithet, "international Judas of the cinema".

It was not hard to predict that Eisenstein's relations with the Hollywood industry were doomed to collapse. Yet with many open minds, some of them inevitably pro-Soviet, plugging for him, he obtained an independent contract from Mary Upton Sinclair to do the Mexican film. But what happened the moment Eisenstein and his collaborators, Tisse and Alexandrov, set foot on Mexican soil? The three were arrested and hustled off to jail. Miss Seton explains that Eisenstein, officially considered, "was the most dangerous agent Moscow has ever sent on a mission". A "mission"! In a world where such things can happen, an artist (all appearances to the contrary notwithstanding) must remain a kind of stranger. Nevertheless, Eisenstein proceeded –

as I find myself repeating in this book – to make the plastic thing a work of film art should be; at least, he went a good part of the way.

The eventual upshot, after he had accumulated thousands of feet of precious film, is so well known as to require only casual account here. He was enjoying the luxury of a "studio schedule" which he, and he alone, commanded from day to day, and which inevitably cost many, many American dollars; those dollars he considered should not rule, but serve, the cinema. It is not too trite to record that he was like a schoolboy on a holiday; literally, he was an artist on a spree in which he could enjoy the constant "rushes" of film as if they were so many debauches of the filmic sensibility. This did not mean he lacked the usual serious planning. His scheme, in fact, took a majestically radical form: he would show the whole Mexican people, not sentimentally or statistically or superficially, but at the ultimate depth of poetic comprehension as accessible to the film camera. Every "reality" would be seen as it is, but on the most primitive and universal levels simultaneously, where life and death join in the soul of man, where man is carved or painted in the image of his gods, where spirit vies with flesh in human destiny, where people love, kill, die and give birth. Eisenstein, at this time, was the only film man in the world with such

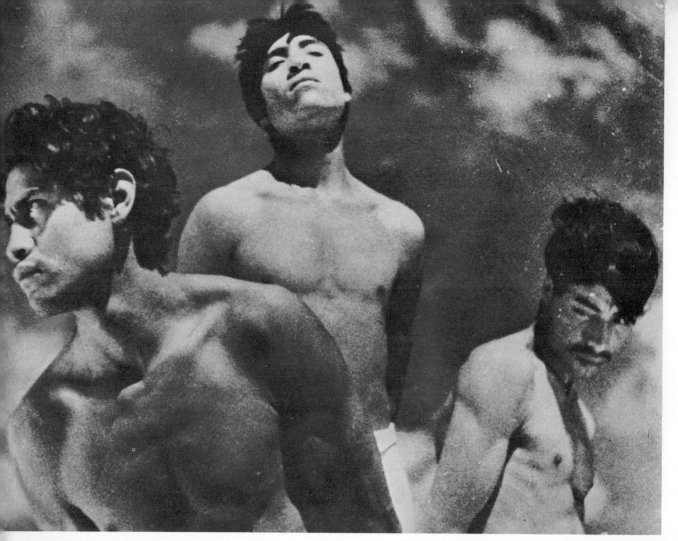

The most famous of Eisenstein's three-figure compositions: the fugitive peon ("Christ between the two thieves") has been caught by his master and will be buried chest-high in the earth and trampled to death by horses' hooves because he has dared to protect the chastity of his peasant bride.

a programme, together with (he thought) the means totally to realize it.

He was wrong. Oh, he was wrong! Not in intention (he was sublimely right there) but in his belief in his star of destiny in conjunction with what may be termed those stars of financial investment to which his own star was fatally hitched. His proven method of sketching out each film scene on paper, as if it were a painting or section of a painting, had now an unqualified liberty. Inspiration for motifs was at hand in native art both ancient and modern; he drew from both. Eisenstein's full-length scenario was approved by the Upton Sinclairs, who after all were many, many miles away, as well as by the Mexican government, which was quite near, but whose official watchdogs got along beautifully with the visiting director from the Soviet Union. He felt free, in short, to treat humanity as the "actor" it is: in the acts of love and marriage, in the act of bullfighting, in its death struggles and religious acquiescence to death, in the round of the day, the night, and the round of time that trims down man's individuality to a birth and a death. He would show the bullfighter erect and taut, smiling as the bull's curved horn grazes his side; the passing caress he gives that horn; then the crowd's

"outburst of delight". He would show the terrors and the torpidness of a peon's life: its pathos, silence and repressed animal intensity, its fight to live and consummate life under oppression. No stroke, no path, was too wide or too narrow to show the abundant gesture of nature and its shaded truths: the grace of chiaroscuro, and also its weight, as these were reflected on the film reel's sensitive surface.

As shown by this work alone, Eisenstein had a deep instinct for man's religious nature as form-producing: the array of symbols found omnipresently in Mexican life. These were essential to Mexican being, the life of the body filled with spirit, the life of the spirit filled with body. No wonder he should get the idea of cross-cutting film in a very modern style-sense; no wonder he planned his most daring montage for *Que Viva Mexico!* Symbols of Christ's crucifixion, as the *Penitentes* were whipped, would blend with the merry-making of a feast day, and appropriately dressed-up

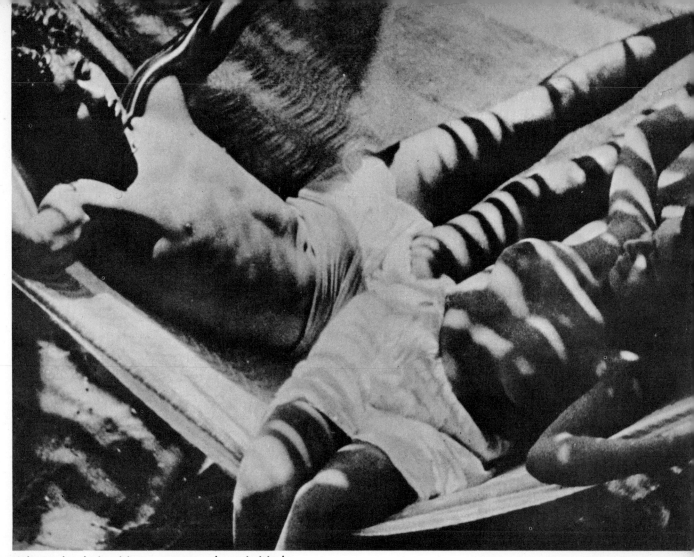

Eisenstein's tender lyric vision compasses the primitively erotic at home: the sarape itself, whose "violently contrasting" stripes seemed to the film-maker like "the cultures of Mexico running next to each other", must have evoked this intricate, masterfully sharp moment of chiaroscuro.

skeletons would be filmically cross-referenced by views of Mexico's political demagogues; the "martyrdom" of the three peons, buried in the earth up to their chests and trampled by horses' hooves, would automatically evoke the penitential images of Christ and the two thieves on their crosses. Like all poets, Eisenstein revered the supernatural powers: their images glowing with the instruments of the pain man inflicts on man, whatever the cause of the infliction: social, economic, or religious. It is religion by which humanity reorders and harmonizes the brutality of death and even death's injustices: that is, the domains of religion (as in the cult of self-inflicted pain) where man achieves and renews the ecstasy of sex, birth and death in the nameless marriage between pleasure and its contrary.

I do not myself assert these things as explicit and immutable truths; I assert them as the known basis for *Que Viva Mexico!* Little more than conventional sequences of the film ever saw the light of a projection machine. Peremptorily demanded by the Sinclairs, after what they considered much too long a delay, the legal rights to Eisenstein's film fell into their hands; the physical reels of it had been sent them in instalments. When the film-maker was denied the right to edit what had been made of his film, public pressure was organized—largely by the liberal-minded Lincoln Kirstein— to induce the Sinclairs to surrender the work to him. However, negotiation finally became impossible. Eisenstein left American shores in a bitter mood, without hope of ever repossessing his film to finish it; in due time, his hopelessness was confirmed. Yet, according to Marie Seton, an entirely new filmic theory of composition came to Eisenstein as a result of this Mexican project. While each of the known fragments, mentioned above, were professionally edited (one by Miss Seton herself), stills from Eisenstein's footage give one a good idea of how thorough, how exquisite, was the plastic conception animating this work. *Que Viva Mexico!* remains the film world's sole abortive and indisputable classic to date: a "tragedy" not only for Americans, but also, more justly put, a "tragedy" for world film in its first half-century.

Don Quixote

Fyodor Chaliapin, famous Russian bass, is overwhelming as this film's Don Quixote: as lucid and fabulous a presence as in any of his stage roles. Facial lines, hair, moustache, even a jutting eyebrow, contribute to his comic yet noble characterization of the Knight of the Mournful Countenance.

Don Quixote de la Mancha, Knight of the Mournful Countenance—mournful because convinced in his old age of the world's injustice to the world and because committed, not without consciousness of anachronism, to righting that injustice. It was the theory of *noblesse oblige*, already outdated by new views of statecraft, but clinging to life in the courts of princes. It is hard to decide, in our era of dominantly democratic (or at least republican) thinking, if the rule of an enlightened few or the genius of an individual leader is either efficacious or ethically "proper". However, to instrumentalize the past, as history or myth or both, has been the individual's privilege (and, on occasions, his art) even up to the present, as I think some films in this book prove; G. W. Pabst's version of Miguel Cervantes' famous novel is one such film. A few years before, the German director had made the whimsically off-key *Threepenny Opera*, modernized by Brecht to be a satire with wide social implications, and grim where Gay's original opera was just that: gay. But here the view of life required an heroic scale that was beside the point of Brecht's theatre piece.

The place of the film in Pabst's career brings out a curiousness not wholly unlike Cervantes' frustrated and risky fortunes as these were embedded in the auto-biographic testament that critics have admitted his *Don Quixote* is. As one commissioned to make a modern film, Pabst could undertake the work as a director known for his epicurean taste. Yet surely he had the humour to perceive the *true* humour of the masterpiece he was adapting. The reason for suspecting his motives lay in his habit of shifting his allegiances after the Nazis came to power; he certainly gave evidence of sympathizing with Hitler. However that may be, the freedom of artistic expression, its frequent irony toward the facts of contemporary reality, is well known. We see from the nature of Pabst's present material, and his treatment of it, that grandeur is here: grandeur and the comedy of grandeur if put in a false position, especially interesting since this false position, Don Quixote's mission, is chosen, not imposed.

The incarnation of the fictional hero by Fyodor Chaliapin was not a mere matter of adding to the film's interest by having Don Quixote sing his part; Chaliapin, on the opera stage, had the authority of the noble presence that is fast vanishing, even in art. Like Don Quixote, like Cervantes himself, Chaliapin was an old man, an old man in whom a magnificently expressive voice survived in the way the ideal of chivalry had survived in Don Quixote de la Mancha. Chaliapin's looks were doubtless somewhat grander than the man whom Cervantes forced himself, bitterly, to imagine, but not grander than the ideal soldier whom Cervantes romantically must have envisioned when he himself had been a soldier. Paul Morand, the distinguished French novelist, provided Pabst with a script quite alive to the alert, insidious irony as well as the large dignity and pathos of the original.

It would be a wretched mistake to think of the Don as a mere laugh-provoking figure, like the antique fops and pedants of Shakespeare's comedies. That function, as Morand and Pabst understood, is specifically assigned here to Sancho Panza, the Don's minion, a peasant whose common sense allows him to discern what Quixote's idealism prevents *him* from discerning: that a kind of world, memorialized in books and pictures, has passed away. Since Sancho's forbears were that world's servants, he is well aware that it has vanished. With it has vanished the classic concept of the knight as a man who worships woman as an idea and a specific woman as representing this idea. Old-fashioned even at birth, perhaps, this idea had governed the conduct of individuals and created (through Tasso, for example) an epic poetry. The knight-errant was trained for individual combat in honour of a woman as symbol of the Virgin Mary, or according to the romantic convention of the Middle Ages, in order to obtain her person: see an alien, but very old, example, in the film *Rashomon*.

Don Quixote takes a milkmaid for his true love and mounts the ignoble steed, Rosinante, to rescue the victims of giants and ogres, to liberate virtue everywhere. That this is a form of old age's insanity is assuredly true; that it is senile, and nothing more, is not true so long as the mind may be considered an autonomous medium of life. In one sense, Cervantes appears to tell us, the chivalry enshrined in a work such as *The Faerie Queene* was always fraudulent in that idealism never pretends to correspond with given realities in nature; it is also true that chivalric deeds, as proved by an enlightened view of history, were not always ethically pure, but on the contrary, were masks for practical economic and political motives. Yet chivalry had moved sincere hearts and led to personal, uplifting deeds of heroism; above all, to a culture of the élite. A great epic poem, a great painting, was never a *moral* lie.

Practically considered, it was absurd, and in fact calamitous, for Don Quixote to impoverish himself by acquiring the wonderful library which converts him to his creed of idealistic deeds. But human fate is a notably ambivalent thing: tragic heroism may be preferred to abject passivity. That even the illusion—that is, the literary concept—of that heroism may be preferred, the testimony of this conspicuously lovely film tells us. It is significantly "detached", a work of art not so beautiful in structure, in severity of idea, as in its sensual fleshing of the world's sights and sounds: sights and sounds "de-

An atmosphere at once lush and crystalline is created for the Spanish countryside that is the story's background. A sluttish milkmaid, idealized by the Don as his Lady, Dulcinea, exchanges gaff with Sancho Panza, played by the British comedian George Robey.

ranged" in the mind of an old Spanish nobleman exactly because their luxuriance, their sensuous beauty, hold no reward apart from sublime natures and high-minded acts. He himself, with his delusion, exists just as truly as the nature around him. Here lie the beauty and drama of Cervantes' idea, if also its cruelty: it points to the "existential" gap between an individual and external reality.

Pabst's photography of the Spanish countryside catches the lushness of the commonplace: priest and peasant girl, farm and domestic beast, field grass and straw—all the languor of proliferant nature. A crystalline allure is conferred on things as if seen magically, luminously, somewhat hazy and immaterialized, within mirrors. But is not the camera, through its lens of glass and its medium transparent to light, fitted to do exactly this? What, after all, prevents the Don's appreciation of the animal appetites and their satisfaction except his *age*? Ambiguously enough, something else may contribute to this disability: the existence, perhaps, of a youth whose prime vigour has been itself too "idealistic". The Don's renewed vigour issues, it may be, precisely from this tardy inspiration of vital energy; at his age, it

The ageing Don has been called to his mission to right the world's wrongs as a result of saturation in a marvellous library, whose acquisition has impoverished him. Here is a close view of him armed for the field; he has taken farewell of Dulcinea.

must seem to be bookishness misapplied. Anticlimactic, it is the "sin" for which he is punished.

The differences between the film and Cervantes' novel are not so important. Pabst's work is a creative interpretation rightly based mainly on the all-powerful apparition of a strong Don, not a silly one; a frustrated "Samson" of romanticism, not a posturing relic. Every feeble move by Chaliapin—his strange shuffling gait is especially fine—is strength in disrepair and redeemed gloriously by the voice of vision, to which is added a real voice trained in the transcendent truth of song. The film's music is by Jacques Ibert and Dargomizhsky contributed an aria: "Sierra Nevada". The Don, astride Rosinante, takes sheep and a windmill for giants and fearlessly charges them; he is unhorsed, made ridiculous by nature and man, who laugh and wonder, pity and retire (if they are noble) into remote compassion.

Meanwhile, the complaining Panza is the vigilant demon of common sense. When his master returns home, a defeated knight, his own relevance disappears. The burning of Quixote's library, poetically signifying the destruction of illusion, has a searing contemporary reference to the Nazi edict that ordered a similar conflagration. The flaming books occupy a long scene, dissolving into marvellous patterns of perishing matter as the camera shows us fire changing books into smoke and ashes. Here is an eternal object of human contemplation, a parable of man's own extinction as a physical body. Pabst is perhaps *too* lyrical in this closing passage; the glowing, shimmering patterns may seem too decorative. Yet the tragic voice of Chaliapin tenderly singing the Don's piteous grief as his life expires, this sound floating over the mirage of imagery, gives the end the dimension it called for. Films such as *Don Quixote* enter the hall of fame as evocations of human history.

The full-length figures of Don Quixote and Sancho Panza, mounted for their heroic adventures, make an inspired illustration-in-the-round for Cervantes' classic novel.

The world's casually met objects, presenting the mirage of giants to the Don, invite the retribution of his lance: he will be unhorsed, manhandled by a windmill, sorely wounded and humiliated. He returns home, finally, to die and witness the burning of the library that held his chivalric dreams.

Pure genre: the situation between César, a café proprietor, and Marius his son, in love with Fanny, lies in this level, man-to-man look across a table; besides being essentially comic, the situation becomes critical when Marius (ignorant of Fanny's pregnancy) decides to go to sea.

1932-1933 · FRANCE

Marius Trilogy

Marius

Fanny

César

For French genre, *pure* French genre, for keenness of insight, gift of sure execution and care of character-drawing, nothing on film can compare with this fondly remembered trilogy produced by the author on whose plays it was based, Marcel Pagnol. With the directorial assistance of Alexander Korda on *Marius* and Marc Allegret on *Fanny*, the whole proceeds with an audacious leisureliness inspired by a respect for its literary origin. The trilogy's use of the newly developed dialogue film was thus most distinguished. This set of films is all the more fondly remembered by connoisseurs, I should

guess, because the story was lately remade by other hands in a single-feature version expressly for international consumption; this new version, whatever its arguable merits, is not in the same class with its precursor, and luckily, since the original films are available perennially through revivals in art theatres, we do not have to depend on their "modernization".

In the evidently affectionate adaptation from page to film, realized by Pagnol and his collaborators, we see a serious sort of comedy recalling at times Balzac's *Comédie Humaine* and at other times the simpler portraits of the French common people in *La Femme du Boulanger*, also a work made by Pagnol into a film. Pagnol is a more light-hearted storyteller than Balzac, one less analytical and visionary. Pagnol's film theatre, as such, is always subservient to the end of a given content. True imaginative content, if in pre-existing form, invariably resists tailoring by up-to-date requirements and other technical tamperings. Pagnol the film-designer was not put under the necessity of such handicaps. With Raimu as the lead, César, a Marseilles café owner and father of the hero, Marius, as played by Pierre Fresnay, and Orane Demazis as Fanny (who bears Marius' illegitimate child), Pagnol had just the acting talent he needed, and to full measure. The logic was to effect the transposition of characters created on paper, for the stage, to characters who must be endowed with a new fluency of movement and speech toward the idiom of the dialogue film. Pagnol's success brought to light a decided cinematic flair quite lacking in reverence for the "pure" film narrative.

Our characters here, having room to move in a trilogy, even appear to dawdle at times . . . How much precious footage was intentionally saved from the cutting-room floor! The *brio*, the flavour as of bouillabaisse, would otherwise fail to linger on the palate of memory. Marius, Fanny and César, besides convincing us in many ways they are thoroughly human, actually seem to perspire before our eyes. The trio of leads, with Charpin playing the man manoeuvred into making poor Fanny an honest woman, wear their humanity like the national tricolor: they are as "juicy" as the excellent roast lamb of their country, and as tender of its acting honours as that finest of roasts of the gourmet's approval.

Marius is a young man-about-town in love with Fanny: the two take, when tempted, the ancient path. Fanny's pregnancy, when her lover has to absent himself, becomes the sort of moral nuisance which, on every social level, is weathered by Frenchmen with an incorruptible *savoir-faire*. Among the upper classes, this *savoir-faire* is governed by "the rules of the game" (see Renoir's film in these pages), but in César's waterfront world, it is simply a fact over which to triumph with as little cost in money and as much dignity as possible. Raimu is the presiding genius of a real, picturesque milieu, its philosopher, its "bouncer", its judge, guide and dispenser of wise forgiveness. As the man for whom matrimony with Fanny is ready-made cuckoldry, Charpin has a chance to practise his superb style as a character-comedian, and does so without blemish.

The versatile Pierre Fresnay never seemed less of an "actor" than here. Of course, it is obvious that he, like Mlle. Demazis, wears make-up calculated to make them seem younger than they are; in a day when film studios had fewer technical resources, this detail transpires rather egregiously. Yet such casual demerits have very little influence on the total, as pleasure-giving as it is. One of the most touching reconciliations between lovers that I recall in films is that between Marius and Fanny when, at long last, he returns to claim her as his wife.

Spruced up, debonair, Marius, the man-about-town, has proved irresistible to Fanny, who has to withstand the blow of his leavetaking: natural causes then produce natural effects and she finds herself a healthy, unwedded mother.

César has his social position to maintain: he is the waterfront's luminous spirit and never slow to assert this high rôle even if it entails holding a baby on his lap.

The situation must be saved: César, deep at work on the problem of preserving Fanny's happiness and honour, is aware that humour is a great help, too.

The solution in person: a gentleman of means and reputation, after some amusing difficulties, willingly consents to make Fanny the honest woman that all are agreed she deserves to be.

A delicate matter is that now his son exists and Fanny's "husband", Panisse, has grown so fond of the child as to consider him irrevocably his own. But human sweetness (aided, naturally, by the will of God) manages to solve everything in the twisted affairs of Marius, Fanny and César, with a consummate chuckle and a care for

When, at last, the prodigal lover returns in uniform, César's human kindness rises to the new situation: its solution is just as desirable, after all, as it is awkward.

romantic justice. This sense of justice has permeated the spirit of the collaborators all the way to the camera men. That erring humanity is endowed with a saving grace is what this trio of films nobly commemorates: what a boon at a time when true quiet and true wisdom are the objects of hungry soul-searching!

The reunion of the lovers: the true solution comes about in one of the most eloquent and touching reconciliation scenes to appear in the history of the film.

Zéro de Conduite

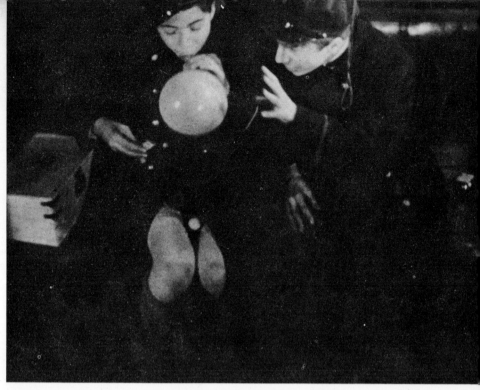

In a sequence unparalleled for forthright simplicity and candour, Vigo's film opens with a train ride taken by two military-costumed students of a French school: the boys demonstrate innocently suggestive gewgaws to each other.

Naturally, true rarities in the film-making world are rarer than in the world of other arts; this fact is so striking that when a true filmic rarity does appear, however modest its outline, it is guaranteed a special niche in the esteem of those who cherish classics of the film. When Jean Vigo, who died of tuberculosis in 1934, appeared on the scene in France and made his few contributions, film experts there and abroad never doubted the lastingness of his work. Of his two principal films, *Zéro de Conduite* (1933) and *L'Atalante* (1934), it seems to me that the former by all odds is the superior, both for originality and execution; in sum, it is more of a piece with the personal genius of its maker. The film is an unquestionable, indeed an incomparable masterpiece—for its informal ease, its pure eyesight, its unabashed imagination. As with certain instinctive artists, Vigo's personality seemed to attract to it all needed materials, and to render them on film with a directness, simplicity and unity that only the most fortunate artists acquire and enjoy. "Enjoy"! Sheer enjoyment, blanketing a sly satire, is the flesh and blood of this work, whose black-and-white medium and ungymnastic camera have the overwhelming efficacy of innocent children to stimulate and transfix the heart.

In no other film, with the possible exception of *La Maternelle* (where younger children are involved), have children in a theatrical medium seemed so natural and—I shan't say "so innocent", but "so purged of the idea of evil"; this, despite the fact that they are all schoolboys, who in France, at their spindle-legged age, are governed entirely by men; and despite the fact that the film's hilarious action turns on the successful plot of four of the boys to overthrow the school's government. But it is precisely *because* of those facts that this exquisite farce, at once gentle and lively, is a believable fantasy. A French friend of mine once remarked, smiling: "Why is *Zéro de Conduite* considered so extraordinary? It's just like every boys' school in France!" This was really a tribute to Vigo's pure grasp of the subject matter from his own poetically transfigured view of it.

Doubtless, getting boys of eight to twelve or thirteen to behave like amusing little barbarians, who yet are so much human gold, requires a kind of magic; for if any of the action or portrayal tended to be stagey or self-consciously exaggerated, the illusion would go *poof*! Only that magical quality called empathy endowed Vigo with the ability to create what remains a unique triumph on film: a group of bizarrely imagined impressions bent on parodying the world of schoolroom and dormitory by presenting it through the eyes of the pupils. The school principal is a boyish-looking midget in formal clothes, a black beard and preciously simulated dignity; the headmaster and the spying monitor are stiff human puppets, respectively nicknamed Fishface and the Creep. The athletics master, who draws

Their school is out of this world: the adult spy known as the Creep catches the athletics instructor (who meanwhile can draw a caricature with a pen held between his teeth) entertaining the students.

Four students form a ring to assassinate school decorum: here the dormitory is wrecked with a lyric passion appropriate to ancient saturnalia as well as modern Surrealism; the riot is ineffably climaxed with a processional dance in slow motion (above).

caricatures with a pen held in his mouth while standing on his hands, imitates Charlie Chaplin during recess in the schoolyard. He is the only teacher enlisting the boys' sympathy.

To the dormitory, where the tyrannical headmaster sleeps in a curtained-off bed, a night of terror comes when the whole school, led by the four little conspirators, wreck the premises. Pillows fly, mattresses are ripped up, beds overturned; all decorum is raped while the headmaster leaps about in his nightshirt making futile protests. The climax is a triumphal march of wild, half-naked boys up and down the ruined dormitory, paper lanterns aloft on improvised standards and white feathers thickening the air. Suddenly, to thin, eerie music, we see the march in slow motion, its rush turned into a ritual dance. I cannot think of any filmic effect more irresistible than this majestic image of childish ecstasy; one's eyes brim with its poetry and one's heart bows before the justice of its naked riot. All the previous impish humour, touched with small-boy obscenity, issues in joy like the glad processions of the old Greek mysteries . . . Natural comedy, becoming lyric drama, unveils a glimpse of the soul's legendary rebirth. For purity of purpose, for unforgettable marks of a humanity exalted by children, *Zéro de Conduite* is virtually in a class by itself.

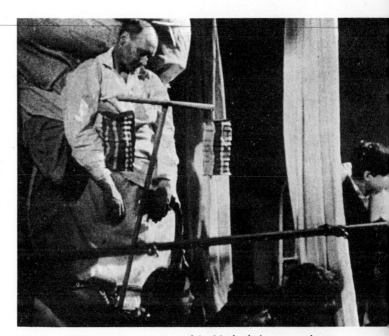

The dormitory master, prostrated in his bed, is set up in a mock-crucifixion scene that remains an unforgettable emblem for the film: below him are the four victorious rebels.

A lull before graduation ceremonies, next day, to be presided over by the Director (the midget in the centre): the ceremonies will be broken up with objects hurled from the roof by the four conspirators, who have hidden in the attic; serious yet hilarious, unique, the film deserves 100 for conduct.

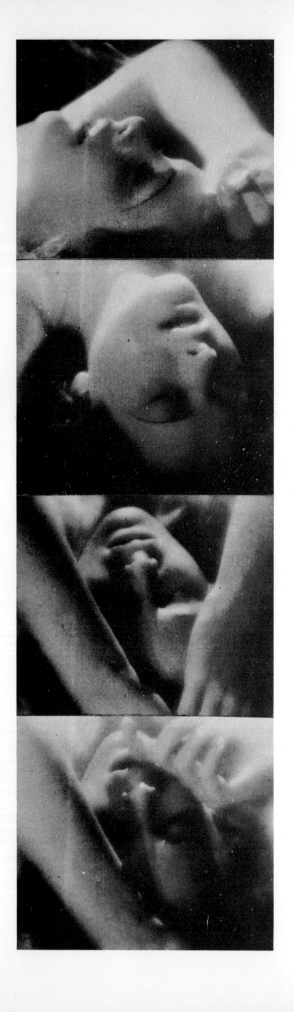

Ecstasy

Ranking this film as a classic, rather than as a curiosity remembered for aesthetically dubious reasons, may seem to some open to question. I should like to note *Ecstasy* as a minor classic, not important as a finished work of art but arresting as an unusual gesture, in an unusual direction, at a moment when its subject—viewed seriously as I think its maker viewed it—required courage to film and offer to the general public. Uniqueness, in fact, is one of the criteria making films eligible for inclusion here. The year that *Ecstasy* was made by a well-known professional Czech director, Gustav Machaty, was not propitious. It was 1933, no upcoming year anywhere in the world except in Germany, where the Nazis had emerged. Sound, moreover, was just voicing its siren chorus, though somewhat less actively in European studios than in American. Machaty, however, was inspired by the person of Hedy

Taken directly from the film reel, these single frames show Hedy Lamarr in the film which gained her international attention and led to her Hollywood stardom; the ecstasy she epitomizes is golden through being neither elusive nor obvious. On this page, her face appears in the positions in which it is seen in the theatre; on the following page, all four views are uniformly reversed to show how images, when seen from different viewpoints in space, may evoke subtly different feelings.

Lamarr, who was then Hedwig Kiesler, and did not acquire her famous surname till she became a beauty, vying in Hollywood (at least *visually*) with Garbo.

Miss Lamarr was a genuine beauty, one of the fairest, I think, ever to grace a film frame. There is some poetic justice in the fact that *Ecstasy*, offbeat as a commercial film, was also offbeat in featuring not Miss Lamarr's best asset as seen by Hollywood, her face, but her best asset as Machaty saw it, her figure. The truth was, her lower legs were thick and her hips wide; she never seemed to reduce and transcend—as Garbo reduced and transcended—those conventional defects. Nevertheless her figure was lovely in 1933 and was documented by this film with a chaste discretion—a discretion to which, perhaps, censorship added. The plot, termed by one critic "a psychological study of a sex-frustrated young wife", is surely credible enough if at the same time it falls wide of either depth or subtlety. That poetry, not plot, is the pith of the matter, is evident from the work's general looseness of structure.

Its scenes of most interest, filmed with a charmingly naïve photographic zest, show the heroine floating nude in water and slipping through the woods in the same natural state; the camera follows and watches her somewhat like a voyeur, but more like an aesthete thrilled body and soul by having stumbled on a lady who has just undressed for a dip in the water. Machaty's handling of film as an art form is a little cavalier and yet by no means without conscious responsibility. This quality is still a result more of inspiration than of routine, subterfuge or apology. *Ecstasy* is not a cheap film and was not conceived and produced merely to make money. Its casual sound effects—all off-screen except one sequence of directly synchronized speech—seem special contributions to a labour of love.

I fancy that, as an impressionistic poem rather than a modern triangle drama (being, as the latter, weak), *Ecstasy* has influenced the world's experimental film movement more than is suspected. Public attention was first drawn to it, naturally, as a censorable article, a status whose mesmeric charm seems reluctant to leave it; truthfully, it remains an epicure's item. Despite its professional methods, it has the flair of a camera made candid as if spontaneously, through ardour, and thus "amateur" but not "amateurish". Machaty never made a film nearly equal in fame to this one and seems permanently to have dropped from the film-making scene. But this memorial to his unique impulse should not soon be forgotten. To illustrate its classic nature, the coherent group of images taken directly from the reel faultlessly conveys the unabashed eroticism implied in the title. In films of very recent years, we have been treated to so many brutal, and brutally convincing, aspects of women in sexual situations that this vision of Hedy Lamarr seems one of lyric enchantment, and for this reason, if no other, earns representation here.

Redhead, the shame of a rustic French household, makes mute appeal to the sombre coldness of his mother, who has borne him illegitimately and for this reason lives with her husband in complete estrangement.

A prophetic pair: Redhead and his five-year-old sweetheart, to whom he "marries" himself in a charming Spring ritual, anticipate the two children of a later, also memorable French film, *Jeux Interdits*.

Poil de Carotte

1933 · FRANCE

This is not an "important" classic. To state this, I know, is to invite the question: "Then why is it here?" No film is here without a reason which I think important to the interests of culture and to filmic potentialities as well as realizations. As with minor literary classics, a film may hang in the memory for an episode, a scene, an actor, or a rare, unpretentious style. Yet I think such isolated elements would not be remembered if they had appeared in stupid and irrelevant contexts. Nothing is brilliant in the indisputably *large* sense in *Poil de Carotte* (*Redhead*), though it is directed by the notable Julien Duvivier with exemplary taste. The whole is suffused with a fine humane poetry, the sort of poetry we associate with France, with a society starred for its instinctive tolerance for human frailty, human vices. "Immoral"? The French have earned a world reputation for being immoral, but that reputation has been so salted and sweetened, served up in so many beguiling dishes, that it is blended with the time-stream we know as Culture.

I choose *Poil de Carotte* as an example of Culture with quite specifiable beauties emerging from a situation which is sordid in its tragicomedy and yet ends on a very tender note of harmony, the sort of revelation of human grace that marks the "sad story with a happy ending". Again we find French sentiment proving itself unsentimentally. This national trait comes through an ordeal of agony without the emotional fireworks of the Germans (see *Maedchen in Uniform* or *Metropolis*) or the moral self-consciousness of the English (consider, for example, *Pygmalion*). The French film says there is a strong, very simple, lyric spirit in life: never slight it, for it is part of the backbone of all culture.

The little hero is first seen martyred to an "immoral" situation between his ostensible parents, a corrosive situation that might spoil the future of any very young individual. The community is small, rustic, ingrown with the usual bourgeois prejudices. He is illegitimate, his mother's offspring by her adultery, and has lived since birth in the midst of a feud between the lady and her husband, who have kept respectable appearances only

Boy, candle, chiaroscuro and composition lift this film moment out of its context to the status of an independent still image; seen in context, it becomes an equally fine cinematic image.

Poetic pathos saturates the efforts of Redhead to overcome the cruelty of being a burden of dishonour in his home. He and his little friend pause in the doorway of an inn where later his supposed father is told that Redhead means to hang himself.

by remaining together upon rigidly estranged terms; she might be the housekeeper of a taciturn recluse. When the film opens, the lady tries to break the ice in sheer yearning for human companionship, but to no avail. Both adults regard the boy as symbol of their marriage's failure and a community shame. The truth has been guessed by the village because the boy has inherited his red hair from a memorable fellow-countryman.

The famous Harry Baur, as the cuckold, is somewhat "heavy" and un-French but so forceful an actor that he builds up conviction out of his inherent powers. Robert Lynen as Redhead has an eloquent personality whose only proper description is *poetic*. The boy is infinitely saddened by living a hollow, embittering life as "son" of this household; his status is half a lie and holds nothing but inhumanity; his strategies to escape it, to bring fertility and pleasure into living, have the genius of poetry. The five-year-old girl who dogs his steps becomes partner in a beautiful idea. For why, one spring day, shouldn't they be ceremoniously married to each other? A child's game becomes an exquisite ritual of serious meaning when Redhead decks himself and his little friend with flower garlands and they parade through the fields. Many besides myself must treasure this episode because of the lyric simplicity with which it is acted and photographed. But daily despair reasserts its grip on Redhead as he grows increasingly aware of his home's cruel aridity; in a burst of childish grief, hopelessly deprived of love, he decides to hang himself.

Racing home, the stricken man (Harry Baur) cuts down the boy in time to save his life. The reconciliation between them, with its reversal of the family situation, is dramatically moving.

His supposed father, notified just in time while drinking at an inn, races back home and cuts him down from a rafter in the attic. Their reconciliation creates the glow essential to all "magic" reversals of feeling.

La
Maternelle

A French day school: cause and setting for *La Maternelle*.

It will be hard ever to forget this celebration of mother love made in France in 1934 and often brought from the archives of film museums to be seen again. Strikingly enough, its subject is the yearning for mother love in a little girl abandoned by her real mother, a prostitute, and seeking a substitute mother in one of the maids working at her school. What could have been trite and sentimental, or harsh and moralistic, is handled with a direct and scrupulous tenderness seldom found in film studios anywhere, any time. The setting of the French day school was more than a "setting" for Jean Benoit-Lévy and Marie Epstein, who made the movie; it was a cause—the marrow of the matter. As an achievement, the film remained unique in the career of Benoit-Lévy, also distinguished as the author of a book on film theory. *La Maternelle* proves that motion pictures may be the medium of a vocation as earnest as that of experts in all fields of child education and yet produce a work of the imagination.

A prostitute is tempted to abandon her little girl, one of the day-school's pupils; the child anticipates her tragedy.

Filmically, *La Maternelle* merely keeps step with the staticized convention of telling a story that came with the arrival of the "dialogue film". There is no fast action or melodramatic shock to diversify the mild pace or make the spectator jump; quite the contrary, the action drags, self-concerned, along. Though everything is done artfully, at times "stagily", each detail rings true through honesty of intention. We never doubt this is a real day school before us and these very young children its actual pupils. Seldom are we taken far from the school itself; the camera seems to embrace each child, leaving it with a caress, while each is singled out as a "type", with beautiful feeling for the chunky and cute, droll and grotesque, pathetic, helpless, poetic thing a small child may variously be. Most of the children are from poor homes; there is the undernourished little boy who never smiles, but from whom the maid, adult heroine of the story, at last coaxes a smile; there is the roguish little boy who swallows a stolen coin and embarrassingly must be purged of it. When the undernourished little boy dies, our emotion is magically replaced with something to smile at; this rhythm of alternate sadness and gladness is faithfully maintained.

The little girl demanding a new mother-love feels such passion that she tries to commit suicide when the maid to whom she is so attached accepts a marriage proposal from a director of the school board. When rescued from the river into which she casts herself, her morbid little figure has begun to glow from the film frame. Pauline Elambert as the child and Madeleine Renaud as the maid (virtually unknown abroad in other rôles) seem identical with the rôles they portray. In romantic fashion, this "maid", as we know from the start, is well educated enough to be a teacher and has taken her job meekly as a means of livelihood after being jilted by her fiancé. Frail but pretty, herself lonely for love, she is warmhearted and has earned the devotion of every child in the school.

This rôle and her little adorer's are cast with an inevitability which makes minor artifice retire and major reality take command. The school's fat cook, its headmistress and a visiting old professor are acted broadly, with a delicate edge of farce that the action breaks down into the overwhelming sentiment of the finale. The brooding, sweet, searching pathos of the two main characters dissolves into what the patience and care of the film-makers have surely built around them: the infinitely touching quality of crude little bits of human life seeking the love that will *gently* initiate them into growing up.

Her solace, a maid working at the school, becomes her obsession. Pauline Elambert as the adoring child gives a performance of genius.

The maid, responding to the child's passion for mother-love, is proposed to by a director of the school board and finally accepts him.

Her jealousy a morbid grief, the child has thrown herself in the river; saved, she is brought back to her foster mother – and to a world of renewed faith and understanding.

Ostensibly made to show off Flemish painting, Jacques Feyder's highly artful film had a momentous political timing: the peaceable city fathers of a Flemish town like nothing better than the lighter side of politics such as having an official portrait painted.

Something to make an artist throw down his easel, however, is the very disturbing news that the Duke of Alba, Spanish Governor of Flanders, is marching on them: a massacre would not be unusual. Beyond camera range, the year is 1934.

La Kermesse Héroïque

1934 · FRANCE

or *Carnival in Flanders*

If there was ever a typical French pleasantry, on film or off, worldly and impervious to all but the right note, the right pitch, the right style, *La Kermesse Héroïque* is it — something I say at the risk of repeating myself. Perennially, the French take the same risk; they repeated it when Paris became an "open city" before another decade had passed. To be sure, in World War II, a resistance movement appeared in France as strong as that in Italy. Yet Paris, when the Germans entered in triumph, seemed in a swoon, while, when Rome was in the same position, one can imagine the Italians seething and cursing their erstwhile allies. Jacques Feyder's famous film, done with true Gallic polish, was made from Charles Spaak's novel laid in seventeenth-century Flanders, and its innocent purpose was mainly, it was said, to recreate Flemish painting with photographic means; in the same act, however, it made "collaboration with the enemy" look like the better part of moral wisdom. *La Kermesse Héroïque*, a product of French art, won French applause when it garnered the Grand Prix du Cinéma Français as well as the medal awarded by the Société d'Encouragement à l'Art et l'Industrie. With unfortunate simultaneity, it was likewise singled out by

the Nazi régime — for then rather transparent reasons — as one of the year's most important films.

Ironically, Jacques Feyder and his colleagues (as Georges Sadoul has pointed out) were among those persecuted by the Germans after their conquest of France. Is it too much to attribute to the French a special chameleonism? — I mean to the French temperament proper, implying that, to some degree, French politics would share this peculiar virtue (or vice)? Personified culture in France, conceivably, is a virtuoso so supreme as to imagine he can play any "tune" and reveal himself an unerring master. Is this the tradition of the conquered state which conquers its military conquerors through culture? France, as a nation soon restored to autonomy by its allies, was not obliged to undergo that precise ethical test.

Human nature being what it is, I cannot but think that *La Kermesse Héroïque* is as much an honour to French ethics as to French art; as the latter, it helps France pile up historically, from cinematograph to Cinerama, its present edge over other film-making nations. Related to the French, while distinct from them, the Flemish play here an amusingly successful game; in fact, a stratagem

The city mothers, after suitable consultation, decide on a daring emergency measure: they will welcome the blood-thirsty soldiers with something to slake, and otherwise satiate, their "bloodthirstiness". The film's gay but naughty political joke reaped a contemporary whirlwind.

A subterfuge in support of the daring measure: The Mayor pretends to be dead so that the welcome being offered the Duke and his army seems a sacrifice twice over from the mourning town – especially from the bereaved Mayoress, played by Françoise Rosay (right).

considered legitimate for the losing side since time immemorial. The Spanish Governor of Flanders is announced as descending fierily upon a serenely peaceful Flemish town, which expects to be decimated in the hallowed manner. But its ladies, led by the Mayor's wife (Françoise Rosay), decide, with the consent of the masculine town council, to resort to an extreme measure to avoid plunder and murder. This is simply to lay out a feast for the invaders and let natural appetites, embellished by courtesies, take their course. After the hectic "carnival" (ambiguously fleshly indeed), the warlike Spaniards will retire like well-fed guests.

And so they do, as if the issue depended on all-subduing cuisine. Part of the comedy, it must be stated, is an elaborate insinuation confusing the actual tracks left by the several appetites. This is like a story told in *The Decameron*, strictly for the amusement of aristocrats who would be vulgar to assume it as applying to themselves. It is surely a mockery of the chivalric tradition: a bourgeois innovation in the moral cuisine. What can be said for it is that it works, and like all triumphs of wit, ought to be regarded, implicitly, as a figure of speech: exactly as are many classical paintings! One feels the Flemish ladies and gentlemen are overcome with self-congratulation when the outwitted "conquerors" leave. Yet Eros, in the eyes of the French, is perpetually a god exacting his due. We see more than one romantic tear shed by the Flemish womanhood. Is

the Flemish manhood really cuckolded? On the other hand, I believe the adage "All is fair in love and war" has never been repudiated, in substance, by any nation.

Madam Mayor proves herself a born enchantress. A shrewd priest (Louis Jouvet) here enjoys the tricky situation; in fact, the tricky situation turns to wassail, more or less genteel but satiating, more or less, the enemy's insatiability.

For the first time in films, the Expressionist exterior is used to indicate passage from the ordinary, sane world to one of mental hallucination. Persons: a severely depressed doctor and a snubbed prostitute.

The doctor, in flight from a fatal medical experiment, tries to drown himself, but is saved. Taken back to the hospital he has left in dishonour, he walks the corridors of another world.

1936 · GERMANY

The Eternal Mask

The eerie passageways of schizophrenia lead him to a man with a face like death: it seems to be the patient who has died from being injected with the doctor's new serum.

This is a film that deserves its status in film history, and thus in this book, not for acting or directing, nor for purely filmic imagination, but entirely for intellectual honesty combined with originality of purpose. Produced in Switzerland from a German script, it treats a subject that, till then, had not found its way beyond the mental clinic itself. It is as though clinical psychology had decided to illustrate its teachings with a scientific fairy tale. Is the point of this tale, as presented, viable? I think that, taking it on broad principles, it is; we need judge it no further than that, for *The Eternal Mask* is a story before it is a case history. With various geometric patterns of shimmering light replacing the painted décors of Cubism, it bears, not implausibly, a family resemblance to *Dr. Caligari* and other films of the bizarre school, both French and German—films which explore the vagaries of the mind solely for their fantasy or entertainment value.

However, *The Eternal Mask* also suggests its strange kinships by being laid in a hospital and, like many

102

filmed "crime stories", it concerns a scientist's obsession. The obsession here is benign, that of a doctor who is determined to cure a fatal disease with a serum he has invented. The opening is the opposite of mystifying or melodramatic; we are in the world of sane reality, scientifically ordered and restrained. Against orders from the hospital chief, the doctor injects his serum into a patient whose disease has reached the hopeless stage; at first the man arouses optimism by improving, but then has a sudden relapse and dies. Inevitably the doctor's action is discovered. In shame and guilt, he vacates his post at the hospital and hides himself from the world.

Much disturbed, he sits in cafés as one bereft and wanders around the city at night, convinced his honour is destroyed, his career at an end. Already the ordinary "sane" world of the hospital has been replaced by a city suggesting the Expressionistic sets of many German films of the past. The doctor has entered the world of mental delusion, and in a fit of despair throws himself into the river from a bridge. His impressions of drowning lead us into the world of hallucination that possesses his mind after he is recovered from the water and returned to the hospital. He has lost his sense of identity and lives in a world of subconscious fears; he is not violent, but he treads the hospital corridors like a zombie.

It develops that the outraged hospital chief, even before his errant doctor is brought back, has learned that the serum can do its work after all. However, only its inventor knows the formula for it. To save the lives of patients still in crisis, therefore, the doctor must be restored to his normal mind. The struggle between his dominating guilt and the efforts of his colleagues, with the help of the dead patient's widow, induce a series of dream states in him in which past events and his present inner conflict are represented by a series of actions in strange-looking and strangely connected rooms that have the distorted, eerie and transformed quality of both dream action and the Expressionist theatre style.

The quiet, conscientiously pursued method of the film is obvious: the bizarre stage-world of Expressionism is here the chambers of the soul, to whose melting, frightening passageways the blow of his guilt has condemned the doctor's mind. The inspiration of a young colleague serves to bring the unmoored identity of the doctor back to itself, to the world it truly desires, by contact with the implements of his science as symbols of doing good. The issue has swayed back and forth even as the camera between the unstable dream world and the firm corridors of the hospital. Moving awkwardly at times, *The Eternal Mask*, which is literally a symbol of illusion, has a chaste and reassuring presence when compared with films showing our current world of infinite moral quibbling.

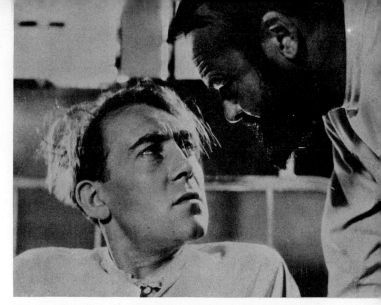

The head doctor, having forbidden the new serum's use, discovers it is really effectual, but only his bereft subordinate knows its formula; he must be brought back to normal to save many lives.

The methods of Expressionist fantasy illustrate the work of psychic suggestion: the doctor regains his normal mind by lifting the mask here to see his own living features.

La Grande Illusion

Six French officers in a German prison camp during World War I muse on the topsy-turvy fortunes of war. The principals: Jean Gabin, left, as an Air Corps pilot, Maréchal, lately shot down while carrying Captain de Boeldieu, (Pierre Fresnay, centre); and Dalio as Rosenthal, right, member of a rich Jewish family, philosophically reconciled to "playing soldier".

La Grande Illusion is interesting, distinguished and important for a whole suite of reasons. Intellectually and emotionally, it is one of the most scrupulous of all films in approach, method and execution; with Charles Spaak (author of *La Kermesse Héroïque*) collaborating with the director, Jean Renoir, on its script, it started with much in its favour and relinquished nothing as it proceeded. It was endowed, furthermore, with the soul indispensable to what it pretended to be and was: an *heroic* film. The "grand illusion" of the title is an illusion only by discourtesy; the motif so described is historically real, and if the chivalry for which this film is a requiem has really vanished, it occasioned here, by a large margin, the tenderest and most towering elegy of its kind in film history.

Renoir was destined to do a more amusing work in *La Règle du Jeu*, but not a greater one. Comparing the two films, a striking fact is accented: each is a differently mooded epic on the theme of chivalry as a disappearing if tenacious value in world society. According to the action of *La Grande Illusion*, World War I became this value's self-conscious epitaph; two career officers (one French, one German) being delegated to recognize the fact, lament it from their personal viewpoints, and act

out its death agony. The *style* with which this is done belongs indivisibly to a first-rate triumvirate: Renoir the director and two actors, Pierre Fresnay and Erich von Stroheim, both illustrious and fitted for their rôles by what I should call historic necessity operating in the realm of film and in the cultural tradition at large.

That Fresnay and Stroheim have the support of another pair of the first rank, Jean Gabin and Dalio, also playing French officers, but of castes different from those of Captains de Boeldieu and von Rauffenstein (Fresnay and Stroheim), meant that Renoir had the acumen and good luck to gain for his film four leads incomparable for what was required of them. The film glitters in the sun of such fortunate casting. Renoir's vigilance toward the nostalgic notation of a style he instinctively admired, and yet whose anachronism his sense of reality forced him to burlesque (as later he burlesqued it in *La Règle de Jeu*), creates the aesthetic warp and woof of *La Grande Illusion*—braids its uniforms and styles its soldiers, confers its medals with solemn finesse and outfits it with the pure white gloves of aristocratic vision. "Aristocratic vision": is this a justifiable term for film style? Well, "aristocratic" pertains literally to the "rule of the best"; I do not know what director or set of actors, with the

These men and roommates are successfully digging a long tunnel to make their escape; the respective characterizations are masterfully done according to the prescription of director Jean Renoir and Charles Spaak, who collaborated with Renoir on the script. The day before the tunnel is completed, notice comes that all the prisoners are to be moved.

help of what writer, could have done any better than those engaged here.

With the graceful behaviour of fortune that at times regulates the course of the best things, *La Grande Illusion* had the luck of acquiring the veteran film translator, Herman G. Weinberg, to convert its dialogue into English captions. *La Grande Illusion* is one of the more than 350 foreign films for which Weinberg, to date, has performed the same office. Along with the Pagnol trilogy, *Marius, Fanny, César*, it is among the most distinguished on which he ever worked; Weinberg was, incidentally, one of the 150 critics polled in 1958 at the Brussels festival to select the world's twelve greatest films. *La Grande Illusion*, made two decades before the poll including it in that number, fairly brims with significance. Actually, it was another swan song for the silent-film-that-was and the dialogue-film-to-be: a pivot where the merits and demerits of each are found blended. Outstanding about its method is its concern for personal characterizations, episodes and individual scenes — all elements which the tendency of film style, since then, has subordinated to fluent narrative and devices of the camera. An odd structural weakness, apparently taken in stride by Renoir, is the break appearing after the French officers, Maréchal (Gabin) and Rosenthal (Dalio) now

fast friends, have escaped from the castle-prison to which they have been moved along with Boeldieu. We take farewell of Boeldieu and Rauffenstein as soon as the latter's duty has compelled him to shoot Boeldieu; thereafter, we follow the fortunes of the pair allowed to escape during the prisoners' planned demonstration.

If we pause for critical reflection, we will not be disappointed. Despite the interests of filmic technique — how little, for example, film should owe established *theatre* tradition — a film artist must hold a musical sense and a pictorial sense among his plastic gifts. Renoir has left no doubt that harmony was a major asset of his; he understood the basic rhythm to be maintained by every art medium, no matter which, and that a fine balance must be reached among a work's given elements, regardless of their category, variety or quantity. When, quite recently, Renoir intentionally abandoned those principles, the result was a shocking deflation of his artistry: *Le Déjeuner sur l'Herbe*. For conscientious workmanship, the present film has few equals among the film's most artistic products and belongs to the superlative "minority" of the classics represented in this book.

Yet *La Grande Illusion* dates itself by its very editing, particularly in its earliest moments when Maréchal is supposed to pilot Boeldieu over enemy territory and is shot down by the German "ace", the old-school soldier, Captain von Rauffenstein. The two Frenchmen escape death, Maréchal sustaining only a broken arm, and are then ceremoniously received by their victorious enemy and entertained at table. In the version I saw lately in revival, not a single shot concerning the flight and shooting down of Boeldieu's plane appears; each succes-

Now at a great, old, seemingly escape-proof castle used as a prison, the three men have met Captain von Rauffenstein as played by Erich von Stroheim, a punctilious old-school German militarist who shot down Boeldieu's plane; here Rauffenstein has the regretted duty of shooting Boeldieu off the castle roof.

sive scene of the action I have just described might, for all its filmic essence, take place on the stage. *La Grande Illusion*, indeed, is a "war film" with a very extraordinary "merit": in the midst of a World War, not *one* battle scene is shown us. Its absence is especially noticeable only because we see the film again after another quarter-century of filmic evolution. One virtue to replace "filmic-ness" here is pure imaginative invention, of which there are many instances. The military dandy, Rauffenstein (supreme in his Stroheimish period glamour) is making dinner-table conversation with his honoured captive, Boeldieu, whom he clearly distinguishes from his inferior officer, Maréchal, when a huge floral tribute to dead French soldiers is brought in for Rauffenstein's approval. In that curiously low, curiously retarded, studiously refined tone of which Stroheim was the master, he apologizes to Boeldieu for the regrettable coincidence.

From step to step *La Grande Illusion* reveals a brilliance of authority which one doubts would exist without the precise formulation of men and their deeds actually passing before the eyes. Stroheim had never performed so well, with such ready-made backbone of character, and never did so thereafter. The metal support he must wear around his neck because of war injuries is an inspired touch, making his ramrod style (he can bend only at his hips) a physical parody of his military deportment. This rôle proves he was best when guided not by himself but another. His politesse, his irony, are matters he had already taken to heart here: in Rauffenstein he lived his own ideal image. Imagine! Rauffenstein and

Boeldieu, German and Frenchman, collaborate under a code of honour binding enemy to enemy—a code which does not exclude the rules of war as a deadly game.

The relations between Boeldieu and his pilot, Maréchal, build up the general crisis when the former elects, by a trick involving the whole prison, to give Maréchal and Rosenthal, a rich Jew and a fervid French patriot, an opportunity to escape. The successful device is fraught with meaning because Maréchal has complained to Rosenthal that while Boeldieu is a "regular guy", a strange intangible something separates them. The case is that, however regular Boeldieu may be (and his self-sacrifice proves this beyond doubt), social caste and all it implies separate him from the Rosenthals and Maréchals, who may be honourable but are not noble, who may have many virtues but lack those of intellect and elegance. He and Rauffenstein communicate on a higher level which, though it may be a dying social value, is ever present to them, makes them and their destinies as high a mutual concern as the patriotism that divides them. This is, I think, a profound human paradox, with a curiously global echo.

When Rauffenstein must bring down Boeldieu with his own revolver as the Frenchman, carrying out his subterfuge, darts among the shadows of the castle's peaked roofs, playing a flute, and when Boeldieu (the German's bullet hitting higher on the body than it was aimed) quietly dies after a very moving interview with the grieved Rauffenstein, we have a touch on life deep yet unexaggerated, rare yet entirely persuasive; it is the same rich and particular touch we have seen in a previous effective episode when the imprisoned officers, including some Englishmen, have put on a theatrical show in which most of the men dress up as women. The gay performance is in full swing when the news arrives that a certain strategic town has been regained by the French; in a flash, all the wigs come off, and every bepainted Frenchman (and seemingly the English too) stands at attention and sings the *Marseillaise* as the German officers, an invited part of the audience, leave in humiliation and mute anger. It is a lovely stroke, brought off with incomparable nicety, and unashamedly theatrical in its drama. How delicately it prepares us for the tragic atmosphere of the great German castle, to which the four French officers are then moved, and where Rauffenstein now presides like a monkish antiquarian, relegated to a passive part in the war! Boeldieu and he then play opposite each other like master chess players in a championship match and Boeldieu, as it were, sacrifices his own victory to France's. The distinct episode that follows, concerning only Maréchal and Rosenthal, is illustrated here; it is pale, I think, the hollower part of the "grand illusion" that unites a dying military caste with a French theatre whose vitality still goes on.

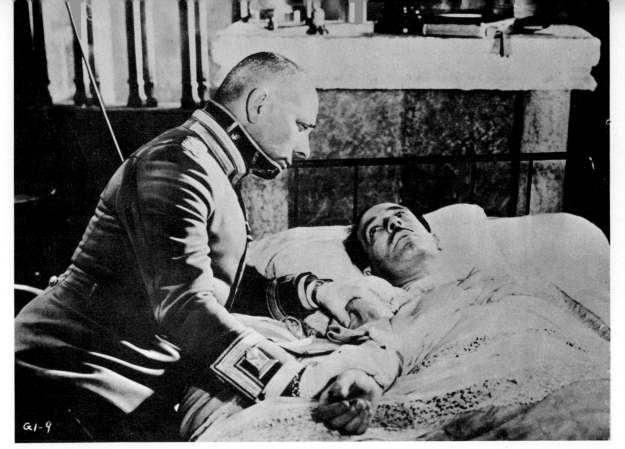

Much that is profound and profoundly interesting has taken place: Boeldieu has invented a way to let Maréchal and Rosenthal escape; in the above deeply touching scene, Frenchman and German, as Boeldieu dies, know they are part of a requiem for the fast-vanishing code of chivalrous warfare.

The sequel: Maréchal and Rosenthal, having suffered bitterly while making their way back to France, chance on a ministering angel in a German farm woman, who falls in love with Maréchal. But the war is not over and Maréchal returns with Rosenthal to their country still in peril, rounding out a finely wrought epic of nobly humane values.

One of the dazzling shots introducing us to the heroic staging of the 1936 Olympic Games in Berlin: Sizzling flame is almost tangible in this close-up of a gigantic torch.

1938 · GERMANY

Olympia

Here is unrolled a paean to the human body in action, to athletics as a modern ideal, an obsession with the out-of-doors. Conceived by Nazi officials as a propaganda film to be made from the Olympic Games held in Berlin in 1936, it was issued in several versions suitable for export to participating nations whose winners were respectively featured. As Nazi propaganda, the film harmonized with the exceptional passion of German scholars for Classical culture. Enlisting the finest photographic skill in Germany, it had the further asset of supervision by the talented Leni Riefenstahl, an actress turned director-editor. *Olympia* survives as one of the grandest documentaries in world film archives and it undoubtedly is the most impressive film ever to deal with field sports. Regarded aside from its political function, it provides a fascinating study of its innate content: whole-souled, harmless physical competition.

Reel-washed of its Nazi motivation, it can even rate as a sincere tribute to the Greek ideal as still perpetuated in the Olympic Games. Fräulein Riefenstahl tried systematically to make her film as "classical" as possible. It opens solemnly with multiply exposed views of the temple colonnades and shifts fluently to a torch being lit by a runner at Olympia in Greece, following the torch as it is handed from runner to runner, till the last one, in long, easy strides, enters the huge, decorated Berlin stadium. Considering that any existing version is apt to have haphazard editing, these Games emerge as an exciting, dramatic and even lyric expression of the beauties of physical being in the flush of

competition among champions. The diving contest, in thrilling montage, is treated as a poem of human flight, while the high jump, filmed glamorously at twilight, is a marvel in slow-motion. Innumerable cameramen, as well as many editors, are responsible for an Homerically-scaled collective piece of film-making.

One can discern national traits in the performances as well as the looks of the athletes. The American Negro, Jesse Owens, is a portrait in swift, highlighted black and deep force. Glenn Morris, American winner of the Decathlon, seems to bring to kinetic life the ancient statue of the Discus Thrower. The obstacle race for equestrian Army officers shows each national entrant at the same hazardous jump. An incredible tension is built up as, time after time, each national entrant is announced, and we witness his and his mount's effort to exalt their country's honour. The German officer who wins, clearing the jump successfully with perfect aplomb, forces us to gasp, while the Italian officer's spread-eagled fall from his mount wrings a howl from every throat. The climactic Marathon, won by a Japanese, is accorded the elaborateness due its high prestige; now the camera becomes the very eye of Mercury, hovering over and encouraging the winner, even seeming to touch his head and ankles, making it clear why, in winning an Olympic event, each athlete becomes the heroism of a nation incarnate. Nazified Germany, in having to grant athletic supremacy to the United States in the 1936 Games, could mark up one supreme conquest of its own: the by-lines on this film.

Alexei (surrogate for Maxim Gorky as a child) has two horrid, selfish uncles who quarrel unceasingly over their inheritance. At a welcome-home for Alexei and his mother (just bereaved of father and husband), the two greedy brutes spoil the affair with a bloodthirsty fight.

1938 · U.S.S.R.

The Childhood of Maxim Gorky

Unfortunately ignored in some standard books on the film, *The Childhood of Maxim Gorky* is still shown widely as a Russian classic and deserves every word of praise ever bestowed on it. Subtly contrary to the aggressive formalism for which Eisenstein is noted, this heartfelt presentation of the Old Russia, made in 1938, is wisely, beautifully, spontaneously candid, though the idealism of the New Russia obviously motivates its post-Revolutionary note of hope for the new social order. Its director, Mark Donskoi, unhesitatingly accepted the Russia of his country's fiction masters, Gogol, Dostoevsky, Tolstoi and Chekhov; yet, unlike Dostoevsky, who in *The Possessed* had arraigned the New Russia with burlesque irony, Donskoi portrays, by way of Gorky's own authoritative story, the drive toward the Revolution as man's insistent desire for an enlightened human consciousness. Surely, whatever the situation today, the bespectacled, bearded adult friend of the boy Alexei (Gorky's surrogate), represents the early hardships of those plotting to overthrow the stifling, hopelessly out-dated Czarism. At the end setting forth to "conquer the world" like a boy in a fairy tale, Alexei encounters his former friend, a convicted revolutionary, on his way to prison in manacles.

Yet the luminous substance of this film does not lie in revolutionary idealism, least of all in the pretentious formula known as Socialist Realism; it lies, rather, in a wonderful feeling for human truth, good or evil, despicable or admirable. A masterly portrait of a struggling provincial tradesman's class is exposed through a human glass with ominous shadows and tenderly preserved nuances. Classic Russian "moodiness", the intoxicating sunlight of merriment crazily alternating with the gloom of beastly greed, cruelty and despair, emerges at the start with the behaviour of two grown heirs to an old man's modest fortune. His sons fear he will make their sister a gift of his "wealth" as her dowry. The gay-sad party welcoming her return home with her son Alexei, following her husband's death, is wrecked by a brutal fight between her brothers, superbly rendered

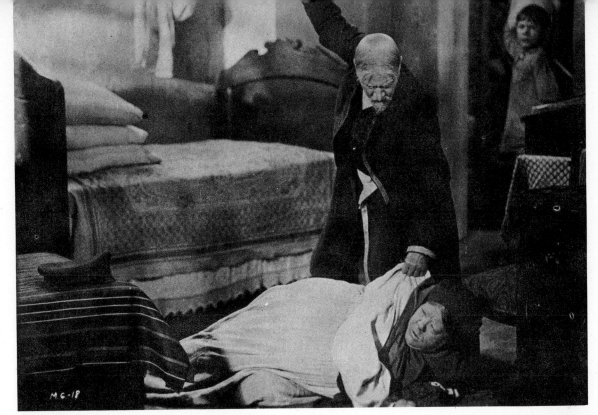

The two heirs, not without some dark chicanery, finally wrest the remains of their father's real estate from his unwilling hands; in turn, the evil-tempered old patriarch beats his wife, Alexei's grandmother, an angelic soul untouched by the vileness and degradation around her.

Alexei's grandfather, actually a childish simpleton, has his benevolent side, instanced when the boy shows his surprising aptitude for learning.

A sunny little cripple pinpoints the film's dramatic mixture of the world's sordid gloom and poverty with humour and innocent goodness.

by impeccable camera work and magnificent impersonations.

Madcap tricks by both child and adult come into play: spiteful little things that act like fuses to powder cans. The ferocity of the Russian temperament, home-destroying and self-destroying, assumes a horrible truthfulness, its edges softened and sweetened, however, by unsullied kindness. The latter is concentrated in the testy patriarch's wife, Alexei's grandmother, acted by an old woman who suggests a great painting brought to life; her broad, flattish, humorous peasant face, the large, compact, suffering female body, have the look of the most ancient visible things—monuments natural or man-made—a face of experience to support those who claim that goodness, not evil, is the product of mature human understanding. Her husband, owner of a dye works, is finally manoeuvred out of everything by his unscrupulous sons, in whom greed has become a demoralizing vice. The old man himself is an almost terrifying picture of human weakness in a male of given time, place and class: giddy, selfish, whining, childish, cruel and stupid—not by turns but all at once! That the

spectator feels an iota of sympathy or pity for him is due to the twin miracle of acting and directing.

Inveigling though not brilliant, the film's forthright style has unusual nicety. Inspired touches of visual angle, characterization and human essence blend together unpretentiously but surely; take the crouching Alexei's view of another small boy's whipping through the boots of a pair of men, or his grandmother's ritual gesture of crossing herself, interrupted in its horizontal by gliding into a gesture of impatience with him because he is not yet asleep. The death of another adult friend of Alexei's, a young peasant whose "golden hands" are employed in the dye works, is brought about through a revolting trick engineered by the vicious heirs. It is done with the visual effectiveness of scenes whose method had already been postulated in works by Eisenstein, Pudovkin and Dovzhenko. Strangely like it, in substance and pictorial effect, is the scene from *Earth* in which the murdered peasant's corpse is carried over a hill to its burial place. The boy Alexei's friend, the young worker, is enjoined by his uncles to carry a huge wooden cross to where it must be planted; venomously cruel, they only pretend to

112

Perennial frieze of outcast boys in Czardom's heyday. Maxim Gorky's surrogate, becoming their hero, bids them goodbye to make his way in the world just appearing on the horizon.

help him with the load. Reaching the top of the hill, he falls and is fatally crushed by it. Alexei is inconsolable. One thinks of the medieval Dance of Death as Ingmar Bergman photographed it in silhouette on a hilltop at the end of *The Seventh Seal*; likewise, of course, it recalls the burden of the cross carried up Golgotha.

Now Alexei, living with his impoverished grandparents and going to school, strikes up a friendship with the local gamins, those "boys of the road" whose reformation has been a prominent theme in Russian and Italian films. Reduction to abject poverty is the most touching theme in this film; it sears, and wilts the very heart, but the heart is revived with the lifeblood of gaiety. This gaiety is the sweetness and goodness of what we may be allowed to call "natural man": the grandmother, the sunny young peasant employed in the dye works, the little orphan, a cripple, who believes "a mouse can be fed to the size of a horse"—*there* is Russian romanticism for you! If certain sentimental "sound" conventions (such as the invisible female chorus sending Alexei off on his journey at the end) are reprehensible, they can be forgiven in a film having such persuasive powers of showing good and evil on equal terms in human society.

La Femme du Boulanger

or *The Baker's Wife*

The Baker (the incomparable Raimu) and his Wife (a typical young French actress) make a couple from a contemporary morality tale.

La Femme du Boulanger has the ideal simplicity of something sanctioned by sheer primitiveness, by belonging to times so remote (this has nothing to do with the year it was made) that it flouts time and seems to have existed always. With time, it grows larger, not less; for things around it have vanished. Though I have not seen it for more than two decades, I did not need, as I did in some other cases, refreshment on its plot. *La Femme du Boulanger* is as broad as a mountain whose outline greets you every morning through a window; as elastic, yet intact, in its structural certainty, as the best classical statues whose names everyone knows. That its title

suggests the personnel of nursery rhymes is no accident, nor was this point ignored by Marcel Pagnol, who had found such a sympathetic theme in Jean Giono's novel that he might have invented it himself.

Perhaps no nation can seem so much at home as the French in a language, before a camera, or with a mere "rôle". Surely, of all the actors and actresses I have ever seen, none more than Raimu has given me the impression of being master of the situation. Only Louis Jouvet, besides Raimu, had an assurance seeming to issue from the very centre of his being; yet Jouvet was also a bit haughty, a bit frigid, with the superiority of the "high style", self-conscious and speaking as from a platform. Jouvet and some others are doubtless gourmets of the emotional palate, but usually they "let on" they are; not so Raimu. If other actors, including the

The Baker's Wife, so the tale goes, meets a lusty young pagan who looks at her in no uncertain way: love-stricken, he tarries over a purchase.

French, can be "noble", it is because they rise to a rôle or an occasion, they deliberately reach toward the heights. Raimu, warm as the sun itself, was noble through a nameless, classless sort of human dignity, which he wore as casually as a birthmark or used like a handkerchief. He was as elementary as the bread he is supposed to bake in this movie; as hearty (and inevitably as heady) as the wine he drinks, the wine in which he overindulges when a strong, good-looking fellow persuades his wife to run away with him one night. Stunned with grief, the baker, day after day, neglects to bake his bread; as the only baker of his tiny village, he innocently threatens the welfare of his com-

One day before dawn, the Baker rises as usual, only to learn that during the night his Wife has eloped with the young pagan; whereat, besides getting silly-drunk, he swears not to bake any bread till she returns.

While the naughty lovers hide their pleasures on a little island, the villagers are in a quandary: bread is the staff of life and the Baker still declines to bake any.

munity: his wife's infidelity becomes a public calamity.

What is especially happy here is that the runaway couple express the French respect for *l'amour* at its pure animal level—something that most French films, like most French novels, insist on as though it were one of morality's most sacred maxims. The sinning woman (artificially made-up, like all women in French films) seems far too pretty to be married to a plain, middle-aged man, but this fact makes her adultery all the more credible. The couple take refuge on a little island, and indeed like animals, make their abode in a cave. As if we had some primitive morality tale before us, this island is where the village priest (carried on a peasant's back so his skirts won't get wet) penetrates in order to retrieve the erring wife. Her lover, a cross still dangling on his naked chest, takes flight in fear as the priest approaches . . . and social order, with the help of re-

ligion, wins the day; that is, the baker gets back his wife.

The story is beautifully, faultlessly comic, one even forgets it is a movie, and as such is dated both in moral attitude and aesthetic method. The camera dwells artlessly on its passing imagery, the action moves at a pedestrian pace. Yet *La Femme du Boulanger* is a classic exactly because classics are identified and reverenced for their capacity to ignore time and technique and everything else that goes under the disguise of being fashionable.

The Village Priest decides he must act; he routs the young pagan (really a Christian at heart) and returns, as below, with the Baker's Wife – what would have happened if Raimu hadn't been the Baker?

Two lovers, a rich girl and a poor student, silently and secretly communicate during a religious ceremony at her home.

1938 · POLAND

The Dybbuk

No negative print of *The Dybbuk*, I am told by its 16-mm distributors, is believed to exist any more; no 35-mm positive, apparently, is available in America. Thus, "duped" positives provide whatever currency it has in the U. S. Its sound track, especially the dialogue, has suffered more than its imagery, so that it no longer exists as originally created, but, like sheer fable, remains a beautiful anachronism. To me, and I am sure to others, the original impression of it is unforgettable. I think it one of the most solemn attestations to the mystic powers of the spirit the imagination has ever purveyed to the film reel. Directed by Michael Waszynsky, and featuring A. Morewsky, R. Samberg and M. Libman, it arrived untouted from that rather tempestuous, ambiguously situated country, Poland—the scene, memorably enough, of one of the most criminally deliberate attempts in history to exterminate Jews. During World War II, there fell on the Nazi-isolated ghetto of Warsaw (remember *The Golem*!) a planned,

wholesale annihilation by the German army. *The Dybbuk* is medieval in its spirituality, dimly historic in its Jewishness. It utilizes a medieval view of witchcraft, its powers and cure, but a universal view of the spirit of holiness opposing itself to sacrilege.

Numerous stories of witches have appeared on the world screen (including a fanciful documentary), some of them meaningful, more of them frivolous jokes. But the focus in those films has been on the *professional* witch, male or female. In *The Dybbuk*, the "witch" is the love passion itself, and so a protagonist in the timeless battle staged in human beings between God and the Devil. S. Ansky's play, on which the film (released here in 1938) was based, is the most famous in the Yiddish theatre and was already known internationally. New York stages have held repeated performances of it; my guess is that we shall see still further productions. As a film, the dark, bewitching, passionate beauty imbuing it is upheld despite the fact that the movies consistently hesitate to expose a "dim view" of life, death, and love so fatally intertwined as here.

It is an *internal* rhythm of things which the collaborators have understood and maintained; the basic pattern, however, is very clear, very old. A young student, exotic with a handsome Semitic face and curly sideburns, is fascinated with the old scripture of esoteric

116

The girl's father rebukes her for not greeting the father of the rich young man she does not wish to marry.

Her marriage spoiled by the *dybbuk* of her lover, who has committed suicide in order to enter her body, the girl is taken to a great rabbi for the *dybbuk* to be exorcized. The gesture made by the rabbi is a masterful stroke of portrayal.

wisdom, the cabala. But he is very poor and so the lovely girl with whom he falls in love is forced by her well-to-do father to engage herself to a rich man's son (the rich man being a blood-brother of his); at this point, convinced by his command of magic learning that he can become a *dybbuk*, and thus enter the body of his beloved in spirit, the student commits suicide. His *dybbuk* thereupon enters the bride's body just as the wedding ceremony is about to take place. The girl loses her reason and speaks only in the student's voice; naturally, the wedding ceremony becomes impossible.

A very powerful rabbi, a Hassid, is besought to restore her by exorcizing the *dybbuk*. The film reaches its most haunting sequence when the wise old rabbi performs this sacred office in a synagogue. No pyrotechnics or novelties of vision are needed: the spirit of the thing is enough. Jewish life and all life is seen at a medieval distance. The peculiar, rhythmic dignity of the action is incarnated by an allegoric figure of Fate, a pilgrim whose magic materialization out of thin air is the only "device" resorted to in order to establish the film's visual authenticity. This pilgrim keynotes the whole style; even the sensual practice of the student in the public baths appears transfigured by the noble struggle between good and evil. At the close of the agonized session in the synagogue, in which the taxed spirit of the rabbi is supported by a chorus, the *dybbuk* obeys the command to leave the living with a touching, most reluctant sorrow. One of his responses, like a terrible groan, has been that his beloved's body is Heaven to him. Our last view is of the girl, crouched alone on some steps in the synagogue; she raises her head from her knees and sighs. This sigh (hers or his?) is one of the most moving things I know in the poetry of the theatre: it is the liberation of the crushing burden which love inflicts on the body.

The rabbi consults a book to make certain of the precise rules for exorcizing a *dybbuk*: the spirit of the dead capable of possessing the body of the living.

The girl, exhausted from the terrible ordeal of exorcism, lies in the synagogue, while the fateful figure of the Pilgrim stands by.

At first glance a casual film shot? Starting this Russian epic of the thirteenth century, every angle on this landscape was composed by Eisenstein, figure by figure: these are Tartar soldiers guarding a tribute of Russian peasants destined to be slaves.

1938 · U.S.S.R.

Alexander Nevsky

It would have been hard to present the classic *Potemkin* as the work of a film artist who is, everything considered, the most intellectual the world has ever seen; it might have been hard to give even *Que Viva Mexico!* this special function considering the dismemberment of that stillborn film. But coming to *Alexander Nevsky*, released in 1938, though not seen till later in the Soviet Union, the film itself along with its maker's parallel attitude reveal that Eisenstein was as earnest about sheer ideas as about art. In *Alexander Nevsky*, we find the rebirth of this artist's formal aims taking place on the historic level, knitting Russia's past and present into a timelessly grand expression of patriotism; incidentally, *Russian* patriotism, inevitably *generic* patriotism. At the same time, *Nevsky* had a very modern application in being directed against one of Russia's old European enemies, Germany, once again on the warpath. The Teutonic Knights of Livonia and their cohorts, crushed by Grand Duke Alexander and his army in 1242, are made to appear as arch-villains, totally unre-

lieved by any appealing quality but that of proud conquerors brought verily to the dust. Eisenstein accomplished this, apparently, with heartfelt zest. But when the Soviet-German pact came on the heels of his film, he was uncomprehending and deeply embarrassed; after all, he was an artist, not a politician. *Alexander Nevsky* could not be put on public view till a year and a half after it was ready.

Hundreds of biographic facts attest to Sergei Eisenstein's intellect as pre-eminent among film directors. Because of it, rather than despite it, he is the most sorely tried man in film history. His absence abroad, and his failure there as climaxed by the abortive *Que Viva Mexico!*, put him in bad odour in the Soviet Union. His rigorous concentration on "method" had always exposed him to suspicion and he had to struggle, on his return to Russia, against bureaucratic criticism and the rival claims of some strong directors, including Pudovkin. He was told that despite all his demonstrations of ability, he had never fully represented the profundity

Russia's historic crisis: the city of Pskov has been betrayed to the Livonian army and the Pskov patriots suffer martyrdom under the gaze of the Teutonic Knights. An example of Eisenstein's famous three-figure composition.

of the change wrought in Russian society by the Revolution. After attempting to remedy this in *Bezhin Meadow* (1935-1937), a film that was forever denied public circulation because of its religious mysticism, Eisenstein understood that he would have to resort to totally different tactics. He then took Russian history, so to speak, by its forelock.

He found himself, aptly enough, looking into the eyes of the Grand Duke Alexander Nevsky, the great prince who became a national hero when he defeated the Swedish invaders on the Neva and then so decisively rid Russia of the threat from Germany in the famous Battle on the Ice, lengthily depicted in this film. Eisenstein only had to turn his glance toward history to see his great opportunity: history presents an exotic face whose elements, in the style sense, compose automatically, while historical material is as freely manipulatable by the artist as modern material. His approach to his new film was the antithesis of the usual "historical" formalism, which mainly relies on the pageantry of costumed figures, individual and massed, but all tagged with glamorous names and deeds. Without eliminating pageantry, costumes, or glamorous names and deeds, Eisenstein proceeded to create the plastic thing a work of film art should be.

"Formalism" as the ideological charge against Eisenstein is finally revealed by *Alexander Nevsky* as a myth. If it exists in his work as a handicap, it lies precisely in his obedience to the political patterns of his country, which he had to obey as a "matter of form" whether

reinforced by aesthetic substance or not. He developed many ways of transcending politics, a few of avoiding it. But he was invariably punished for every unacceptable "artistic licence" he sought to exercise. This became true all the more paradoxically because he had built a concrete aesthetic method on Marxist dialectics as officially endorsed by the Soviet government. The flaw in the crystal lay not in the aesthetic method, however, but in the political merger. In art, form surrounds and incorporates itself with substance; naturally, the "crystal" thus produced remains impervious to any shift, sudden or gradual, in political tactics.

True enough Russian history, true enough Russian patriotism, *Alexander Nevsky* is a classic because of Eisenstein's intellectual and artistic integrity. Another contingent truth had proved a source of inspiration; this was the person of Nikolai Cherkassov, who became the most distinguished of Russia's film actors through Eisenstein's skill. Eisenstein conceived him as the ideal knight, saviour of his country and bravest of heroes. The film's dynamic panorama infallibly centres on his figure. Fair-haired, of true princely stature and mien, with a noble, lucid gaze, Cherkassov might have, in theatrical parlance, "stolen the show" as may easily happen if an actor is better than the director and the film. But a proof of Eisenstein's sound method was that Cherkassov is kept in proper ratio as the work's domi-

Nikolai Cherkassov as Alexander Nevsky: a personified legend consciously wrought by Eisenstein to dominate his epic. No national hero has ever been so simply and vitally rejuvenated for a film.

nant symbol and never bursts his bounds as its "star".

His ratio was established partly by a right balance of the plot as such, developed by Eisenstein from both legend and the historic record. The prince of princes, Nevsky, would be a spirit that imposed itself *on* history and *through* history, a spirit growing directly from its struggles, from the confidence and admiration of the people in Russia's moments of crisis. Thus, representatives of this popular admiration themselves occupy the story of the film and take their turns filling the screen. This had nothing to do with orders from the Kremlin but was the shape and proportion of art as dictated to Eisenstein by observation of life and study of history.

The traitor from Pskov: a typical figment of Eisenstein's rich evocation of history. This director made the banal film spectacle come alive with zest for detail as well as for structure.

Eisenstein's uncanny gift for type-casting is expressed by this citizen of Novgorod: one of a good-natured pair who vie on the battlefield for the hand of a young beauty.

In contrast with the happy, open humanity of his Russians, Eisenstein designed such aspects of the German enemy as this: a blank, dehumanized grimness that the Germans themselves had pictured in *Metropolis*.

The texture of Medieval pageantry: Eisenstein went to end-
less pains to evoke imaginatively the Russians' formidable
enemy. Note the symbolism topping the monumental helmets of these Knights.

Stalin was enchanted by the result and it was perfectly logical that he should have been. The triumph of *Alexander Nevsky* in official quarters was especially fortunate for its maker because it gave him a free hand when he came to film *Ivan the Terrible*.

How had Eisenstein brought about his artistic coup? Not, essentially, by emulating the cult that Stalin had personally installed in Russian history but the one that Alexander Nevsky (and then Ivan the Terrible) had installed there centuries before: the cult of the semi-divine hero. Ironically enough, the representatives of the pan-Germanic idea were exploiting the German mythology and its cult just as vigorously and successfully; its prime artistic expression in the theatre resided, as Eisenstein well knew, in the grand operas of Wagner. Only two years after *Nevsky*, Eisenstein created a one-man production of *The Valkyrie* at the Bolshoi Theatre, instructing his actors how to do everything but sing. All his life, regardless of medium or incidental theme, this artist was dedicated to what he termed "the internal unity of sound and sight".

Sound dialogue and the music track had arrived at just the right moment in Eisenstein's career. *Alexander Nevsky* became the vehicle of what its maker termed Vertical Montage, or absolute control of image, speech, sound effects and music on simultaneous planes. A musically fine score was provided by Sergei Prokofiev.

There are scenes on the actual snowy sites of the Battle on the Ice that might be transferred to the stage without alteration. This was not to minimize, to revert to the stage, but to go on to greater artistic definition of the cinema spectacle. To review the way Eisenstein's historic figures move, the way they are costumed and otherwise rendered symbolic as well as real, might be to conclude that he uses human beings as if they were puppets; even as the chesspieces that the great helmets of his Teutonic Knights suggest. But what is in question here is neither art nor reality, but style. Eisenstein's style, in *Alexander Nevsky*, began purifying itself of naturalism and courting the extreme artificiality of *Ivan the Terrible*, his last film.

If we examine the facts, we find that this tendency has a perfectly logical origin in Nevsky himself. Who is Alexander Nevsky? He is a medieval man and a medieval prince; he has the simplicity (as we know from the opening episode) of the life lived by everyone; he also has its pious faith, its fierce one-sidedness and its primitive innocence. That is, as an aristocrat, or leader, he epitomizes and refines the virtues of his time and place. Though impersonal in his grandeur, he is "humanized" and "personalized" by two lesser heroes, "men of the people", who are rivals for the hand of the same beautiful young woman. Three private stories are worked by Eisenstein into the contours of history and

122

The famed Battle on the Ice: a Russian contingent comes to the aid of Russians battling the Germans, turning the tide through one of Alexander's strategies. His nation's saviour, Alexander defeats the Master of the enemy Knights in single combat and then enters the rescued Pskov in triumph.

one public story (that of Alexander) is worked into the same contours, while every incident and every minor character are worked into the main action: the advance of the Livonian forces and Russia's peril at the fall of Pskov, preparation for the great battle, the battle's duration and Alexander's ensuing triumph.

In this film, the theatre style that was to dominate *Ivan the Terrible* had not completely saturated its material but the emphasis is here: in the awesome and sinister array of the elaborately armed and decorated Teutonic Knights, in the use of dramatic symmetrical and asymmetrical formations of group and filmic design, in the self-conscious panoply of war as climaxed with Alexander's entry into Pskov with his humiliated prisoners. Naïvely stagey? Even platitudinously romantic? Let us shift the focus and apply these broad, psychologically uncomplicated cultural moulds, medieval in

character, to contemporary Russia. In type, it is the very image of the Soviet Union's true cultural aim, *circa* 1938, whether or not the bureaucracies realized it prior to, or during, World War II. Was this aim not to unite the highest, the leaders, to the lowest, the common people, under a new system, "Communism", which (at least *formally*) called for a radical simplification of social conditions, a simple faith, and the kind of monolithic symbol into which a Stalin and a Nevsky might seem to fit with comfort to both? Yes, Alexander Nevsky seems to have an intimate, happy and lordly enough relation to the Russian people. But this *entente* with Stalin lies mostly in Eisenstein's film. As for Eisenstein's film itself, it exists among the free, living forms, as dateless as it is factual, far more a piece of human history than Soviet history.

Confrontation at the house party: the Marquise greets her pursuing lover, the aviation hero, as the polite panderer (Renoir) stands by.

1939 · FRANCE

La Règle du Jeu

or *The Rules of the Game*

Today one wonders if Jean Renoir, having passed his seventieth birthday with some forty films to his credit, really grasped the widest, deepest relevance of this "society farce". Taken as more than a sex-gamble (pun intended), it was strictly for connoisseurs when a cut version appeared in New York in 1950 and remains so now, when it has been restored to its original length. Testimony to its high esteem lies mostly in the fact that in the 1961-62 poll of international critics it was named among the world's ten best films. On reseeing the film after my own vote was cast, I am in emphatic agreement with its choice. Renoir's film has the true starch of creative intelligence: a particular intelligence that recognizes the depths of social veneer and in what way its post-World War I quality sustained the chivalric tradition at the expense of what is known as human honesty. Leave it to the French to be grossly ironic about the virtues of caste and high style. The most

fastidious and insistent in cherishing sheer sentiment, the French see most clearly and penetratingly behind the screen erected by sentiment—that ambiguously sweet, generous and heart-warming human something—around the basic passions of mankind. The laughter and coarseness of French chivalry are seen in the farces of the Comédie Française; its blooded, inviolate survival abides in the still-performed tragedies of Racine and Corneille.

A rugged young French aviator has fallen for a Marquise he has met in Paris and dallied with. She is Viennese-born with a relaxed feminine style shaped by her native Austria and beautifully defined by the acting. This Parisian Marquise is like *Liebeslieder*. That no one, servant or master, loses either personal or national style throughout *La Règle du Jeu* is part of the rules; it shows what a percipient, scrupulous artist Renoir, son of the famous Impressionist painter, is.

In a hallway of the château, more confrontation: a lull in the tangle of aristocratic adulteries; it's past bedtime.

The stylish sportsman's game; its rules: wild rabbit and fowl are conned into being sitting ducks.

Elegant laughter and sheathed nails: the Marquise and her husband's mistress know how to be debonair when it's woman-to-woman.

All personalized types in this film, from gamekeeper to retired general, are as carefully embodied in dress, execution and resolution-in-action as are those of the *commedia dell' arte*. Yet *La Règle du Jeu*, on its first introduction to New York, proved such caviar to the general that a free-lance critic such as myself (most daily reviewers having greeted it with sniffs) was canvassed to provide a needed blurb for the theatre front.

Now restored to its original form and length, the film has outlived most of the then-current successes. Our Marquise, actually faithful to her foppish Marquis (an Old-World eccentric whose passion is collecting antique mechanical toys), does not go to the airport where her adoring lover has just flown the Atlantic in a one-better on Lindbergh's historic achievement; the poor lad, mobbed on his arrival, breaks up before the microphone because she is not there. His consoler is none other than a bumbling salon-bohemian, a rough but kindly parasite played by Renoir himself as the piece's "evil genius". I do not invent the last ascription; Renoir once confessed he played the "villain" of the piece at a lecture where I was present. Part of this bittersweet, uproar-destined farce is "good intentions", principally its villain's good intentions; for he intuits that the Mar-

The solution? A masquerade, of course! Our passionate aviator as a Spanish gypsy to the left, the now-aroused Marquise as a Tyrolean peasant, and the mischief-making Renoir under bearskin.

quise, whom he too adores, returns the aviator's love, though she is reluctant to think of him as more than a frivolous young man who is trying out his powers of seduction.

During a phenomenal house party at the Marquis' phenomenal château, the cat scrambles out of the bag to the raucous tunes of a chase, brawls, universal commotion and actual music. Everybody concerned is habitually alert for adultery. It is an accepted fact and one which, according to the rules of the game, must be kept as quiet as possible. The two lovers, masquerade costumes parodying their passion as if they were Harlequin and Columbine rather than a Spanish Gypsy and a Tyrolean peasant, almost elope—but, as that would be breaking the rules of the game, the heavenly powers protecting this decadent aristocracy prevent it, although it is at the cost of the aviator's life. Renoir has set his tragi-comedy so ingeniously amid the classic customs of upper-class luxury society that it all makes a hectic, if strangely believable, mirage.

Madame's pert, pretty personal maid—acted with a polish that could only come from the wisest theatrical traditions—is as French as her mistress is Viennese; the soubrette has a husband, the Germanic gamekeeper, Schumacher, whom she plans to cuckold with a lusty little game poacher (a monstrous sort of Eros) suddenly added to the domestic staff during the house party. The gun-shooting antics at the masquerade, caused by the gamekeeper's frantic jealousy, mix with the tangled amours of the gentry: the Marquis happens to have a mistress who obstinately refuses to be discarded. The result is half a René Clair chase, half those scandalous mishaps indigenous to international farce. How well Renoir knows his elements, how well he reuses them! His way of realistically overlapping conversation and action in one vivacious fugue, making life at a revelling house party flow at its true flux, much outdistances Orson Welles' efforts in this direction.

The seriousness Renoir brings out on the erotic side defines the pathos of a corrupt class clinging to its "honour" as the Middle Ages clung to the Chivalric Ideal. But the hidden animalism of civilized man operates from top to bottom of the house, from below-stairs in the great kitchen to an upstairs bedroom, where the

127

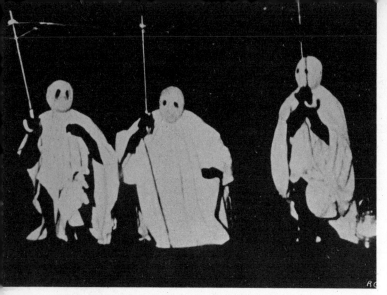

The Skeleton Dance is a significant counterpoint to the shenanigans as everybody gets drunk – and desperate.

Marquise and her husband's mistress have an unmasking tête-à-tête in which they philosophize on the realities of the flesh. We have seen, in the château's reception of the public hero of the moment, the aviator, how hypocritical and how witty our fine people are. The plot's development, with its deadly erotic vengeance (the chase) seeming like another party stunt to the amazed guests, shows what a vulgar rumpus may scar the most gorgeous, most authentic of châteaux. The gentlemen launch into fisticuffs at the drop of a woman's honour, slapstick becomes the criterion of manners, and chaos (deceptively part of the "act") reigns unchecked for a while.

Dalio, an actor whose ambiguous gloss is perfect for the lord of the manor, is a genius at defining a bored, worldly character by the way he walks downstairs to greet a guest. Even were this film's telling less brilliantly energetic, its casting would be a feature of genius. Renoir, directing it, is no *deus-ex-machina* behind the camera but an honest clown in front of it, functioning as the plot's catalyst. The two great sequences are midway and at the end; the former is the hunting sequence where rabbits and fowl are beaten from their coverts to be "sitting ducks" for the rifles of game-crazed, stylishly outfitted sportsmen; the carnage is like the most pathetic human battlefield: an unforgettable inspiration and achievement. At the end, the poor, love-smitten, honour-honouring aviator (having had a man-to-man explanation with his host, whose wife he is stealing) becomes another such sitting duck. The "sportsman" is the jealous gamekeeper, who mistakes the Marquise for her personal maid (his wife) and shoots the aviator on the presumption that he is our good, simple-hearted panderer, Renoir, bent on a clandestine rendezvous with Madame's pretty maid.

Suppose we compared this film's characters and plotline with the same elements as they compose and animate some stories of love and intrigue of recent years. Moral and immoral motives, defining human character, now dissolve themselves in free-form ambiguities that desperately truncate the action or perversely leave it in suspense: observe *Les Cousins*, *Last Year at Marienbad*, and *Jules et Jim*. Dignity and intelligence, lust and love, are not apt to be *judged*, ironically or otherwise; everything evident is submerged in neurotic taboos, every issue tinged with doubt, every "value" designed as grotesque or dated. Plot structure, emotional drive? Useless, silly affectations (says this new school) swept away by the implacable "flow of life".

In this film we have a healthy, Mozartian resonance. Was it not Don Giovanni who exchanged cloaks with his servant, Leporello, to forward an unholy errand and elude pursuers—and yet was finally trapped by divine vengeance? Lisette, the maid, has handed Madame her own Red Ridinghood cloak to make a rendezvous in the greenhouse, and the aviator, to keep it, shields his own identity by flinging a raincoat over his head. No one can conceal the sound of the shot or the resultant corpse. But honour is rescued by the Marquis, who ceremoniously informs his awakened guests that a "regrettable accident" has taken place. The retired general, every inch a knight in his bathrobe, remarks of his host to another male guest, aside, "Ah, but he has *class*—he has kept the rules of the game!" It is like a salvo to a king, and delivered with that sublime, confident ambiguity we know as style.

Madame's personal maid, smitten with a new domestic, snatches this lover's tidbit during the general entertainment. It is probably unique in the annals of filmdom's *erotica*.

The Marquis, about to be cuckolded, slugs out the fine point with his successful rival, the aviator. But this priceless period piece has only come to a semicolon.

The amorous quibble becomes a public ruckus as the maid's husband, the gamekeeper, chases his successful rival with a rifle.

The sobered panderer at the farce's tragic anticlimax: the aviator, triumphantly keeping a rendezvous with his Marquise, has been shot dead, in error, by the gamekeeper's still vigilant rifle. Renoir's face is a beautiful study in puzzled unhappiness. Only "the rules of the game" have escaped unchastised.

129

This scene, grave with black and white yet elusively refined with the touch of the hanging embroidery thread, introduces the elderly husband, young wife and young stepson in Carl Dreyer's second feature film in sound; the wife falls in love with her husband's son.

1943 · DENMARK

Day of Wrath

Carl Dreyer is surely one of the most distinguished film-makers ever to take up the medium, but one that, for better or worse, seems to have earned, starting with his *Passion of Joan of Arc* in 1928, the enviable and un-enviable reputation of being a film artist's film artist. *Day of Wrath*, much admired by aesthetes, solidly confirmed this reputation. Made and released in the war years, the film reasserted its director's solemn preoccupation with the human soul that is tempted to achieve its desires illegally, outside official religion and in defiance, if necessary, of both man and God. It is the virtually timeless revolt of the individual against the world and its legitimate ways, conceived by Dreyer in terms of a special human personality, today socially outmoded (at least on the surface) but still a mesmeric legend of feminine powers: the witch. Allied in some ways to the vampire (who, like the witch, may be male) the witch stands on an ambiguous borderland of human morality; as a female, she may be glamorous, perhaps the very virtue of Venus, but still—as the old movie vamp was a token—she may be malign, an enemy of both sexes, potential stealer of husbands, an instinctive adulteress, destroyer of men's souls and bodies, and perhaps her own soul and body.

In *The Passion of Joan of Arc*, Dreyer had found a figment of sacred myth: a woman accused of witchcraft

130

Composed as meticulously as a Dutch painting, this scene shows the pastor, Absalon, Anne's husband, sentencing an old woman charged with witchcraft to burn at the stake; Dreyer keeps the theme of *The Passion of Joan of Arc*.

and burned for it, though later, in a dramatic reversal by the Roman Catholic Church, canonized as a saint. Dreyer well understood the profound ambiguity of this same reversal and that, beginning with pagan times, it was related to all tragedy. Joan, in his film, is a suffering tragic heroine; one who is oddly close, in fact, to the equally obdurate Antigone, whose blazing family faith was punished by a king with death and then glorified in legend. The drama of punishment, to which Dreyer confined himself in his earlier witch film, he abandoned here for a more plausible and humanly commonplace story, laid in Denmark in the seventeenth century. The tragedy he sets forth is not merely the pathetic agony of a witch, as in Joan's case, but the tradition, as it were, of female witchcraft: how, specifically, love may imbue a woman with the dark power of obtaining her personal desire by destroying anyone who provides an obstacle.

That in this story the "witch", Anne, cannot prevent the simultaneous destruction of her own happiness, seems to be art's submission to the law correcting all supreme excess, rather than an instance of the old "morality tale" ending in which evil is punished and good rewarded. When Anne, crushed, stands by the coffin of her former husband, Absalon, an elderly pastor whom she has "wished" dead because he stood in the way of her love for his own son, Martin, nobody is raised to happiness, good has triumphed in no sense. Martin, her lover, deserts her when, beside the pastor's laid-out corpse, Absalon's mother accuses Anne of bringing about the pastor's death by witchcraft. Ruined, yet somehow proud, Anne does not deny the charge but stands grim and upright, apparently ready to accept any judgment that will come; so the film ends its sedate, retarded flow of beautifully modulated, sombre pictures.

Dreyer's art had become, in itself, rather puritanical, accurately shading every photographic tone and composing each shot as though engaged in a series of austere paintings in black and white. It is as if he had been inspired by the Dutch school of measured chiaroscuro and Baroque lighting, making everything funereal here by depriving it of all colour, including chiefly the gold of sunlight. Previously, an old witch has been con-

131

With a strange feeling of compunction, Absalon asks the half-crazed woman to confess so that she can escape torture; she persists in refusal although evidence of her guilt seems to exist.

demned by Absalon to torture and burning in a sequence that reproduces the general pattern of *The Passion of Joan of Arc*; dying, the old witch cursed both her executioner and her judge and soon both curses are lethally fulfilled. St. Joan's memory was redeemed in the rosiness of resurrection as a saint. But the flames destroying this Danish witch are more significantly made of a black-and-white chiaroscuro: they are the lowering greys and sooted whites of an evil fate's palette.

Light falls on the formal white collars, the black suits and dresses, of these Danes as if it had some portentous kinship with the frigid weather of northern Europe, the prevalent external cold in which the most burning passion, figuratively as well as literally, would wrap itself, at times finding there a providential cloak against detection. This "burning frigidity", deliberate and formal, is Dreyer's sensibility, his aesthetics of film and the imagination; it is a significantly slow burn, too, like the desire gradually occupying Anne's heart to will the death of her husband, whose guilt in taking her for wife, against her true consent, she intuits as a weapon that will help destroy him. No film artist has a steadier eye for his own values than Dreyer has here, a greater immunity to the idea of success through crude tour-de-force. As his camera had its own scrupulous nuances, his heart had its own obscure, delicate but determined intents.

Stoically, she is carried to the stake; stoically, the pastor accompanies her. When the wood is lighted beneath her, however, she screams deadly curses at her torturer and her judge, the pastor; soon, both men die.

Dreyer's artistic film is brought to a final chord of majestic chiaroscuro: Anne, whose love for Martin, the pastor's son, has caused her to will her husband's death, loses her lover when accused by Absalon's mother of being a witch.

An attractive but hysterical young woman, a sensitive and good-looking student: a mystery in her life helps bring them closer yet poisons their relationship.

The mystery is this sadistic schoolmaster, as mercilessly hard in the classroom as in the privacy of his hidden vice: Alf Sjöberg's film tells a clean-limbed, beautifully photographed story of the student's tragic emotional ordeal.

1944 · SWEDEN

Frenzy

Frenzy came at a moment when its merits as a film from Sweden, a nation then still obscure in world film, were doubly welcome. Its happy emergence was an occasion of the postwar international film festivals. Obtaining the Grand Prix at Cannes, it bristled with fresh talent of a kind that, since 1944, has grown a little stale and stereotyped under the constant ministrations of Ingmar Bergman's film-repertory system. Bergman himself wrote an original script for Alf Sjöberg's direction of *Frenzy*, which is altogether closer to his own films than his later collaboration with Sjöberg, *Miss Julie*. One may note that despite the irrefutable virtues of Bergman's actor-repertory system, it has developed no bright particular star, no highly eloquent personalities such as *Frenzy* had in its two leads. The increasing *literary* inflection of Bergman's themes (when he made his own films) placed the chief burden on ready-made characterization.

Acting personalities, of course, can be made to count in a film more or less as the director pleases. Alf Kjellin and Mai Zetterling, the young leads of *Frenzy*, seemed born for their parts and, besides that, were really new

"faces". Unfortunately their faces have aged or grown dim, their owners having been lured away into undistinguished, money-making careers. But this film has framed them in their bloom. Paradoxically, *Frenzy* is a film that etches on the face of youth its very first withering, creating permanent lines of experience, lines which, in the boy's case, come into being before the naked eye. Kjellin, as the adolescent student who prematurely learns the role of sex in life the hard way, gives one of the most remarkable performances of the kind in film history. Under Sjöberg's hands, he suggests, in fact, the triggered responsiveness of the young Barthelmess and Robert Harron to D. W. Griffith's touch. But Jan-Eryk is a more revealing part, a more complete portrait of a budding man, than anything comparable I can think of. It is as if Kjellin himself had discovered the sheer pathos of sex, its hurt and its mysterious desire, while still, like Jan-Eryk, receiving his scholastic education.

In the same process that he is ruined in school, failing to graduate, he becomes involved in the innermost misery of sex and shares its public scandal, confronts its naked body, both horrible and sweet, and yet manages to squeeze from its heart (one feels at the end) the compassion that will save him. The cost of his moral education is greater to others than to himself; to his affectionate but blindly uncomprehending parents, from whom he breaks completely at last; to a sexually hysterical young woman, whom he pities more than he loves; to his puritanically prim Latin teacher, a sadist in sex who has

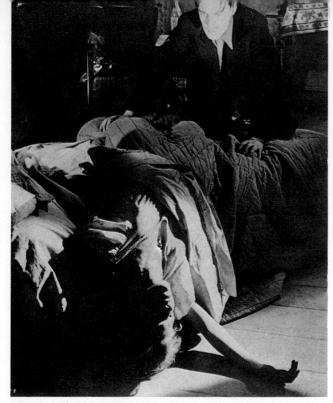

Climax: the persecuted girl, whom the student has grown to love, is found dead of heart failure; minutes later, the schoolmaster is found cowering in a corner of the apartment.

Engrossing dénouement: the shocked student, failing to graduate, is accosted by the repentant schoolmaster, whom he has denounced; the young woman's two lovers, in equal despair, face unknown futures. But the student's real life is beginning; the schoolmaster's is over.

secretly been victimizing the young woman, Bertha. Jan-Eryk is a sort of Eros submitted to a life-or-death ordeal. He knows all along that the sobbing, drunken Bertha he has found on the street, and accompanied back to her room, is being persecuted by an older man; he wishes to save her yet has no notion of how to do so as she keeps his identity a secret: she stands in dread of the man's attentions and yet (as Jan-Eryk guesses) finds them irresistible, even indispensable. It is a convincing portrait of sex as a motif of suffering.

Least involved physically, most involved spiritually and intellectually, Jan-Eryk uncovers the meaning of the terrible situation and its tantalizing masquerade when he finds Bertha dead in bed and his Latin teacher (ominously named Caligula) cowering behind some hanging clothes and whimpering, "I didn't kill her, I didn't kill her!" Caligula's identity is all the more appalling under the circumstances because he is the school's strictest disciplinarian, feared and hated by all the students. The mystery at last penetrated, it almost, but not quite, annihilates Jan-Eryk's sanity. In leaving him the strength to denounce Caligula to the school's principal, it seems to grant him the means to find the truth that is selfhood and the calm that such a realization brings with it. The medical autopsy on Bertha's body, stating she died of a heart attack, exonerates the sadistic teacher, who now, like his dead victim, turns into a hysteri-

cal whimperer, pleading for sympathy from Jan-Eryk himself.

As if fully to comprehend the tragedy and its meaning, the strangely illumined student has been standing in Bertha's room, thinking of her. He must take in all the past perfectly, every sight and every breath, to be rid of it and create a future to replace it. Perhaps only in this film, in *Miss Julie* and in Dreyer's works do we have properly exacting, really clear, portraits of the curiously frigid passions of the North European temperament. Whatever role environment may have in it, this temperament is distinctively "morbid" in its moral responses to the sexual drive. Sexual expression never attains ease, gaiety or the status of a clear-headed "game", natural to man and not too offensive to God; it tends to "drag down", its wrestling-matches are never dissociable from the wrestling-match with Death. One may say that these mythical, semi-ritual patterns of sexual experience are, after all, universal and reflect themselves in the films of all nations. True . . . But *Frenzy*—its very title helping to emphasize the point—proves that *moral tone* is what ultimately defines a national or personal experience. Sensual delight is a poor and agonized thing within the limits of this film of Sjöberg's. And think of what a bitter, antithetical feeling is infused into the orgiastic doings of Sjöberg's other film considered here: *Miss Julie!*

135

An act at the popular Théâtre de Funambules, Paris, early nineteenth century: a cocotte turned "goddess", Harlequin amorously triumphant, Pierrot amorously crushed; it is a charade for what happens in their private lives.

1945 · FRANCE

Les Enfants du Paradis

If *Les Enfants du Paradis* earned such extraordinary acclaim, it was partly because so rich and rare a film could hardly have been expected from French studios during World War II. It has the opulence that comes only with worldly experience, the feeling that men and women—and only men and women—have created the world of health and joy, grief, mishap, disaster and revelation that entwines them and utters their direction as from a stage. Elsewhere we find a like abundance of being, of moral shape and personality with the stamp and authority of works of art, only in great novels, great plays, great statues. True, a French poet of decided gifts, Jacques Prévert, supplied the original story, his second film script for the director, Marcel Carné, un-

der the German occupation of Paris in the last war. Carné's film creation, not released till 1945, is still a commanding example of French style, luxuriant with charm and human wisdom. If it somewhat lacks the masterly transitions that finish off a great novel or painting, it is still cinema of rare power and luminosity, various as the world, solid gold in each of its acting performances. Considering the place held by this film in the mind, it signalizes that nameless thing, sometimes called theatrical persuasiveness, that forces us to acknowledge life as a matter of fine points, inescapable fine points; all the points are fine here because they are, first, sheer theatre, beauty-marked.

Its perspective opens with a vision that, for richness

136

Garance (Arletty) has found a simple-minded true love in the potentially great mime, Baptiste Deburau (Jean-Louis Barrault), who seems a moony milksop till he trounces this bully.

of presence, is like an orchestral prelude: the stream of humanity flowing down the Boulevard du Temple in Paris in the somewhat less cynical, less politically advanced days before 1840. Beyond the cameras stood monitors, sleepy-eyed with self-importance and the thrill of victory: the Germans who had humbled Paris itself, who controlled a city and a nation in all ways but the essential, the governance and proliferation of spirit.

"Children of Paradise": they are the French people, watching the blossom of its life while the theatre enfranchises it of the responsibility to the real, to the stifling humiliation felt by all France. French film cameras never took in true life more heroically than when everybody dressed up for his part in *Les Enfants du Paradis* and played the evil and loss bizarrely present in himself and his haunts. The occupationists were so mesmerized by their own deluded present that they could not imagine that the past could symbolize the present . . . How little they knew of art's tricks, the resources of a wilful culture; or if they knew, they did not care.

We are in the peopled thoroughfare, I said, of Paris and humanity, holiday-spirited. Time and eternity clocks all: camera, story and death. Arletty (Garance) is pointed

out in the crowd; naturally, she has a lover, a frustrated author, vulgar enough to stoop to crime to make his way meanwhile. But for Garance, love is *"terriblement simple"*. There is the difference: she is the power of Venus, disguised. Arletty, who would not care to mention the years she has worked in films, never earned the clamour of publicity rendered a Garbo or a Dietrich. But I think she is more authentic than they: woe to the woman who must stand before news cameras and answer the questions of reporters! Arletty has never been in American films; I daresay her breasts are too small. But she is a beauty, as far back as I can remember; she has feminine mystery and knows it; as the demimondaine, Garance, she is elevated by the timely love of a Count, barely escaping arrest as the thief Lacenaire's accomplice. She can be grand, dressed as nobility or a streetwalker; it makes little difference except to the breathless way she testifies to being arrayed like a Countess, not a courtesan.

Human aims, enriched by egos, connect like things in a test tube. An orchid of the people, Garance stops to watch a performance before the Funambules, Paris' historic theatre whose "dictators" are the gallery gods, the "children of paradise", who throw oranges, who

Yet Baptiste's passion unmans him and Garance turns aside to the ready virility of another upcoming actor, Frédéric Lemaître: their faces here have the fruity eloquence of images in a master painting.

Garance receives serious attention from Count de Montray in her dressing room; tempted at a critical moment, she rises in the world as the Count's mistress.

A symbolic figure of fate taken from life, Pierre Renoir as Jericho, the old-clothes man, takes evil pleasure in reading the unhappiness predicted for Baptiste's wife: she is played by Maria Casares – several years before she appeared as the "vamp", Death, in Cocteau's *Orphée*.

stamp and immortalize with their outcries. Outside in the daylight, an all-white clown in traditional costume is recognizable as Jean-Louis Barrault, playing the youthful but already matchless mime, Baptiste Deburau of the famous acting family; Etienne Decroux, who trained Barrault in pantomime, plays his father here. Baptiste's soul-faced sadness has a theatrical wisdom as old as greasepaint and makes the doldrums of Pierrot seem like clouds or shadows painted by Watteau. He seems simple-minded, too, something like the *castrati* (those of the enchanted silver voices grown in Italy), but he's a man, a young man longing to love and be loved; now he fixes Garance with the deceptiveness of one performing on a stage. Next to her, in the watching crowd, a bourgeois has his wallet lifted by Lacenaire. Garance is accused. Without words, Baptiste exonerates her by miming for the crowd how the crime was really accomplished by a man. It is beautiful as a dance, a dance made more beautiful by having a moral purpose.

So much space given to the opening of *Les Enfants du Paradis* is a tribute to its original length of over three hours, curtailed to the two-and-a-half-hour version made in England and only partially restored, recently. That is, it has the rights of a classic fragment whose invisibility survives as part of its tangible glamour. Elsewhere, I refer to what I name as the high-life of the mind. Too precious? But one of the qualities of that life is leisure; another, spaciousness. These are, to this high-life, as her eyes to Arletty, his gestures to Barrault's mime, the Funambules to history's myth. That Garance becomes an actress hopelessly worshipped by Baptiste, his passionate soul outstripping his lithe body inarticulate in love; that the stage of the Funambules becomes the arena of his agony, she a "goddess", he her frustrated adorer, losing her to Harlequin; that he fails to consummate his love on a stolen night with her and that next morning she finds the arms of a normally virile man, the rising actor, Frédéric Lemaître; that the helpless Baptiste then husbands a humble little actress who bears him children: all happens with the serenity of lucid nature amid the unseen confused politics and dirty dealings of war, isolated from time and the temptations of the real.

Words-at-arms: the French theatre has never produced a more brilliant genre scene on film than this lethal encounter in a Green Room; Garance's lovers (here including the discarded Lacenaire) have it out as nobility of caste and profession put down the ill-bred fellow who still aspires to Garance.

Dénouement in blood at a Turkish bath; in this still, the vengeful ruffian and his confederate arrive ahead of schedule to murder the Count, whom they catch while naked in his bath.

Finally, in the carnival crowd, Baptiste loses Garance forever, but the gallery gods demand the performances go on; life has been like a play ... yet we know it is life.

The real is an intrusive ghost here: the peddler, old "Sleep-Alone". Ah, the peace of buzzing cameras and the sacred perspiration of actors who have learned the life of the "unreal"! This is the learning that makes real and whole statues that have lost their limbs.

Les Enfants du Paradis is suffused with authority as if with the exquisite filaments of a huge electric flash-bulb that turns into a sun. Garance blooms from a box in the Funambules like a flower from the ground; Baptiste's little boy visits the box; this chance meeting is esoteric, touching as the survival of a period Valentine. Meanwhile, all the men's passions have been aroused. Blood, answering the call to arms (then a contemporary anachronism in Paris) flares up; there is a stunning scene in the Green Room of a great theatre. Garance's former lover, Lemaître, superbly impersonated by Pierre Brasseur, is now a celebrated tragic actor; he jests with the Count de Montray over the impudent pretensions of Lacenaire, who is bitter at his loss of Garance and poses as a gentleman. The upstart is put in his place by wit, Garance defined by innuendo as quite beyond his class. The soul of a fop, a dandy's clothes and the libido give Lacenaire his arrogance; he challenges de Montray to a duel on the very staircase of the Count's home. But

he is low-bred: de Montray can fight only a gentleman on the field of honour.

So be it. Carné would be a world-ranking director with this film alone. Did he originally model his action more carefully and is editing (possibly in the U.S.) responsible for the tacit, abrupt sequence that still ends the work? De Montray, naked in his booth at a Turkish bath, is murdered by the vicious Lacenaire and a confederate. He "goes out" like Paris symbolically bending the knee: an "open city". There may be a chilling contemporary reference here. No matter! Paris, too, is still unspoiled. Another rendezvous takes place between the heart-hurt, yearning Baptiste and his passion, Garance, and everything seems consummated. But his abandoned wife appears to implore her to release him from her spell. Garance drives away in a carriage, alone, in a carnival crowd so thick that the poor, bleating mime cannot fight his way through in pursuit of her as confetti and streamers rain down on him. Garance is lost—to him and to time. So it will be, and has been, this wily cycle of an art ending as it began. Why not? Men, such as they are, noble or base, have been men; women, likewise, women. That is no cliché. But when the curtain comes down as if by accident, the gallery gods protest . . .

141

Man and woman of the people in German-occupied Rome during World War II: this film introduced Anna Magnani, here rather prettified, to international fame; she was a heavily made-up glamour girl in prewar films.

1945 · ITALY

Open City

or *Roma, Città Aperta*

The New York Film Critics Circle discontinued its awards to foreign films during World War II, but when they were resumed in 1946, the first to be honoured was a film from rejuvenated Italy, Roberto Rossellini's *Open City*. The work was so recently vintaged that it had been a project even before the Germans had vacated Rome and had been made under very difficult conditions—a fact that partly accounts for its authenticity. Also gaining three Grand Prizes at foreign film festivals, it took command of Italy's new film trend, and with de Sica's ensuing *Shoe Shine*, started the international influence of the style called Neo-Realism. The hallmarks of Neo-Realism became a deliberately ragged photographic look, an informally aimed camera, a brutal facing of certain common enough facts (yet a tender appraisal of them) and an espousal of the interests of the underprivileged classes. Postwar conditions naturally consolidated this attitude and gave Neo-Realism a convincing complexion, if also one that, unavoidably, was fated to be overdone and sentimentalized, both politically and artistically. Yet *Open City* was strong in its clarion candour, fresh in its coarse truths about those

enduring poverty, misery and shame in German-occupied Rome. Its relentless focus was on the heroic action of the Resistance Movement of the people.

Not the least striking among the film's "heroic" angles was the presence of the actress Anna Magnani, to whom it brought an international fame equal to Rossellini's. Like Raf Vallone on the male side, she photographs "heroically" from no matter what angle; however informally aimed or carelessly poised, the camera seems to do both actors justice. Magnani became a star playing "a woman of the people". Yet she has a quality none of the great glamour queens can claim: a basic womanhood that exists beyond conventional beauty of face or figure, no matter which kind of beauty be the standard. *Her* elegance is, in fact, without standard and of no social identity. As a result she seems the quintessence of the feminine even when not suggesting bed and its delights, though at will she can suggest these, too. While here she is her rougher, ungainlier self, Magnani taught us how overwhelming her sort of dignity can be: it is the Generic Woman seen apart from the pagan and post-pagan ideals in art. This makes her, I should say, *Open City*'s rarest achievement by far.

Because Rossellini's film is, like *Potemkin*, so earnest, so concerned with the changing fate of peoples at its basic level, it nevertheless registered as imaginative

142

propaganda. As an individual work, it is by no means so pure or distinguished in form as *Potemkin* or as another post-World War II film, *Bicycle Thieves*. Like *Potemkin*, like *Metropolis* and the flood of vision undammed in Gance's *Napoléon*, *Open City* expresses, it is true, a very recognizable and omnipresent force: the force of aroused masses, the might that may be military, armed resistance, or unarmed, popular combustion, but always the might by which the collective pushes history toward the future. In great national peril, especially when the home nation is laid low, caste distinctions tend to fuse into one organic action.

This is *Open City*'s moral emphasis and Rossellini puts it in blunt, blackboard terms by having a priest sacrifice his life to the Resistance cause. The story itself is brusque, unaffectedly and even cornily melodramatic;

The other side of the Roman coin: the German Army maintains its espionage agency now intent on tracking down a daring Resistance leader; this woman agent provides a vivid contrast to Magnani.

The woman agent teaches a female traitor how to finish up her job: the Resistance leader, as a result, is caught, and Magnani, as a woman in love with his friend, is shot down as she runs after the Germans carrying away her lover.

The noted Italian actor Aldo Fabrizi takes the role of a priest who bravely aids the Resistance. After the Resistance leader is tortured to death by the Germans, the priest is executed by a firing squad.

evil is identified with luxury, obvious vice and treason, the good with the poor, the honest and the downtrodden. Manfredi, the Resistance man, is betrayed and tortured to death while Magnani, as a woman carrying in her the child of his friend, Francesco, is shot down running after the lorry taking her lover away; the fearless priest, apprehended as an arm of the Resistance, dies before a German firing squad. The conventions of the popular film of action received, here, new lifeblood from history itself. Melodrama seemed to thrust its stereotyped spies and intrigue, its popular lone-wolf heroes, into the immediacies of daily life.

Ivan the Terrible, Eisenstein's masterpiece of masterpieces, begins with the coronation of Ivan, Grand Duke of Moscow, as Russia's first Czar. Nikolai Cherkassov, who played Alexander Nevsky, is a peerless Czar; always heroic, he grows old, gaunt, lonely, demonic with the film's progress.

1946 · U.S.S.R.

Ivan the Terrible

Parts I and II

It was not for nothing that in February, 1948, when Sergei M. Eisenstein's ashes were carried in an urn to be buried in snow-covered Russian ground, he was reborn even to estranged friends as the Old Man: the Grand Old Man of Russian film-making, though he had just passed his fiftieth birthday. In 1941, while preparing his first book to result from his twenty-year practice of the film art, he had received the assignment to do *Ivan the Terrible*; at once he had been allowed to resign from the post he had assumed in 1939, the head of Mosfilm and supervisor of all Soviet film production, to devote himself to what he correctly anticipated would be his supreme work, an unquestionable film masterpiece. At that time, writes Marie Seton, his biographer, he was wearing several decorations, chief among them the Order of Lenin, since in 1938 his *Alexander Nevsky* had completely redeemed him from his period of disgrace.

After *Nevsky*, Eisenstein had produced a number of propaganda films made by his two collaborators of long standing, Edmund Tisse, photographer, and Grigory Alexandrov, script writer and director. Now faced with a new creative work to do, the artist who had made *Potemkin, October, The General Line, Que Viva Mexico!* and *Alexander Nevsky*, expected his old associates again to put their invaluable talents at his service. Personally estranged from Eisenstein for a couple of years, Alexandrov had come to admire him again, and readily joined Tisse to make up the former team; moreover, Prokofiev, the composer, had made a fourth member in *Nevsky* and now his collaboration was also guaranteed as soon as he found Eisenstein determined that the new film should follow *Nevsky*'s precedent: the music, that is, should be "an active participant in the drama ... fill it with a parallel developing action of emotional sound." Eisenstein, already learned in Russian history, soon started work on the scenario for *Ivan*, visualizing it in two parts.

Both parts of the scenario were published in an English translation in *Life and Letters Today* (London), for November-December, 1945, and May-July, 1946.

The powerful Boyar Princess, Euphrosinia (marvellously incarnate in Serafima Berman), is Ivan's hostile aunt who wishes to replace him with her own feeble-minded, effeminate son seen here beside her. The sumptuous costumes and textures denote the unlimited material resources which Eisenstein's prestige had earned him.

Prince Kurbsky, Ivan's bosom friend, to be made chief of Russia's army, is led by the hand of Ivan's bride. Kurbsky, constantly rebuffed in his desire to seduce her, plays a game of intrigue against Ivan that ends with his handing over the Russian forces to Poland.

Ivan's absolutist policies isolate him from the Boyar nobles and excite the opposition of a Boyar whom Ivan raises to be Metropolitan of the Church: an example of the beautiful plastic means interpreting the macabre and violent drama of Ivan's success as Czar.

It was clear from them, even before Part I was seen in the United States, that Eisenstein had completely reversed his position on historic heroes of Ivan's calibre; this sort, he had said, "was a personality in the manner of Edgar Allan Poe", a conception which, he went on, "would hardly interest the young Soviet worker". Yet even in Part I, the contrary signs were definite enough. His Ivan was to become an exact semblance of the personality Eisenstein had taboo'd as "a Mephistofelean figure, a Czar who was a wild beast". After Eisenstein was dead, Alexandrov and Miss Seton agreed on an explanation for the change-over. Eisenstein, having matured since the year of *Nevsky* (1938), was reaching toward new heights of imaginative splendour, more enlightened, more comprehensive. The truth was that finally this film-maker understood that no great hero of actuality should be idealized exclusively as an instrument of social forces, as a simple measure of his nation's glory. Coexistent with the image of an historic hero, thus defined, must be his image as an individual hero, a humanized image concerned with the inner drama, the private fate, of a personality of his special kind.

The evidence shows that Eisenstein's view of Ivan the Terrible, precisely from this encyclopaedic angle, converted his film into a dialectic between Ivan the ruler and Ivan the man; furthermore, as if reaching for a vast fourth dimension, this dialectic was expanded to reflect

himself, Sergei Eisenstein, a greatly honoured artist, in Ivan Vasilievitch, Grand Duke of Moscow, who in the sixteenth century was the first to bear the title of Czar. Eisenstein knew perfectly well that "Mephistofeles" and "wild beast", the labels he had given Ivan, also applied to *himself*, to the history of his career as man and film artist. Ivan is shown growing lonely, despondent and childlike, feeling in his dark isolation that he is hated, that the great of his own land are ever ready to betray him.

In *Nevsky*, Eisenstein has succeeded in making a work that conformed with the pattern of "official" Soviet art and yet was a sound creation in the filmic medium. Now, in *Ivan*, he would really dare the enraptured heights of art, and would still, he believed, preserve the outward appearance of the official art. Or did he ever hope to achieve, at the outset or toward the end, this complex tour de force? It is impossible to say with certainty whether he did or not. As his biographer fully demonstrated, *everything* about Eisenstein can be put in some doubt, with testimony for and against a stated proposition, except a single and constant fact: *he always did his utmost to be loyal to himself as an artist*; yes, even when he formally recanted his treatment of the second part of *Ivan*, and promised to correct it when its exhibition was banned in Russia and he was publicly censured.

Readers may not know what a provocative enigma

146

His rule intact, but newly threatened by the Boyars' growing rage, inflamed by his aunt, Ivan listens to the wily and brutal advice of a devoted henchman: a perfectly controlled and harmonious pantomime, from close-up to long shot, pervades this lengthy film.

Ivan risks his throne and his life by having three important Boyars secretly executed for treason; here, afterward, he ironically humbles himself before the unyielding Metropolitan: probably a parody of Eisenstein's own compelled submission to the Soviet film bureaucracy.

Euphrosinia and the Boyars have taken desperate counsel together and decided the only recourse left is to have Ivan assassinated: a simple youth is sworn to stab him at midnight Mass. Eisenstein's wonderfully flexible actors, upright or in diagonals, responded to the biomechanics taught to Eisenstein by Meyerhold.

Eisenstein might appear as man and artist. In Mexico, when making the film commissioned by the Upton Sinclairs, and in the Soviet Union, when he had made *Bezhin Meadow*, he had gained a clinging reputation as a "bad actor"—a genius who had an arrogant, perverse streak and could indulge it without conscience. He is said to have taken great interest in obscene aspects of popular life while in Mexico, to have filmed scenes in bordellos, and to have staged ribald Russian folk comedies on the open road, himself participating in them as a loudly declaiming actor. However all that may be, such acknowledgeable facts, if used to discredit Eisenstein's films and the sincerity of their artistic motives, are entirely inadmissible.

By 1941, the heroic sense had ripened and sunk deep roots in Eisenstein. Yet his own personal looks and manner helped the paradoxes involved in his reputa-

tion; at the time of *Ivan*'s completion, observers, who also remarked the two clownish tufts of hair that reared up from his vast bald forehead, termed him "an amoral gnome, a miniature and intellectual satyr". Yet the man who produced this impression had already created the incomparably powerful and mythical figure of Ivan the Terrible! Eisenstein had come into the open as a man of world culture, a stylist who was utilizing in the medium of the film, and perfecting for it, Meyerhold's biomechanics theory of acting, of which he had been a student from the very beginning of his career. This explains why all the actors in *Ivan the Terrible* are fabulously responsive human mechanisms, guided by an infallible dynamics of plastic design as well as human emotion. For the first time in an Eisenstein film, every foot of *Ivan*'s two parts attest the strictest application of the Meyerhold Method—the opposite, be it noted, of what is known as the Method today; that is, the Stanislavski Method.

Like Marxism itself, the film script for Ivan was a programme to be followed point by point in letter and spirit. Far from repudiating or neglecting the dialectics

Ivan, meanwhile, has suddenly discovered that Euphrosinia poisoned his wife; he then recalls how, as a child ruler, he witnessed his dying mother's spasms after being poisoned by the plotting Boyars. In this sequence, Ivan's legs do not touch the floor when he sits on his throne; see a photograph of Eisenstein in similar position elsewhere in this book.

which the example of Marxism had taught him, Eisenstein employed it more rigorously and richly than ever in *Ivan*. As likewise, along with so many intellectuals in the modern world, a student and admirer of Freud and James Joyce, Eisenstein gazed simultaneously into the psychological and imaginative depths of Ivan's childhood, seeing there a double dimension: the private and the public life of his hero. Once, as a boy of eight, Ivan, the puppet ruler of his nation, heroically determined to become ruler in fact as well as in title; in this episode, fantastically recreated from historic annals, Eisenstein dated the birth of Ivan's supreme will to save both himself and Russia from threatened defeat. Doubtless, this identification between Ivan's personality and his acts is subject to dispute by historiographers, but as Eisenstein's symbolist device for illuminating his own human depths through a known historic figure, the identification is quite valid. After all, it is precisely what Shakespeare, so far as interpretation of historic record goes, did in his histories of the kings: those dramatic works notably vulnerable to historical criticism yet invulnerable as human documents and works of art.

Eisenstein's enigmatic nature held a very demonstrable dualism: a trait that pointed toward great legends of dual personality as reinforced by modern psychology. Marie Seton was Eisenstein's very close friend for several late years of his life; her biography provides a highly convincing analysis of the Freudian nature of its subject's relations with his mother, and how these were reflected in Ivan's relations with his aunt, Euphrosinia, who, although a woman, was the most dangerous of Ivan's Boyar enemies; this princess' demonic aim was to rid the Boyar nobles of Ivan and place her effeminate, feeble-minded young son, Vladimir, on the throne of Russia as the same sort of puppet Ivan had been as a child. Vladimir thus becomes Ivan's alter ego, and by another remove, Eisenstein's. There is myriad evidence for this in plot and characterization, testimony that looks oddly specific in the view of the boy Czar,

149

Ivan and Prince Vladimir are surrogates for the mature man, Eisenstein, and the susceptibly childish nature he always tried to expel from his character: Ivan invites Vladimir to a revel preceding midnight Mass.

Ivan, seated in full panoply on his throne with dangling feet off the ground; two such photographs exist of Eisenstein when he was making *October* and show him, once with feet similarly dangling, on the Czar's throne in the Winter Palace. One of these photographs will be found in this book.

Having just completed the montage of *Ivan*, Part II, Eisenstein was honoured with a party celebrating the award of the Stalin Prize First Class to Part I. While the celebration was at its gayest, he collapsed with the heart attack that he owed to the strain of completing his most ambitious and demanding film. Yet he was still in the hospital when the banning of Part II was announced and an official statement condemning him was published. Due to the gravity of his condition, his friends long kept from him the calamitous news; when finally he should learn it, as inevitably he must, they feared it would bring on a morbid, lengthy, and now perhaps fatal, inactivity such as that which followed the banning of *Bezhin Meadow*.

But, Miss Seton says, Eisenstein's will to live and work, far from slackening when he learned the news, grew stronger. He wrote his formal recantation of the historical misinterpretations which had been imputed to *Ivan*, Part II, and instantly began work on books and other plans with truly amazing energy for a man whom the doctors had pronounced on the brink of death. Why should he not have gone on with fresh courage and no

shame? The sufferer from a fatal *angina pectoris*, though often breathing in gasps and in continuous fear of sudden death, had triumphantly shown history in his own personal mirror. Though he had promised to amend this inacceptable image of history, it remains to us today, miraculously, very much as he intended it. All he himself did later to revise it was to reshoot the final sequence of Part II *in colour*, thus underlining rather than withdrawing the *mea culpa* whose tragic meaning, to human history and to him, was beyond the comprehension of the film bureaucrats: that is, if any of them intuited its truth, they were compelled to disdain it. What the film bureaucracy termed only "court intrigues" in Part II actually reveal Ivan's authentic struggle to erase the power of the Boyars, which kept the nation disunited, and to institute a central rule which would enable Russia to outface her surrounding enemies. How good, ultimately, this policy was for Russia and the world, may still be a matter for conjecture by some. But that historically it appears to have been Russia's very lifeline, was technically and exactly, in 1946, the assumption of the official supervisors of Soviet art. It was merely Eisenstein's emphasis on Ivan's story that was the object of censure. Surely, *this* is no place to argue the case against Eisenstein's emphasis. His "emphasis" left us the most perfect of all films, if film be valued as an art ever-aspiring, self-sustaining and with a will not to compromise.

In symbolic travesty, Ivan "crowns" Vladimir while the young leader of the Oprinichi (Ivan's private bodyguard) appreciates the irony. Ivan then asks the simple-minded prince to lead the procession into the church.

Thrilling catharsis of a magnificent film drama: Vladimir, disguised as the Czar, has been killed by the deceived assassin, and Euphrosinia gives herself up to mourning him; this final sequence brings to a point the most complex tragic design ever to appear in a work originated by a film artist.

These two boys, seen in the distance in the next picture, are inseparable chums. They supplement their honest earnings with black market fees in order to buy a horse that makes them an equestrian Damon and Pythias; innocently they are snared in a blackmail operation.

1946 · ITALY

Shoe Shine

or *Sciuscia*

The Italian title of Vittorio de Sica's film, *Sciuscia*, was a phonetic rendering of the phrase adopted by shoe-shine boys to address American GI's in Rome: "Shoe shine (sciuscia), Joe?" The *ragazzi*—Italian for "boys" in the familiar sense of "kids"—had already attained a focus of filmic interest in two distinguished Russian films, *The Road to Life* (1930), later made into an American version, and *The Childhood of Maxim Gorky* (1938; see elsewhere in this book). As his first important piece of direction to follow World War II, de Sica gave us this *ragazzi* film. Insidiously tender, if also violent and bitter, it came on the very heels of Rossellini's *Open City*, and as if on purpose, began on the note with which *Open City* had closed: the *ragazzi*, having witnessed the priest's execution by the German firing squad, drift back to their futures in the Italian capital.

In our era the so-called juvenile delinquent has been, of course, a major social problem, and from 1946 to the moment in which I write, has occasioned a host of films, more or less serious, devoted to him as a human agent challenging the peace and quiet of the civilized future. A number of such films, like *The Road to Life* itself, have expressed a romantically optimistic view based on institutional reform. The Italian reformatories, as revealed by de Sica, evidently had not then achieved (whatever they are today) a real enlightenment comparable to the reform seen in Russian films. The end of *Shoe Shine*, brutal and charged with shadow, defines its two boy heroes as compelled victims of the adult system of crime and punishment.

The world issue of the delinquency problem is both complex and controversial; with due recognition of that fact, I should call *Shoe Shine* the most realistic and representative of all the *ragazzi* fictions on film. Italy produced several more and each nation's industry seems to have made its contribution, although Germany's, before World War II, was an explicit arm of Nazi propaganda. *Shoe Shine*'s edge on its rivals is due to what I consider an undeviating, heartfelt awareness of what it means to a boy to be an unformed creature in the hands of "delinquent" adults. A waif, unmoored from family and education, he becomes society's problem child.

Here two of Rome's shoe shine boys, a Damon and Pythias of the streets, are united in possessing a dappled white horse bought with their earnings in a Black Market operated by adults, one of whom is the younger pal's brother. The horse seems a realization of all the ease, splendour and gallantry imaginable to the boys. Twin centaurs, they are innocent tools in a new blackmail racket emerging from the Black Market. Recognized by

"Shoe Shine, Joe?" It was the Italian boys' formula for addressing American GIs during World War II in liberated Rome. It begins the most notable of the films about *ragazzi*: "kids" who could become juvenile delinquents.

The victim has identified them, they have been arrested and sent to a reformatory where typical prison intrigue wrecks their friendship. The larger boy is Franco Interlenghi who grew up to be an internationally known lead in Italian films.

the elderly female victim, they are arrested, taken to a reformatory run like a prison, tragically separated and "grilled". Deceived by the "humanely" faked thrashing given his little pal, the older boy squeals on their adult confederates, thereby losing his pal's loyalty and stigmatizing himself. Both are victims of an evil bully who then plants a file in the boy's cell, hoping finally to disunite the two. Punished for possessing the file, the older boy somewhat reinstates himself in grace (and the eyes of his lost friend) when he thrashes the bully in a first fight.

The obvious, tarnished plot comes alive with de Sica's fresh, sympathetic understanding and the extraordinary naturalism he coaxed from boy and adult actors. A humble new art of candour and humanity was being born to the cinema. A scheme by the bully, to effect his cell group's escape from the reformatory, coincides with a riot started when a film projector, in a movie show held by some priests, catches fire. The bully and his stolen pal are the only two to escape: they go directly to the stable and take the horse. The betrayed boy guesses as much and in an agony of jealous rage offers to lead the reformatory men to the stable. The horse is gone, but now grasping a lead pipe and stealing away, the boy catches the two riders crossing a little bridge. The bully flees as a guilty little Damon faces an incensed Pythias. The gesture with which the latter imitates his warders by reaching for his belt to thrash the smaller boy is truly tragic. Young blood is just as logical in its maimed passions—and just as fatal.

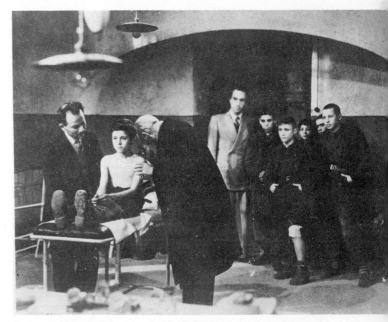

Remarkably candid, remarkably delicate and sympathetic, de Sica's handling of the trite plot elements turns his reformatory drama into something much outclassing the usual juvenile delinquent melodrama.

The older boy, wrongly stigmatized as a squealer, whips a bully who has finally succeeded in separating him from his smaller pal: the evils of the reformatory issue into an escape, a pursuit and finally a tragic confrontation between the two pals that ends in the accidental death of the younger.

Cocteau's fairy-tale world of the past is a thing of finesse; its human beings are as exquisite as its costumes. Beauty wonders if she can love a mere handsome young man.

La Belle et la Bête

1947 · FRANCE

or *Beauty and the Beast*

In Cocteau's first film, *Le Sang d'un Poète* (1930), space was a set of symbolic interiors, closed, going from the studio and the bedroom to a theatre, and interrupted only by a memory-vision taking place in a public square. During the time that intervened before his next film, *La Belle et la Bête* (1947), Cocteau's artistic activities were slowed down by the war years; besides, his active interests in art were various, his media including plays, poetry and drawings. *La Belle et la Bête*, releasing his film art into the supernaturally enclosed world of the fairy tale, is unforgettable for its exacting poetic spirit and must be regarded as one of its creator's imaginative hallmarks. To it, he brought the great rarity of an inventive connoisseur of images. The lion-mask of the Beast, designed by Christian Bérard (also responsible for the costumes and most of the settings), is based on the actual features of Jean Marais, who plays Beauty's lover, magically transformed into the Prince from the Beast; the Beast is shown as half-cavalier, half-lion, and the three persons are one and the same actor. Marais' casting was a decisively important element of the film's pictorial rightness. The features of the Beast

make a leonine mask of pure ardour: "beastliness" as a vessel of erotic rage which inevitably sheds tears of tenderness. Equally essential was Cocteau's choice of Josette Day to play the rôle of Beauty: a woman who had to be young, natural and yet a perfect "Princess".

Cocteau had his own theoretic reasons for refusing to call himself a "film-maker" (see the book *Cocteau on the Film*), but here I think these reasons can be disregarded. The truth is that he, like others, rejected the "conjuror's tricks" with which very early films exploited cinema, in order to seek out his own magic of film. This fact is crystalline: he was the first film-maker consistently to develop, on a large scale, an art that neither expanded nor converted the novel or the drama form (as became the conventional thing) into the film form, but directly replaced all poetic devices of literature, whether on page or stage, with corresponding filmic devices, doing this, moreover, within the given dimensions of the myth form.

Of course, he knowingly betrayed his own creed, as an established practice, in the case of filming his play *Les Parents Terribles*; on the other hand, he completely

Life, as in all fairy tales, becomes a dream: Beauty's father loses his way while in search of a rose she desires; plucking it in the grounds of an enchanted castle, he puts himself and Beauty in the Beast's power.

revised another of his plays, *Orphée*, to present it in a film version. The merits of *La Belle et la Bête* hardly depend on its literal plot. Cocteau's film, made from the classic French fairy tale, is a pure re-creation, in which he resolved to rely on incessant invention, lynxlike attention to the existence of lovely images: their movements and their identities whether those of person, animal or thing. Courtliness is very much a part of the "fable" of *La Belle et la Bête*; it is, in fact, the very essence of its symbolism. This noble account of female innocence, for which the father and the lover become merged into a beastlike, partly threatening, partly promising, physical presence, only to be turned, as suddenly as in a dream, into the lover's ideal image (the Prince), is something which everyone, young and old, grasps intuitively. Cocteau's art, avoiding vulgarity, naturally makes a certain demand upon movie-goers in general. To honour his film, properly to enjoy its refined moral portent, one must be an initiate in the forms of poetry as these are universalized in myth.

Rather than have her father sacrificed to the Beast, Beauty offers herself: this is a parable of the chivalric ideal that love is sublime rather than earthly.

In attempting Beauty's rescue from the Beast's power, her human lover is pierced to the heart with an arrow aimed by a guardian statue; his death transforms the Beast into the Prince: the lover for whom Beauty is destined.

Cocteau proves a master of visual enchantment: the Beast, Beauty's captor, is so kind and devoted, so great a cavalier, that she is almost mesmerized into loving him.

Monsieur Vincent displays the historic noble caste of France (early seventeenth century) in all its material richness and imparts to it its highest spiritual value.

1947 · FRANCE

Monsieur Vincent

Gracious, tender, and true is this movie, and also, I should say, great. Jesus died in honour of the idea of making all men great, not necessarily in an afterlife but certainly in this life. It is simply that His immense action has been differently interpreted. But till His idea has been wholly accomplished, human beings as a race can feel neither perfect nor happy. According to man's nature, physical suffering helps degrade him and may create despair. It was the overmastering intuition of this fact that made the humbly born French priest, Vincent de Paul (born in 1576 and sainted by the Church in 1737) leave the ease and luxury that had been his in a noble household to go among the poor and ill, to succour them in the face of all the risks involved: contamination by disease, social contempt, the anger of high patrons, and sharing the lives of paupers.

The film's actual production, which Maurice Cloche, a leading French director, had been thinking about for years, came only after the end of World War II, which had laid a taboo on what already seemed a project of formidable costliness. The history of this project is itself most interesting. Today, we may notice, religion is fighting to hold on to its ancient prestige. This is no aggressive "agnostic" statement of the facts. Of the utmost significance, I believe, is that after Cloche, conceiver and director of *Monsieur Vincent*, had consulted the archives of the Lazarist priests (the order founded by St. Vincent) and sought the advice of an historian, Maximilien Vox, he switched—at the close of the war—to a more practicable means of financing and realizing the abandoned film project. He proceeded to acquire the support of the Office Familiel de Documentation Artistique, which organized a successful appeal to the religious world to finance the film. Shares worth 1,000 francs were to pay dividends after the production earned back its expenses.

At the same time, with success in sight, Cloche secured the enthusiastic collaboration of the noted French playwright, Jean Anouilh, who collaborated on the scenario and wrote the dialogue. As if impelled on one direct course of inspiration, Cloche then induced one of France's most accomplished actors, Pierre Fresnay, to impersonate the historic Vincent de Paul. Fresnay's portrait of St. Vincent is as much a miracle as the great saint's own existence; there are images of St. Vincent throughout the film that literally rival painting on its own ground; they are nothing less than sublime. No critic attuned to aesthetic and spiritual values resisted the result on the film screen, from which emanated the spirit that infuses and justifies the great religious impulses, the great religious lives. At the Venice Biennial Exposition, Fresnay as Best Actor took away the Grand Prix International; the film won the Grand Prix du Cinéma Français and the Grand Prix de la Presse Belge; among its seven other prizes was the Academy Award.

Vincent de Paul, who created the first foundling hospital, shadows the birth of his great aim: a mother, in this silvery scene haunted with the golden thread of pity, plans to leave her illegitimate son on the steps of a cathedral.

Vincent de Paul's genius for the spiritual has made him the favourite of a great lady who bribes him with a costly gift to leave the provincial charity work (for which he has deserted her) and return to Paris as her Confessor. Vincent sees the chance to advance his aims, leaves his soup kitchen on the spot (and two provincial ladies of rank he has won over) to enter the larger phase of his work. Monsieur Vincent emanates a glow of humility and love for the poor that fascinates the feminine spirits of honest ladies of rank and wealth who divine in the lot of the wretched and abandoned a parallel with their own, disguised, inarticulate unhappiness. Yet Vincent always deals with them directly and innocently. Fresnay's conception of the rôle has the mastered form of simplicity brought by great professionals to every rôle they take.

Step by step, Vincent is self-induced to surrender all personal advantages though he is raised in rank by Cardinal Richelieu himself. Lands and serfs seem superfluous and a shame while human beings rot in misery, while the old and sick die like dogs. About him is organized the work of the Ladies of Charity, its members the cream of Parisian elegance. That he induces some of them personally to share his menial tasks as well as to give money is part of the miracle. Appointed chaplain to the Comte de Gondi, and present by his side while his oarsmen are whipped to bring up their strokes to win a race with another nobleman's galley, Vincent rushes to the aid of a fainting slave and even takes his place. Only the purity of his known holiness exempts him from the consequences of this transgression of form.

Yet the shock of the experience arouses him to renounce all accumulated and inherited wealth as a fatal barrier between him and his dedication as a servant to the poor. In this radical, unparalleled action, he draws to him simple girls who, in nunlike spirit, wish to imitate him. To breathe the same air as the very unfortunate, those distorted in soul and body by circumstance, becomes a new religious ideal. To witness in person the horrors of slum life—disease, prostitution, illegitimacy and starvation—attracts Vincent like a magnet; eventually he saves the life of a foundling left in bitter cold on some cathedral steps. But the swaddled infant is an object of horror to the Ladies of Charity. Vincent's spirit almost collapses when all—even his loyal nurses—turn away from the "ugliness" of the child-of-sin.

The film's vision of the lowly and desolate, in the France of its time, is just as richly created as its vision of the high and prosperous.

The film's sure touch on conditions in the seventeenth century, its wars and riots and plagues, is unrivalled for verisimilitude rooted in a faultless taste. A scene in a primitive hospital, as two sick and dying men fight over the right to a bed just vacated by a corpse, is beyond words and beyond tears. It almost loses Vincent his first noble convert, Louise de Marillac, whose garments are clutched by cursing sufferers in this scene of panic. Yet Vincent's spirit is a flame, and it endures, so that even Mme de Marillac is won back. Growing very old, hunched and frail—rather like a crumpled leaf—Vincent lives and dies to see his vision of social charity a triumph.

Closeted with the mature Queen of France, he is informed by Her Majesty that, with every girlish dream realized, she aches with a great emptiness and feels she has done less than he. His reply is that he himself has done too little. The simple grandeur of their talk speaks directly to the heart. Her bosom covered with jewels, her proud face a study of sorrow mixed with happiness, the queen and the wizened saint offer a sublime image perhaps possible only, in its ultimate polish, to the French theatre. Too weak to continue, Vincent excuses himself from the royal presence in order to give personal instruction to the newest young nurse. The pith of his advice to her is tremendous with the rarest human wisdom. Charity work has a secret: the poor must be induced to *forgive* you for the bread you give them. The idea of charity is invested with a great new irony.

A very great lady, a very unfortunate sufferer: St. Vincent de Paul, whose life story this film recounts, brought this dramatic contrast between social symbols into real, vital human relationship.

Exhausted by the pace necessary to win a race between magnificent galleys, a slave faints: Monsieur Vincent, at the risk of offending his noble patron, rushes to take his place in one of the film's many moving scenes.

A worker, whose job is to plaster up posters around Rome, spends an idle moment with his wife and the machine that means their livelihood.

1949 · ITALY

Bicycle Thieves

This famous film, given the New York Critics' Circle award in 1949, was polled internationally, at the turn of the century's sixth decade, as among the world's ten best films; it evokes, I think, a human situation of comparable stature. *Bicycle Thieves* is a victory for Natural Man—a mere common worker with restricted intellect and culture—who establishes contact with the eternal nature of good and evil through immediate experience and wholly without institutional guides. Without question, this film, an inspiration of the team of Vittorio de Sica, director, and Cesare Zavattini, script writer, who based it on a contemporary novel, became a summit for the so-called Neo-Realist school of Italy, and it remains, I hazard, the same summit it was. It contains none of the lush filmic or high-life blandishments used by Fellini and Antonioni, later comers to Italy's top-ranking film-makers. It keeps rather to Rossellini's earlier standpoint as stated in *Open City* and de Sica's as stated in *Shoe Shine*; visually and spiritually, it has the burr of the candid-camera view of the world.

Cleave to the people, says this view, to the bread and the staff of human life, not sentimentally but with stern respect for harsh reality, for in the latter lies the greater truth of what we call the human adventure. One does not find it necessary to agree with this explicit dictum to enjoy the available merits of this de Sica-Zavattini film. Like other Italian works, its largeness of gaze is city-wide, uncritical, uncamera-conscious, and deals with humanity at its heroic animal level. Its true strength, all the same, lies in a place usually unacknowledged (or unknown) by many advocates of documentarism who praise it to the skies and beyond. *Bicycle Thieves* is a lucid moral fable (as I have pointed out in previous years) and bears the stamp of the ancient sense of life as an initiation rite.

A worker has his bicycle stolen while on the job; it is part of his means of livelihood because he plasters up posters around Rome. In hoping to get the machine back, he is quite willing the thief be arrested and punished as a bad citizen. Seeking the usual channels of recovering the stolen vehicle, and companioned by his small son, the worker is snubbed again and again by official indifference: the police regard the theft as a

160

Himself as simple in message as the poster he plasters up, the worker will turn around in a moment to see a thief madly pedalling off on his bicycle.

routine affair of no moment. The Church—as a casual incident hints—has no material relevance in the case. The poster-plasterer's union is willing to help, but the organized machinery of crime, taking apart stolen bicycles and reassembling them so as to disperse the original machine, stymie, in effect, all efforts to recover the bicycle. However, its owner has seen the thief who pedalled away with his machine. The thief eludes the searching worker till the moment when the latter has visited a fortuneteller, an old woman, whose answer to his query is, "You will find it at once or not at all." Issuing from the fortuneteller's house, he sees the thief (bicycleless) on the street and gives chase.

Having collared him at last, and a policeman being summoned, he is informed, however, that there is no evidence by which the young man can be arrested, much less convicted. So the thief, of whose identity the worker is certain, goes free. The worker and his little boy (rather like the blindfolded child who served as guide in the old mystery rites) then sit desolately on a curb, in a scene beautifully imagined and filmed. De Sica had chosen professionally inexperienced actors for the two rôles and they come through like gold. Nearby, on the large square where they sit, some popular sport in a large stadium has just been concluded, and now its spectators pour out and pedal away on hundreds of bicycles: a common feature of Roman life. The poor worker's hopes could not be more crushed now, he could not feel more ruined and mocked by unhappy, unjust circumstance. He has glimpsed a parked, untended bicycle down a side street. He is tempted. He yields under the very eyes of his small son.

But the owner has been providently watchful of his property, starts the hue and cry, and is joined by some bystanders. The stolen machine is jammed among the great flux of bicycles being pedalled away from the stadium. The worker, now himself a bicycle thief, is caught. In a thrilling yet rapid, and perfectly con-

161

Having begun a gruelling search for his precious machine, the worker and his small son chase the thief, suddenly recognized, through the streets and into a church.

vincing dénouement the present bicycle's owner (more affluent than the present thief) seems to read the worker's forlorn, cruel predicament in his face; at any rate, he decides in a split second not to prosecute him—and so the worker-thief is as free as the professional thief whom he has recently been forced to release. The course of the reversal is completed by a climax dazzling for its naturalness, honesty and human kindness. Such is the beauty of *Bicycle Thieves*, based on what is imaginatively neither complex nor rare nor theatrical nor, on the purely intellectual plane, elevated.

It is a sizeable achievement to have shown mankind, materially underprivileged and simple of soul, so nakedly clothed in true modern circumstances. Like a great morality tale, the worker's "obstacle race" through the bicycle market, a church, and then a whorehouse, to corner the fleeing thief, the desolate and incriminating dénouement where the burden of guilt is lifted from all men's shoulders by a single act of forgiveness, this melodrama made of economic facts has been given a directness and clarity of figure that could not be more apt or revealing of the basic sweetness we call "human good". De Sica had a sure camera eye, Zavattini a sure mental eye, for realizing an idea and making it (rarely enough) look like nature unfolding its minutes and its hours as we watch. For this reason, I believe, *Bicycle Thieves* is an unchallengeable peak of what we may take to be the art of motion pictures.

After cornering the thief in a whorehouse, the worker finds himself threatened by those perpetually on the side of the underdog; anyway, a summoned policeman tells him there is no charge on which to hold the suspect, of whose identity the worker is certain.

Worker and son make a picture of solemn human desperation on a basic social level: fate frowns and then smiles in a thrilling dénouement showing the commonalty of human guilt and the sweetness that pardons it.

Stills can be only modestly indicative of the superb flair for beautiful and picturesque action which carries along a hectic liaison between a Swedish Countess and her coachman in 1888: it begins at a barn dance held on Midsummer Eve.

Miss Julie

1950 · SWEDEN

From the beautifully controlled rhythm of *Day of Wrath*, like a slow-starting smouldering fire, to the beautifully controlled *allegro brillante* of *Miss Julie* is a big step for Scandinavian film in every way. We are taken from a far past to a near past; from the temperament of a film-maker, Dreyer, to the temperament of a dramatist, Strindberg; from a film medium where dialogue is muted, somewhat "dispensable", to a film medium where dialogue, despite much headlong physical movement, is the heart of the matter. Dreyer's later witch theme, in *Day of Wrath*, has a certain wintry bareness and frigidness of gaze to which the burning of the old woman as a witch is an antidote, an incendiary release. It is a legend on the lips of a storyteller in pictures. But in *Miss Julie*, dextrously modernized in multiple filmic ways, we are compact with the terrors and morbidity of the *modern* North European conscience, sensual yet straitened, its witches having turned into blood-inheritance, its struggle between good and evil taking place in an arena which can be observed firsthand as of today.

Nevertheless, the setting, characters and morality of *Miss Julie* maintain a certain conscious period "distance". The play (originally called *Julie*) was written in 1888 with a contemporary setting, and is probably the innovative Swedish dramatist's masterpiece. Unlike his Expressionist-Symbolist works, *Miss Julie* is firmly welded into the patterns of real life. Actually, what this marvellously-surfaced, thrillingly-paced movie does is to employ some of the magical techniques used by Strindberg in other plays to recreate the family history which made its heroine, Miss Julie, what she is.

What *is* she? She is vibrantly delineated by Anita Björk, who basically has too fresh, too clear a face to be so complex and tragic a character, yet who is the mistress of her rôle. Julie's beautiful, perverse mother, now dead, has caused her father, a count, who is still alive, much grief. The Countess was a man-hater, betrayed her husband's bed, humiliated him socially, and gloated over bearing him a daughter instead of the son he wanted, rearing the girl as a boy till overborne by the Count's outraged interference.

Miss Julie, the Countess, possessed by famished erotic impulses, provokes Jean to make love to her even under the eyes of his fiancée, the cook: the mad revel goes on all night.

The early background of Miss Julie's strange perversity is revived in the unreeling of the work's present-tense action, which opens with Miss Julie, a countess by title, conventionally joining her large staff of servants in revelling on Midsummer Eve; the gay ritual, also a debauch, starts with the erection of a tall Maypole and continues till sunrise; shortly afterward, the pulsing film is brought to its gruesome climax. From the first, it is plain that Miss Julie's deeply desperate trouble is seeking an erotic outlet. Still a virgin, she has just become formally disengaged from a colourless young man whom she was accustomed to induce, as she did her dog, to leap over her riding crop. Her father being away to celebrate with friends, she is alone on the great estate with the exception of her troop of servants and field-workers. She has stayed behind, it seems, with some ulterior thought; it is at once apparent what this thought is: to seduce, in her own way, her coachman, Jean, a good-looking, well-set-up fellow, whose shyness at her provocations is wholly the result of his inbred sense of being a servant.

The skill and beauty with which the revel is shown, outdoors and indoors, on the calm, full-mooned night with its encroaching mists, the fluent *esprit*, the outward abandon clothing Miss Julie's fierce sexual intrigue, which she and Jean try to conceal from the riotous servants—all can hardly be overpraised. From the hayloft in the barn where the servants dance, and where Miss Julie first feels Jean's embrace, to the white,

nude pagan statues situated on the estate's lovely park, every contrasting pictorial feature is stated and dramatized as the guilty, panting couple flirt, kiss, mock each other, and keep fleeing a jealous peasant girl and the eyes of Jean's fiancée, the "queen" of the kitchen. At last, Miss Julie achieves her desire in Jean's bedroom, where the two are forced to hide, while next door to them the cook is snoring and just outside, in the kitchen, the revellers are getting drunk.

It is a fatal act for Miss Julie, masochistic and mortally final. About to elope with Jean after an agony of mutual indecision, confession and dreadful abuse, Miss Julie hears the kitchen bell which announces the return of her father; she sees Jean cringe and resolve to answer it, though they are late for the train they expect to take: the Count's morning coffee must be brought him! Miss Julie has rifled her father's desk for the money to pay for their tickets and has dressed for the journey. Leaving Jean like a ghost, she walks around the house and enters the drawing-room, where she cuts her throat with the razor Jean has just used, and which he himself, wordlessly, has handed her.

Strindberg was a seer into morbid human passions lying in the precipitous depth where the part-pagan, part-puritan Scandinavian heritage seemed to have weighted, shrouded and bloodied them. What is so re-

Miss Julie and Jean, in unceasing flight from watchers, have found physical consummation when driven to hide in his bedroom; later, tragically remorseful, she evokes her past for his benefit: the film reaches dazzling cinematic levels.

markable about the filming of *Miss Julie* is the sheer aptness with which a first-rate, difficult dramatic text has been freed into real planetary space, into the open air: an expansion which has not lessened its tragic, involved import or made it "healthier", but on the contrary, has underlined the dark powers that operate at all times, everywhere, reaching crescendo precisely when the night is brightest with moonlight. Strindberg's play is set wholly in the mansion's kitchen and suggests the out-of-doors, and what takes place there, with the usual theatrical methods. Where the dramatist revealed the past lives of Miss Julie and Jean through their monologues, the film-makers have taken up the play as a rich programme for bringing the past before us as literal hallucination, and doing this, furthermore, in a daring yet successful way. The technical "flashback" has consistently been used as a visual path seemingly continuous in space through the simple "pan" shot; Julie's mother and events before and after her birth are shown coextensively in the noble drawing room where they once took place, where now she and her lover are seated as she confides to him who and what she is. The same thing has been true as, wandering with each other

over the estate, Jean has told her how, as a boy, he fell madly in love with her.

I know of no technical feat in film just like this one; hence, there is not even a standard of comparison: *Miss Julie* is stark in its uniqueness. Further, I know of no filmic design, at once visually sensuous and psychologically profound, so fully and consistently realized except in the cases of some Eisenstein works. The camera has taken sure command in *Miss Julie* and never ceases to supply a diversity, interest and dramatic surprise of its own. Persons do not run, as groups or individuals, a horse does not gallop or a boat glide in *Miss Julie*, simply to "entertain" us with irritation of the optic nerves; psychological and emotional movements keep pace with physical movements, augmenting each other. Greatness evokes greatness; a great theme, a great author—even a great play, at times, a great movie. With *Frenzy* (winner of nine film awards), 1944, also to his credit, Miss Julie's director, Alf Sjöberg, ranks, in my opinion, above the currently lauded Ingmar Bergman—who, incidentally, created the script of *Frenzy*. *Miss Julie* took the Grand Prix at the 1951 Cannes Film Festival.

Miss Julie and her lover – she half-crazed by her sense of degradation, he by exultation over his good fortune – get drunk, abuse each other and yet decide, finally, to elope together the next morning.

A gruesome climax comes when Jean kills Miss Julie's lovebird because its cage will be a nuisance on their elopement. The act is too much for her and realizing that all hopes of happiness have been crushed, she commits suicide.

The ordeal of Cocteau's fourth-dimensional Orpheus (Jean Marais) soon comes to the point with the Bacchantes, who are a Left Bank café tribe eager to tear him apart for being an artistic bigwig and for suspected complicity in the death of a young poet, Cégeste, darling of the *avant-garde*; he is also bourgeois enough to be in love with his wife Eurydice.

1950 · FRANCE

Orphée

or *Orpheus*

Grossly misunderstood by the press when first seen in the United States, *Orphée* surely has within it seeds of a classic, even if it seems not to be wearing as well with revival audiences as many works which, through the decades, have become assured museum pieces. At the same time, in the filmic perspective, Cocteau is second only to Eisenstein as an artist who utilized film intensively to state his own life story in terms of both modern and ancient traditions of art and culture as they are affiliated to the old mystery religions. Chaplin's case would be comparable to theirs except that he much simplified his cultural means. As an artist living under capitalism, Cocteau was freer than Eisenstein to be personal, and to set at naught the popular insistence that the creative film be "clear" and "realistic" in plot and idea. In *Ivan the Terrible*, Eisenstein had finally worked out a formula whereby, through immense ingenuity, he combined realism with fantasy, private sym-

bolism with public myth, the present with the past. After starting with the esoteric myth of an artist's human destiny, *Le Sang d'un Poète*, Cocteau turned to it again when he felt he had made the ultimate discoveries of the mature artist.

Technically, he was certainly right, for the "poet laureate", the great man of letters who is his Orpheus, holds in himself the transformation from the *avant-gardiste* of Cocteau's youth to the French Academician of Cocteau's late middle age. Of course Cocteau would have denied that he ever ceased to be *avant-garde* in spirit. But the point is arguable and the evidence in *Orphée* is available to the con side as well as the pro. The issue might be settled with a pun to quell even Cocteau's vivacious protests: he was always an Old Pro—a professional ever interested in adapting modern materials to give ancient assumptions about art and life a look of newness while reasserting them. There is a

The case is complicated: the pregnant Eurydice has been kidnapped by the same mysterious crowd which has taken away Cégeste's dead body and so Orpheus willingly negotiates with their representative, who chauffeurs a Rolls-Royce limousine.

straight line, as logical as any defined by Aristotle, between *Le Sang d'un Poète* (1930) and *Orphée* (1950).

The dark-haired young poet, split into stages of experience and symbolic dimensions in the earlier film, is in the later split into two persons—a mature poet, the also dark Orpheus, and the blond Cégeste, a wild young poet whose death takes place under strange circumstances, who is revived by Death in the Underworld and from there establishes an affinity with Orpheus. To some extent, in Cégeste, Cocteau must have been imagining writers whose genius has died early through the renunciation of art, as in Rimbaud's case, or was cut off early, as Radiguet was, through a premature burning out of life itself. In *Orphée*, our magic view of this drama of the artist's inward fate, seen outwardly, is obtained through being situated at the latter end of Orpheus' life span, when everything must be finally settled. The outcome is a triumph for Orpheus, who, unlike his ancient prototype, is allowed, at last, to bring back Eurydice from the Underworld. Here Cocteau simply shifts his mystic ground by combining one legend with another; that of Alcestis who offered her life in place

of her husband's, but was brought back to her husband, Admetus, by Heracles, who had outwrestled Death for her. His problem was to furnish a happy outcome for all the artist's ordeals and to avoid the look of the conventional happy ending of romances. To do this in terms giving pleasure to what might be called the large cultivated audience, Cocteau took risks which left his film with scars made by a safety belt. He cannot avoid enjoying, so to speak, the attitude of the safe, comfortable artist loaded with official honours and the father of a happy family: it is a pregnant Eurydice who is rapt away from her bedroom by Death and a safely pregnant Eurydice who returns to it.

That Cocteau was not married, and not, I believe, the father of children (other than works of art), is grounds for his claim to epic, impartial and objective vision: he means all artists, not just himself. But this is a quibble, as Cocteau well knew, for what is possible to creation is possible to all creators and limited only by choice. Yet he is partly to blame for perpetually taking the poses of a coquette when it came to the true depths of the elements he was manipulating and to supplying responsible keys to those depths. It is as though "telling" wouldn't be playing cricket with the Surrealists, whose criticism he had to disarm in advance. There is a general key to his method and by now it is a cultural com-

The chauffeur (François Périer), no other than Heurtebise, Angel of Death and guide to the Underworld, consents to take Orpheus to the house of Death by way of a mirror in his bedroom: again, for Cocteau, the mirror is a magic threshold.

monplace. I think it might even have been called one in 1950, when the film had its première in New York and Cocteau wrote a note for the programme. Perhaps he took a certain joy in baffling the easily confused and perhaps too it was his policy to handle weighty ideas with the shrug always considered fashionable in such matters. Anyhow, today, culture is one vast thesaurus where a legend such as Orpheus is cross-referenced with a hundred similar legends, whose codes are illustrated in such well-known modern works as Eliot's *The Waste Land*, Pound's *Cantos* and Joyce's *Ulysses*.

Cocteau might easily point, without a word, to the bemused reviewer who cited a line of the film's dialogue as an instance of his rude lack of consideration for his public. It is some advice given by Heurtebise, the Angel of Death who plays Death's chauffeur, to Orpheus. "It is not necessary to understand," he says, "it is necessary only to believe." Philosophically many serious quarrels with this proposition are possible; we have heard quite a few. But it is no impudent *avant-garde* mystique nor an effort of Cocteau's to torture his audience with strange and complicated enigmas. The key to its significance, both in *Orphée* and apart from it, is as apparent as the Parthenon on a sunny day and reminds us that this famous temple bears an ancient religious heritage. The sense in which Heurtebise communicates the statement to Orpheus is the sense in which all mystery religions, including Christianity, have told their initiates that belief is manifest in revelation and all understanding proceeds from this revelation. What is the revelation in *Orphée*? Its events, step by step.

The film is a popularized, and "naturalistically" expanded, ritual ordeal just as the original legend is. The radical fact about it is that the old mystery cults and religions viewed life itself as an expanded, naturalized rite for the good reason that the very structure of their ceremonies, often very elaborate, reduced all experience to a decided pattern forming an allegory. Each mystery simplified existence, its troubles and trials, its fears, its suspense and ignorance of the future, to a given symbolic sequence representing the rebirth of the soul in eternity. Inevitably the happy initiate, emerging from the rites at last, returned to life itself. What happened then? The most natural thing was to interpret everything that happened to one thereafter in terms of the mystery. This is how "mysticism" entered life, that is, in the form of myths and legends, and by the latter, it entered art. Cocteau believed that the artist attains immortality through his works, therefore his art must be related to the mystery religions, which taught that man can attain the birth of his eternal soul in this life. The logic is that simple, and it may be followed, foot by foot of film, in *Orphée* as in *Le Sang d'un Poète*.

Cocteau in many films wished to give the sense of this double dimension of a transient and visible and sensible life, coexisting with a life also visible and sensible but supposedly intransient; at least, if it cannot ap-

The terrible corridor of *Le Sang d'un Poète* receives a variation: again and yet again, the artist must tread it to be initiated into the mysteries of life-in-death. On the right, Cocteau himself appears as an old woman.

pear as a whole at all times, it can always be present in the mind, and its revelations, its ecstasies, can be as systematically sought by the artist as by the saint and the mystic. Film, for obvious reasons (reasons which I believe I have not scanted in these pages), is ideal for creating the simultaneous presences of the double world that all religious myths postulate: the world living under the rule of what science has called the fourth dimension. Cocteau considered the feats of film—I think that, in a way, all artists do—as perfectly good illustrations of this fourth dimension, whether it be called Eternity or Relativity. Film cannot be creative in *any* sense without some intuition of it; nor can any other art form. Film can be great only with a perfect comprehension of what is meant by saying, "It is not necessary to understand, it is necessary only to believe."

And to believe, in this case, what? That serious fictions are candidates addressing eternity; that even artists, facing the last maturity of their vision, must be taken by the hand like a child and guided by accredited authority: the casually incarnate powers of the other world. He must know enough to identify them by appearances; then they will proceed to instruct him in those terms, already at hand, mentioned in Cocteau's programme note, such as the radio in Death's limousine. If he also writes, "Realism in the unreal is a trap set from minute to minute", he means a trap one should

seek, not avoid, for "the blood of the poet", suffering the injuries of this trap, finds there also the ultimate anodyne for his pain. Orpheus suffers at the fascinating apocrypha of his youth coming from Cégeste's lips over short-wave radio in Death's limousine; it is like a foreign language he once adored but has shed forever, replacing it with a more "public" idiom.

Death, whom he is tempted to love after meeting her face to face, is the eternal, intangible "vamp", more a symbol than a woman. She seduces by her immutable repose, her elusiveness; she is mother and mistress in essence, though not wife, since anciently she is the earth itself, the Underworld genius that gives birth to all flesh. Yet her unceasing power of both giving and taking away (she operates here like the glamorous chief of a high-class criminal gang) is subject to that supreme court of fate, as we see, so much like the mystery-story gimmick of the real, inaccessible "master criminal". Again and again, though vulnerable to the heroes of romance, this criminal has been made fabulous on the screen: one thinks of the demonic Dr. Mabuse, who was heir to Dr. Caligari, and of Zeus himself, the supreme Olympian god, whose acts were subject to what the ancients called Fate, which could negate him.

Cocteau revelled in taking whatever "realism in the unreal" lay around the contemporary landscapes: women from the rougher, more radical Left Bank set for his Bacchantes as he had taken Nobilities for the audience of his 1930 Poet's suicide, a genuine movie hero now (Marais) for an impersonated movie hero then (Valentino), a popular luxury symbol, the Rolls-Royce, as

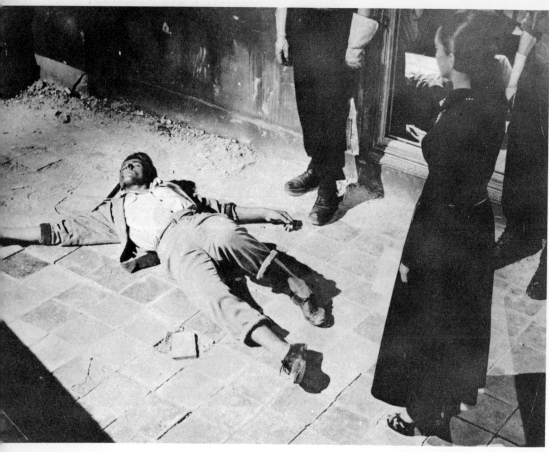

The mysterious owner of the mysterious limousine, who resembles a *femme fatale* at the head of a criminal gang, turns out to be Death; Cégeste lies before her and Orpheus is allowed to witness his resurrection. It shows him how his own identity was once killed to rise to a more sublime level of art.

vehicle of the antique *deus ex machina*. Much of *Orphée* has the excitement of a spy-thriller set amid the higher culture: a Euripidean melodrama translated into terms for the élite film fan. There are other devices just as transparent: the solemn hocus-pocus parodying preparations for hygienic modern childbirth, here parodying and anticipating the birth of Eurydice's child, and the full-length mirror that remains Cocteau's symbol of the threshold to all magic, to eternity and infinity, and the abrogation of magnetic physical laws.

His use of magnificent ruins as the corridor to the Underworld and the haunt of Death turns a modern romantic cliché into tense beauty when Orpheus and Cégeste, his younger self, participate in the rite of mystic rebirth, issuing like divine twins from Death's

womb. Yet Orpheus is permitted to return to the world where he functions in the perpetuation of the race. We owe homage, I believe, to Cocteau's gallant vision which, in common with other classic film-making, transcended the heroism of Cinerama and the 3-D screen. If he was cavalier, playing rather too safe with his imaginative devices, he left us a rare, rare film gift—whose canon is quite complete without the autobiographic souvenir, *Le Testament d'Orphée*, which he finally added with a flourish of his academic bonnet.

Once initiated into the Underworld's magic, Orpheus broods on the charms of the woman, Death, imagines he is unfaithful to Eurydice and listens to Cégeste broadcast cryptic lines of poetry over the limousine's radio. Heurtebise, above, realizes he is in love with Eurydice.

Orpheus receives the supreme favour from Death: Eurydice's life; Maria Casares as Death closely resembles the Poet's Muse in Le Sang d'un Poète (see illustrations for that film). Cocteau elaborately recommitted himself to the creed of his 1930 film: the Artist is hero of a perpetual initiation rite like that in the old mystery religions, teaching him the secret of power over art, life and death.

The priest, the tramp and the wood-gatherer lamenting the tragedy revealed by a police inquest: the wood-gatherer claims to have been its only witness.

Rashomon

1951 · JAPAN

Rarely has a foreign film winning a major award at one of the European festivals failed to appear in the United States the same or the following season. After *Rashomon* won the Grand Prize in Venice in 1951, it garnered the Academy Award as the best foreign film and launched the modern vogue for Japanese films. The U. S. National Board of Review, moreover, gave its director, Akira Kurosawa (already famous in Japan), the title of the year's best director. I should call these successes phenomenal as well as thoroughly deserved. The female lead, Machiko Kyo, needed no prize to be found worthy of recognition as an actress both beautiful and of international eminence. Toshiro Mifune, one of Japan's best known films actors (and, like Miss Kyo, much to be seen in films imported later), gives a very remarkable performance as the bandit. *Rashomon* remains, more than a decade after its début, a film in which it is as hard to detect a flaw as to find anything "dated".

The story is set in the eighth century A.D. An advantage of the historical costume film is that it begins by being already, in a sense, dated. Yet *Rashomon* updated itself by having a very modern view of reality: we are urged to grasp the story visually and morally in multiple dimensions. Superficially a "courtroom

drama", it exposes in the most direct manner a violent event taking place in the isolated depths of a forest, where a bandit happens to intercept the passage of a warrior and his lady. A foraging wood-gatherer then discovers the warrior's corpse, the bandit is captured as his suspected killer and the lady herself, completely distraught, is brought into police headquarters to give testimony with the bandit. Kurosawa dispenses with the circumstantial details of police processes; each witness, without preliminaries, confronts the camera as if it were the examining magistrate, and talks—the dead warrior communicates through a mediumistic priestess. It turns out that each individual story differs seriously from the others. The woman says she was raped by the bandit in the presence of her husband, tied up by the bandit's trickery; the bandit says that she yielded herself willingly after he had worsted her husband in a fair sword fight; the warrior's spirit says that he committed suicide after his wife had voluntarily fled with the bandit. The woman explains her husband's death by saying that, having been refused his forgiveness after the rape, she herself stabbed him while in a state of shock.

With the powerful aid of the traditional flashback, each one's evidence becomes equally real for our eyes.

The tragedy's occasion, the Woman, played by Machiko Kyo, reputedly Japan's most beautiful actress.

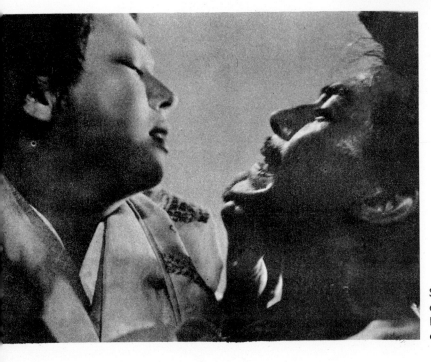

Speaking through a mediumistic priestess, the Man's spirit claims he killed himself after his wife ran away with the Bandit, who had wooed her before his eyes into amorous consent.

Never before was the flashback used with such provocative effect; the truth is enriched by each successive challenge to our imagination. The basis of the film was not traditional but the invention of a modern young Japanese writer, Ryonosuke Akutagawa, who confined the action mainly to what is related above. Kurosawa conceded something to popular taste by giving the original story a "framing" action, in which a priest, a tramp, and the wood-gatherer who has found the corpse, lament the sins of humanity on the picturesque site of one of the great gates of ancient Kyoto, Rashomon, which has been partly destroyed by a civil war. Through this device, Kurosawa weaves in another, shorter tale by Akutagawa, about the robbing of corpses left in the destroyed Gate; in the end, a foundling baby is adopted by the wood-gatherer. Happily, we

can ignore such sentimental hokum because of the way the wood-gatherer's rôle has been organized by the film. He states in court that he has eavesdropped on the whole tragedy, disqualifying the other stories by declaring (as the only "disinterested" witness) that warrior, lady and bandit all behaved in a cowardly, hysterical way, the bandit killing the warrior in a burlesque of honourable combat.

In effect, Kurosawa dared to complicate the already complex for he does not leave the wood-gatherer's integrity intact. When the wood-gatherer catches the tramp trying to steal clothes from a corpse, the tramp reminds him that the warrior has testified that "someone" drew from his breast the weapon with which he had killed himself. The implication is that the wood-gatherer has stolen the valuable dagger, and indeed he

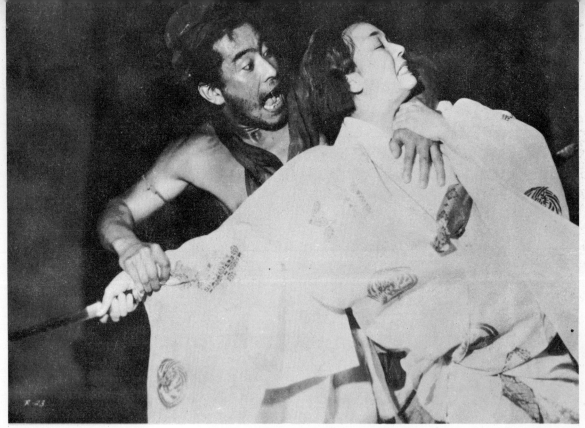

The Woman's version at the inquest: She was raped by a bandit, who had led her husband, by ruse, into the forest and succeeded in tying him up; afterward, she killed her husband in a fit of insanity, she claims, when he refused to forgive her complicity.

looks very guilty and lets the tramp off. So the wood-gatherer's story is also damaged . . . This brilliant film's forthright, unvarying pictorial loveliness, its perfect acting, its use of objectivity to make a richly complex image of truth, not only make it a classic among foreign films but also ripe for inclusion among the greatest films of all time.

Found wounded by the arrows of pursuers, the Bandit too has been brought to police headquarters. Many scenes are lit with the breathtaking virtuosity seen here.

Fiercely, the Bandit boasts that he untied the Man and offered him honourable combat, then killing him in a fair fight.

Who is the truth teller? The wood-gatherer's testimony seems to convict each participant of lying; however, suspicion is cast on the wood-gatherer by a serious discrepancy in his story and the truth remains, after all, an enigmatic quantity.

A stunner in this omnibus film: a young married woman demonstrates the impeccable poise with which she carries through an illicit rendezvous for which there just isn't enough time.

1952 · ITALY

Infidelity

or *Altri Tempi*

Italian films never willingly get very far from the soil: from the image and implicit odour of man's humours, the aspects of his soul as it rises from the sweat of his passions, his instincts, his vices. The present bountiful souvenir, an omnibus film, came from one of Italy's senior directors, Alessandro Blasetti, and is perhaps the finest achievement of his strongly Continental spirit. Suavely competent, its merits put it in a class with the partly Italian, mostly French, omnibus film, *The Seven Deadly Sins*; less trenchant than that, it is deliberately more varied in style. Its conscious object might have been to provide a neat showcase for Italian culture and Italian film-making on its virtuoso level. The episodes range with perfect ease ("framed" in this case by the efforts of a street-vendor of books to sell his wares) from an odoriferous little peasant anecdote to Luigi Pirandello's tight, complex, miniature drama of an adulterous upper-class affair that closes on its victims with an ironic snap.

A nation's laughter is a key to its tragedy and its dominant set of ethics. Italian laughter might be called

an ambivalent laughter of the earth, as a thunderstorm or an earthquake is legendarily, and ambivalently, the gods' laughter and their anger. Italian exuberance and its humour are not like British exuberance and its humour: the Italians never get really wild enough to convert basic moral creeds into sheer theatrical charades; this may be because Italy is the most Catholic country in the world and also (among the non-Sovietized countries) the most communistic. Lust has a sort of chameleonism in Italy; surely, it is sexual, even animal, but the rights of lust there are held to be virtually, so to speak, the rights of man.

This is beautifully brought out in the untrammelled lustiness of *The Trial of Phryne*, based on a legend coming down from ancient Greece and concerning a famous artist's model, a beauty indicted before Athens' supreme court for exceeding the supposed limits of her calling. The case is more concretely put by Blasetti's film, which displays Gina Lollobrigida as a village's reigning prostitute; brought to legal trial for her misdeeds, she is exonerated (as the ancient legend goes)

178

A piece of the ground: that is a deodorized euphemism for what these two peasants are mauling each other to lay their hands on.

"Cut" to a level of human desire that could hardly be in greater contrast to that just mentioned: here is upper-class adultery and it sinks its teeth into the naked flesh of this faithless wife by Pirandellian mischance.

by her lawyer's inspired act of disclosing her physical charms to the courtroom. The frolicsome mood, taking a farcical view of a serious truth, is rendered with apt relish by Vittorio de Sica as Phryne's lawyer, Miss Lollobrigida and everyone else involved.

In what sense Phryne's contemporary trial may be a souvenir of "times gone by", rather than a sly portrait of eternal ethical opinion, is left to the viewer's discrimination. Obviously, one is invited to have the highly portentous liberalism of Athens' wise judicial body. The mingling of the several episodes creates, as it was meant to do, a contagious morality, this morality being, I hazard, mainly that of the aesthetic feelings. As such, it is a token of civilized worldliness: a worldliness no doubt nostalgic but for that very reason all the more serious. Its grace issues best in an episode unfolding with the even tenor of an old photograph album. The awakening of a growing boy and girl to the possibilities of love is set in the same period as Proust's and is so intense and frustrated as to shed over childhood his induplicable touch of beauty and refinement. The quality of this episode is in ambivalent accord with the initial piece: an illicit and quite guileless rendezvous between a self-possessed young married woman and her less poised, unsatisfied lover. It is carried out in a droll, impeccably Continental style. This, beyond quibbling, is the life of pleasure, shamelessly undated and as exacting as the train schedules that, as here, do not always coöperate with it.

A sweeter, more beautifully styled tribute to the eternal legend of childhood love, and the pathos of its unfulfilment, could hardly be imagined within the same space of time.

A dimpling shocker for a climax: two internationally famous stars of Italian films (yes, he's Vittorio de Sica) re-enact a legend to the effect that beauty naked is beauty exonerated of its worst (?) crime.

The Seven Deadly Sins

Splendiferous Gérard Philippe, truly lamented of late, sells more than refreshments in barking for the Seven Deadly Sins, whose odd number he evens up with an eighth, not in the least deadly.

Michèle Morgan's beauty makes a captivating image of the sin of Pride. Is it so bad? It's only self-inflicted hunger.

The Seven Deadly Sins—to catalogue them: Avarice, Anger, Sloth, Lust, Envy, Gluttony and Pride—belong, among other things, to "times gone by", and persist, like the past, through meddlesome intrusions. But leave it to the French to emasculate them by making them look chic. France waited only till 1962 to refurbish them with another set of film vignettes, if only to say that they revise themselves in human experience, and willy-nilly, cause mirth as well as unavoidable misgiving. The new set likewise has different, currently outstanding directors, but this old set, enlisting such proven directorial talents as Claude Autant-Lara and Yves Allegret, is better. Through the persons of Viviane Romance and Frank Villard (still cherished ornaments of French films when this omnibus was made), "Lust" is a come-clean parable of the sexual appetite as it may burst through on any level of social convention; unwittingly, an ordinary mother educates her growing daughter into this deadly condition by example: sex-education becomes a rather blunt quantity. The moral may be that sin is inescapable—here to stay, however it be dealt with.

The French are so catholic in this respect: one must make the best of sin, or anyway the best *art* of it. Those short forms, the true short story, the amusing anecdote, the fable of La Fontaine, are all French specialties. Maupassant was the source of another omnibus film,

Le Plaisir, but the present array, to which Italy contributes, is more varied and ingenious, fine though that Maupassant trio be. Michèle Morgan—so beautiful a person!—plays here, perhaps, her greatest and aptest role because her beauty and assurance are exploited not as sex or glamour but as "Pride", a sin she shares unselfishly with Françoise Rosay as her mother.

"Envy", that curiously *social* sin, is the product of Colette's wordly imagination, just frivolous enough, just serious enough. A true painter, not a dummy of waxenly overflowing passions, is shown living in Paris as painters really live there, absorbed with bed and studio, comfortably fusing sex, work and social relaxation. A lovely girl he meets isn't up to understanding what being an artist means. As his mistress, she cannot participate in shop talk or witty banter and is jealous of a professional model (posing in the nude) where there is no cause. Hence, jealousy is a pretext for envy, her envy of genius and its rightful employments. In stupid revenge, she manages to kill the artist's pet cat and make it appear an accident. But the artist's intuition divines the truth and he simply throws her out.

The Seven Deadly Sins, with a fillip of ultra-worldliness, have tacked on here an eighth "sin". It is the most striking of the lot and indicates how gay and arrogant the *esprit gallant* may be, redeeming sin-as-such by presenting it as false appearance. Who could bind all this together better than the late Gérard Philippe as a sideshow barker? As engaging a male lead as French films have ever had, Philippe combined acting versatility with the most coquettish of masculine charm. Besides playing Fan-Fan the Tulip on the screen, he could impersonate the Cid on the stage of the Théâtre Populaire and deliver his climactic tirade with as much verve and éclat (French terms!) as he uses to make the Eight Deadly Sins into generally palatable attractions.

"Gluttony" is a concise comment on French gourmandise: a stranded motorist prefers some phenomenal cheese as a midnight snack to seducing his peasant host's pretty wife. The Italian "Avarice and Anger" (with Rossellini's collaboration) is rather harsh in its neo-Realistic manners, lacking the quiet French bite. The eighth sin is embodied, apparently, in a fantastic bordello where even priests bring their sailors, but the bordello turns out to be a commercial photographer's studio. This hoax is a peculiarly Continental hint that the cardinal sins, deadly as they are by reputation, may after all, as naughty poets say, "seem" rather than "be". Sheer gaiety and bon-vivantism, as well as the impersonal cynicism of which the French alone seem capable, have probably never been so well fleshed before film cameras. It is as if, on Judgment Day, the Sins will become coy, pleading their cases to a Deity impersonated by Sacha Guitry after being admitted to the Heavenly Presence by Jacques Tati as St. Peter.

Gluttony on tenterhooks: you might think it is Lust from this flirting couple, but Lust is very well taken care of elsewhere.

The giveaway: the stranded motorist, just seen flirting, is scheming to snatch more of that savoury cheese as he begs his peasant hostess to sleep between him and her husband. The Eighth Sin? It must be seen in action to be believed.

Raf Vallone as a Tuscan villager, returning after World War II from a Russian prison camp, has sworn to avenge the death of his brother, a betrayed Partisan; Vallone's magnificent image dominates Curzio Malaparte's film.

1952 · ITALY

The Forbidden Christ

or *Il Cristo Proibito*

Among the strangest phenomena of film history was the emergence of Curzio Malaparte, the novelist, as a full-fledged cinema artist in one stroke; not an artist engaged in exploring formal possibilities, stunts or sensationalism, but in dominating the elements of the talking film so as to produce the edifying thing a cohesive, solid work of art may be. Coming to the medium as the gifted author

of *Kaputt* and *The Skin* (both issued in English translation), he was active in two senses during the last World War, being one of the most striking single personalities to emerge from it. As an Italian journalist with military rank, he was in constant touch with the German fighting forces, their chiefs and their field manoeuvres as well as an honoured guest at their banquets; thus he travelled in Russia, Finland and Poland, functioning as liaison officer with a certain *double-entendre*. His book, *Kaputt*, supposedly a novelized version of the truth, paints him as a much stirred, secretly partial humanist, capable of impertinent irony to his hosts in the guise of banter, and consistently, at heart, sympathetic with those they oppressed. Oddly detached from the horrors he witnessed, Malaparte makes a strange case and a dazzlingly articulate one. In *Kaputt*, whose manuscript was spirited to safety by diplomatic pouch, he is a relentless critic of the German character in its cruel ambitions. Somewhat like a satiric orator at a funeral feast, he employed a savage *délicatesse* in his prose that is revealed here in a quite different dimension.

Perhaps part of his complex emotionalism is due to overimpressionability. This film showed, nevertheless, that he held his ideas under perfect control and then went ahead, without mishap, to work out a beautiful freehand study of human temperament suffering from the universal shock of war. Malaparte appreciated

182

He does not know the identity of the Judas, supposedly still in the town, but expects to learn it from his own family. However, his father, his mother, his sweetheart and even the servant girl, withhold it for reasons he cannot accept.

As director of photography, Gabor Pogany contributes much to the film: this stunning shot shows the avenger's confrontation with a man whom he suspects is helping to frustrate his objective.

A philosophizing friend of the avenger, a sort of hermit, typifies the town's collective will to exile all bloodshed and live in unbroken peace. Note the beautiful illusion of pagan horns on Vallone, epitomizing Man as the ennobled animal.

the paradoxes of spirit, including the collision between major points of conscience as sealed within individual and group. Here the collective's decision tends to dominate the individual's. An Italian prisoner of war, at the cessation of hostilities, returns from Russia to his Tuscan village determined to kill the man who, he has learned, betrayed his younger brother, a Partisan, to a German firing squad. Even with the opening scenes,

rather conventional as they are, one senses that *The Forbidden Christ* has little resemblance to the already established Neo-Realist style. Malaparte, who wrote the script and directed the film, providing even its musical score, had expert assistance at the camera. Yet only a masterful intelligence, dedicated to film as an art, could transmit so immediately the feeling of witnessing something irreproachably designed, balanced in its total framing, musically ordered and profound.

The hero is played by Raf Vallone at the height of his maturity as man and actor, heroic of mould, so noble-limbed of soul and body as to suggest that "think-

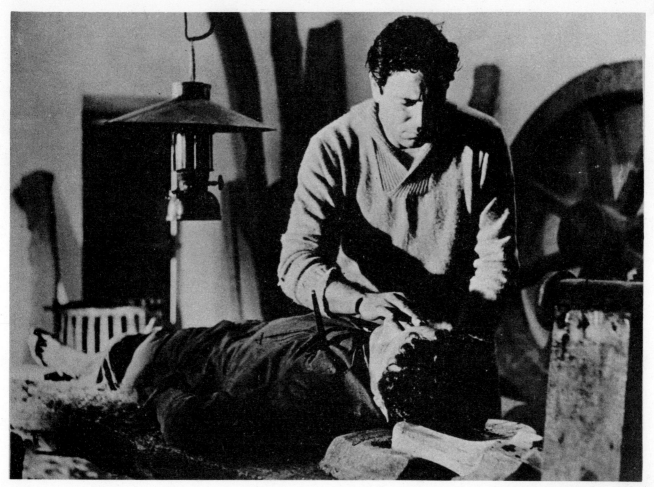

In a lightning-like climax of tragic design, the hermit places himself between his friend and a cowardly thrust of the Judas' knife; with a heartrending cry, the cheated avenger understands: a Christlike sacrifice has wiped the slate clean.

ing earth" which Prometheus, legend says, fashioned to be Man. This family avenger has not been told the identity of the Judas who caused his brother's death, and to his surprise and bewilderment, though he soon guesses it is known, nobody will tell him. The whole town has virtually ostracized the traitor, but this very fact is what protects him. The grim avenger, denied his name by father, mother, the woman he intends to marry and even the servant girl, is stunned when meeting a similar obstacle even in an old friend, a saintlike hermit who used to talk philosophy to him. This man (well played by Alain Cuny) at last explains to him why the town is frustrating him: it has an overpowering desire to have done with all bloodshed and return without blemish to the sacred ways of peace.

Even as in the Orestes trilogy, the moral point is arguable and on a high level. This is dramatically and symbolically underlined when a popular ritual, the Game of the Cross, takes place. A procession carrying banners and grotesque images of death ends at the steps of the Cathedral, where the sexton appears with a huge bare cross and jeeringly dares someone to come forth by choice and suffer Christ's fate there. Though much shaken, the avenger will not give up his vendetta,

which has made him as much a marked man as the Judas himself. We see that the Christian spirit is prevailing through a collective will and yet that something beyond Christianity is also speaking to us. Wanting consolation from his hermit friend, the dark-wrapped avenger goes one night to his isolated house. By now, the Judas—whom we have seen and whose identity we may have guessed—is frightened enough to take the matter into his own hands and tries to plant a knife in the man whose vengeance he fears. But the hermit interposes himself and takes the fatal stab. The perfection of the design, its timeless validity, would not reach us without the most careful handling. Even the avenger's commiserating cry of horror, all his rage spent in it, has just the right pitch. Now, closing his friend's eyes, he cannot kill the Judas, twice guilty by this last crime, because his natural office is to mourn him who has won the Game of the Cross: offered himself like the "innocent lamb" that Christ chose to be.

The above three shots from the opening Maupassant story in the Max Ophuls omnibus film, illustrate one of the most enthralling feats in film history: the whirlwind subject is the ecstasy of the dance.

1953 · FRANCE

Le Plaisir

The roster of foreign directors with brilliant achievements to their credit would be reprehensibly inadequate without token of the deceased Max Ophuls, as zealous a *cinéaste* as von Stroheim, Visconti or Orson Welles, as sumptuous in his ideas as those, yet with idiosyncratic traits placing him in the vanguard of truly visionary film-makers. He was devoted to the mobile camera in the way—to use an expression from a well-known vocabulary—a detective continuously shadows someone to observe his path through space and his every move. Ophuls was the sworn investigator of continuous and extended paths of sightseeing: the marathons of propelled feet and eyes.

This love for revealing humanity through its uninterrupted continuities and propulsions is ideally reflected in the Maupassant stories chosen to make this tripartite film: each of the three has its curious, flowing, penetrating truth, its dazzling point tracing one motif among man's multifarious forward passages—strange, romantic, vulnerable, humorously instinctive and contrary creature that he is when he abandons himself to the fulfilments of his desires. Maupassant was a collector of human curiosities, each ringing true in its oblique extravagance. The opening story has the most superb running-shot I know, being the strict adventure of a man who has lived for nothing, really, but the joy of dancing

in one of Paris' famed cafés of the last century. Without ado, we start with him across the street outside as he dashes, wearing tophat and evening clothes, between arriving carriages, enters and races along a gallery to join his partner just in time for the next dance.

Irresistibly, we are caught up in a visual and audible rhythm: the whole headlong music of human pulse and instrumental music. This is a *passion*: this dance involving body and soul. Only as a sort of double-take do we note that this male dancer has a curiously pale and rigid, handsome, mustachio'd face; everything seems blended into the action as though it held the meaning of all existence. Something wild, a little morbid and even mad, however, comes through this plunge into the midst of a sprightly dance. It is magnificent; we cannot doubt it. Yet we are hardly surprised when the obsessed male dancer suddenly wilts and collapses, to be carried from the floor as in a faint. A doctor, called in, examines him, prostrate and gasping, in a back room; his collar must be torn away to allow him to breathe better. Then an exquisitely anticlimatic discovery is made by the doctor: this scion of Terpsichore is wearing a complete false face of rubber, youthfully smooth, a type face proper to a mask; beneath it, the doctor finds the runnelled, careworn face of an old man whose dancing days, now, seem definitely over.

Flashy town prostitutes are so flattered to be taken as respectable by a country community that their gratitude, while in church, vents itself in sobs: Danielle Darrieux and Jean Gabin bring zest to the occasion.

Taken home, the dancer is the subject of a thumbnail explanation by his mate; even her spare words are hardly necessary. Nothing, either love or marriage, has remained real to this man except the activity of the dance. Under his own roof, he who is a genius of the dance is an enfeebled creature about to give up the ghost. This marvellous hero of a superb fiction might as well remain anonymous: as masked as his destiny. An acid sort of twinkle, in the second story, suffuses the daredevil resolve of a young model to marry her artist lover. Her mating instinct knows the winning move but it is costly to the flesh. The third story is a spirited rendering of the hilarious, disarmingly frivolous, justly classic *House of Madame Tellier*: Maupassant's account of a holiday spent in the country by all the inmates of a town brothel, invited to the Confirmation of a relative of one of the sisterhood. The respectable rustic community is set on its ears while the town gentry (chiefly public officials) pine away at the ladies' shocking absence from their duty. These creatures of easy virtue, accepted as "pure" by the village, dissolve into sobs of gratitude at the church ceremony; their excursion turns into a sort of debauch with the emotion of human charity. Yet business is business; next day, their true stations in life must be resumed. Once back in the nightly routine, however, Madame Tellier finds charity contagious and charges the gentlemen less for the champagne; meanwhile, her obliging ladies become more than obliging and spend their favours with unaccustomed feeling and generosity.

The story's kind, boisterous innocence is exactly suited to Ophuls' sensual and effusive style. This trio carved deeper the niche of the man who also gave us Schnitzler's *La Ronde*.

If you were a pretty model (Simone Simon), would you jump out of a window to snare an artist (Daniel Gelin) as legal mate? Though Ophuls' answer is scenically lush and languidly narrative, it ends with the suddenness of a shot.

187

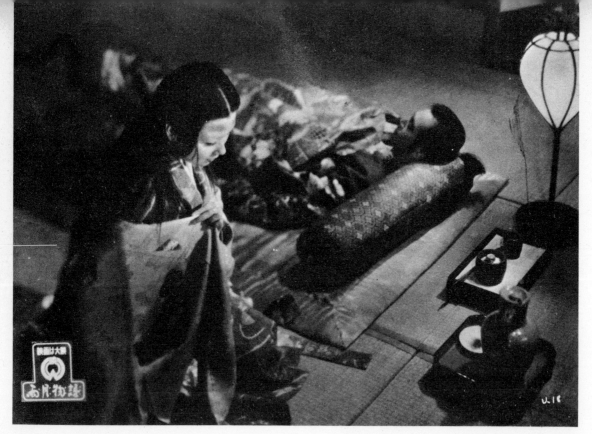

1953 · JAPAN

Two peasants leave their homes and wives to make their fortunes; Tobei to loot with an army, Genjuro to sell his pottery. Genjuro's first customer is the magically beautiful Lady Wakasa, who lures him to her luxurious home and performs a secret ceremony when he is asleep.

Ugetsu Monogatari

In *Ugetsu Monogatari*, the eighteenth-century writer, Akinari Ueda, provided for the well-known director, Kenji Mizoguchi, a source parallel with that supplied by Akutagawa for Kurosawa, *Rashomon*'s director: a vivid tale exhumed from another era. This film took Venice's Grand Prize for 1953 and its presentation in the States was even better organized than that of *Rashomon*. At the première, sponsored by the Japan Society, His Excellency, Sadao Iguchi, Japanese Ambassador to the United States, delivered a speech from the stage. That moment surely marked the height of felicitous cultural relations between the United States and its erstwhile opponent at arms. As leads, moreover, *Ugetsu Monogatari* offered two players already known favourably to American audiences, Matayuki Mora, the warrior husband of *Rashomon*, and Machiko Kyo, that same film's abused and beautiful wife.

The story of *Ugetsu Monogatari* is actually more bizarre than *Rashomon*'s, if both are viewed as fairy

tales. Basically, it is that of the humble commoner who aspires to glory, ease, and happiness only to find them, when achieved, a delusion leading to agony and shame. Here it arises from the inspiration of two peasants to become rich amid the confusion of war, one hawking his wares in the city, the other fighting with the army of a feudal lord. The antique moral is the same as that of the Prodigal Son, appearing here in duet. The two men (one a father) forget all ties with homes and wives. Genjuro consorts sensually with a great lady, who, buying pottery from him, proceeds to lure him to her magnificent house, where he gains all he might desire. The Circe is Miss Kyo, who seems thoroughly to justify the report that she is "the highest-paid woman in Japan". *Ugetsu Monogatari*, as a universal fairy tale in Japanese dress, is perhaps more communicative than other Japanese costume films. The uncertainties of war and the fortunes of the "little" man are all too familiar, in art and in fact, during our own time.

Tobei, the soldier of fortune, becomes a fraud, winning military promotion by claiming the head of a warrior actually killed by another. He and Genjuro, enjoying his unreal paradise, are two victims of illusion that has a psychological pattern close to that of modern

188

Life with Lady Wakasa is a dream-paradise for Genjuro, who does not know she is the ghost of a girl who died before she could make love. He forgets all about his wife, who meanwhile is killed by two starving soldiers in search of food.

Learning from a Buddhist priest the true identity of the enchantress, Genjuro, though still under her spell, is awakened one night by a terrible dream.

warfare, in which soldiers are uprooted suddenly from home and peacetime existence. The unexpected help of a Buddhist priest intervenes to rescue Genjuro from his wicked devotion to love and luxury. As Genjuro forces his way to freedom, only to see the place of his enchantment reduced to a heap of ashes, we have an age-old "morality" ending. Yet it can remind us of the agency of priests in modern juvenile-delinquency films and of a priest's heroic, if ineffectual, rôle in the Italian film, *Open City*. While their husbands are being snared by the world's illusions, Tobei's wife is raped by soldiers and Genjuro's killed by soldiers starving for food. Yet the film's tragic realism, exotic in place and period, retains the magic of the perennially fabulous. Pure and straightforward in style, *Ugetsu Monogatari* evokes the world of reality as the essence of a tragic dream.

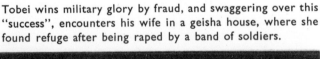

Tobei wins military glory by fraud, and swaggering over this "success", encounters his wife in a geisha house, where she found refuge after being raped by a band of soldiers.

Urged on by the priest, Genjuro madly forces his way out of Wakasa's mansion and, coming to himself, sees that his "paradise" has turned into a heap of ashes. He must return to his potter's wheel, where his dead wife's spirit consoles him.

The acme of fragile grace, Lady Kesa (right), a decoy for the Empress during a palace revolution, smites the heart of her escort, Moritoh, with love.

Gate of Hell

With this film and *Ugetsu Monogatari*, movies from Japan became a cult for connoisseurs the world over. Besides winning the Grand Prize at the Cannes Festival in 1954, *Gate of Hell* began having superlative honours heaped upon it in the U.S., reaping the Joseph Burstyn Award (in honour of the deceased importer of foreign films), the Film Critics' Circle Award of the Foreign Language Press, both for the best foreign film of the year, and a special award from the Photographic Society of America; further, Hollywood's Academy declared its "colour costume design" the best and named it, as well, the year's best foreign film. Perhaps admirers of the Japanese film were relieved to find *Gate of Hell*, unlike *Rashomon*, crystal clear in all ways and more traditionally native to Japan. Lacking (as *Rashomon* did) "special effects", *Gate of Hell* quietly displayed mastery of the film's basic vocabulary, centering on beauties of light

and shade no less than colour, on static design and adagio rhythms rather than precipitate changes of pace and prolonged violence. Not that it fails to excite the emotions with action or to present the spectacle of passion but with these it reaches a severe balance.

For the first time, mass film audiences outside Japan were introduced by *Gate of Hell* to true native theatrical and social traditions: the nobility of disciplined feeling, however strong; the power of outward forms pitted against inward passions with loss to neither. The stylized Noh drama, stemming from ritual as Japan's oldest dramatic medium, is virtually danced theatre, and danced theatre is largely what we have in the measured unfamiliar pantomime of a great married lady, loved madly, illicitly, by a warrior, Moritoh, and the crisis brought about by his persistence, of which Wataru, her husband, is ignorant till the end. The loyal wife (again Machiko Kyo) realizes that some tragedy must take place as a consequence of the frenzied Moritoh's

The lord of the clan, officiating at a great religious shrine, receives word of the riot of men's passion.

The most frenzied is the warrior, Moritoh, impassioned with love for Lady Kesa, though she is happily married. Permitted to see her in reward for his valour in suppressing the rebellion, he finds her determined to resist his desire.

lust for her; so, pretending to assent to his plot to murder Wataru, she cleverly contrives to be fatally stabbed by Moritoh in his stead. The end is suffused with the transcendent grief of both men; all violence, previous and possible, is quelled in the presence of Kesa's sublime self-sacrifice.

Gate of Hell has a more emphatically exotic look than *Rashomon* or *Ugetsu Monogatari* despite the fact that its technical accomplishments as colour film are said to have been learned by Teinosuke Kinusaga, who directed it and adapted it from a twelfth-century chronicle, at the Eastman laboratories and Warner Brothers studio. Japan's flair for things Western, as embodied by its best films, offers impressive evidence of the harmony possible between nations. Experts can detect concessions by native traditions in these transferences: whatever is *un*-Japanese to native eyesight and understanding. But the Japanese nation, at home, has been westernizing itself for nearly a century. Western movie-makers could well make use of some distinctive Japanese formal virtues; among them, the way emotions are reflected in the behaviour of an individual isolated from all eyes in his home's privacy, aiming simply, with dignity and inevitability, at the life or death which fate has chosen for him. An un-Western, un-modern reality? More's the pity!

In medieval Japan, as in medieval Europe, victory in sport or tournament attested to the ardour of a man's devotion to a woman: Moritoh defeats Kesa's husband, Wataru, in a horse race.

Kesa has frustrated Moritoh's plot to kill her husband while sleeping by managing to substitute herself in his bed. The knowledge of her sacrifice unites both men in sublime grief. Only the willing surrender of life, they see, has been able to halt the course of violence. The male's code of honour dissolves in shame and tears.

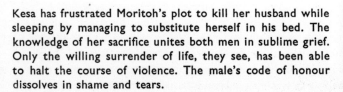

This is an image of consummation – some kind of consummation, no matter what: a true image, a social image, to which Italian film cameras, at their best, are perhaps the best-attuned.

1953 · ITALY

Love in the City

or *Amore in Città*

Italy, among film-making nations, seems to have a decided priority today in at least one department: its films can show most clearly of all the existence of man as the higher animal; not man as necessarily noble or intellectual or passionate, or the opposite, not as sweet or bitter, healthy or vicious in ethical mould, but man as the clean animal presence, holding his precious humanity as in the palm of his open hand. Indeed, love is the *leitmotif* of this set of urban stories from various directors; people are seen treading the lanes of paved streets or city parks, "alone" yet "together" on their errands and at their destinations. All the emphasis on the erotic here is innocent, spontaneous and instinctive, without being consciously or pretentiously so; so exuberant is the pride of expanding consciousness in human bodies that the theme is "humanity in the city" more precisely than "love in the city". Love, after all, is the ideal or metaphoric merging of bodies, but whether ideal or not, it may mean the appearance of one body out of another. The basic yearning of one body for union with another may also be (as here one story touchingly illustrates) a chimera—a dream of the lonely, the ineligible in looks or money, the luckless, the talentless: those who are dispossessed by life of everything but wan hope.

The mere thrill of living bodies that move: this, pre-eminently, is the virtue of *Love in the City*. The "chivalric tournament" which is the modern dance hall, with fleshly union (approved by ethics or not) its sometime climax; the "screening" of love in the folk institution of the marriage bureau; the very private case of a young female neurotic; the animal beauty of mother love aware only of its urge and that urge's simple duty; such, this film reveals, are frequent human predicaments, widely spread human drives. They, or things like them, take place every day, in every big city, without disaster to the human soul or premonitions of the race's extinction. Such valiant, lucidly put humanism is rare enough in our time and among the most optimistic of tokens. To be the *good animal* that is man! This is a quiet thing, the thing the newspapers are dedicated to tell lies about, which journalism renders as sob stories

Delight of the casual eye. Male and female? Well, in this case, yes. Common? That is what life in the city must be. But perfectly natural — nothing to brood over — in the order of the Italian day.

The movies have tried out this image and its appeal ten thousand times. It was never more successful than in this Italian (for-true) dance hall.

or sensational melodramas. Italy, too, is a scene of the melodramas of war and other passions and the crimes to which excessive egoism and ambition lead. But, says *Love in the City* in reply, there are modes of ignoring these matters, even in the teeth of sorest suffering and sorest perplexity.

These modes appeal to the goodness of the animal: the animal contented with same and civilized "devouring". These modes get around difficulties, even horror and despair, with the ease and charm of children; these modes constitute an Italian art—Anna Magnani and Raf Vallone express them in the professional field of films. But so does the hero of *Bicycle Thieves*, whom de Sica picked from among these same "lanes of paved streets" to act his Worker; so does the Worker's little boy, not the most eloquent or cleverest of child actors but possibly the most natural for that very defect; both these non-actors in *Bicycle Thieves* were divine amateurs. The unconceited voyeurism of the streets, fixated on young female breasts and behinds, on the sweet, carnal, consummative contacts of the dance hall: this happy voyeurism, hanging on the threshold of the tangible, is a hope of our modern mass civilization. Culture is another matter; so is art. But culture and art must, and can, take care of themselves. *Love in the City* is the sort of film documentarism which unassumingly enters its classic status. *Joie-de-vivre*, I know, is a terribly flat cliché. But I think it finds apt expression in the lights and shadows of this very exceptional human document.

A glimpse of true care, eternal care, in the city's daily, complex round; children do get lost, people are "conned" and love is destroyed or perverted; the higher animal, man, is healthy enough, according to this film, to outride all such dangers.

A triumph of the documentary view on life is in the swing of this girl's hips; all that is morbid, all that is sorrowful or desperate, is overcome by the design of her dress.

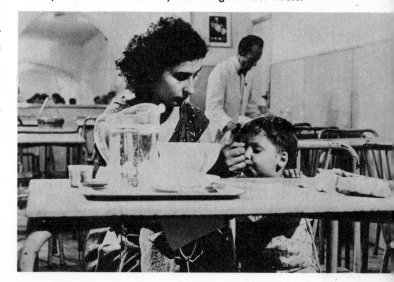

La Strada

A simple-minded adolescent is being purchased from her indigent mother. Her use? To be mate and helpmate to her brutal buyer, who travels through Italy in a motorcycle trailer performing a "strong man" act.

Neo-Realism, so thoroughly installed as a school of Italian film-making, ran into trouble, in the Fifties, when Fellini, having graduated from script-writing and directed the acclaimed *I Vitelloni*, gave *La Strada* to the world. The story, based on human eccentricity, despair and loneliness, and presenting the extraordinary genius of Fellini's wife, the actress Giulietta Masina, was a macabre, if romantic, sort of "Neo-Realism". Merging some moral sunlight with a much more, indeed engulfing, moral sombreness, it was naturalistic enough in tone to suggest, as it were, that *la strada* ("the street") was a simplified image of Italy itself as the degraded abode of a degraded people. The film, though winning the Grand Prize at Venice in 1954, provoked the friendly antagonism of stalwart native Neo-Realists, who were joined by the State in feeling that *La Strada* might deceive foreign audiences into thinking sordidness prevailed in the Italian lower population, where many individuals had sunk, rather than swum, in the unhealthy moral current.

The State, backed by opinion in the film world, desired to assert rights of censorship; at which development, Fellini strategically appealed directly to an authority that saved his film, one Cardinal Siri of Genoa. Some independent newspapers attacked the director's action on moral grounds, while factional colleagues of his claimed that *La Strada* was not really "bad" but "wrong". One might think that Communist factionalism was at work in the foreign public relations field; perhaps so, but the affair was simply a striking instance of the perennial struggle between Church and State, in largely Catholic countries, to sway public opinion. Surely, for example, André Malraux, France's Minister of Culture, is no Communist, yet he too sought to obstruct the export of recent distinguished French films as likely to give the world a false impression of the French people.

What is the issue that should concern admirers of the film art? Fellini's artistic inspiration, granted by his opponents, is still thought properly subject to the State's supervision. If there is to be supervision or censorship of art (says the optimistic breed of Neo-Realists), let it be the State's rather than the Church's. So the basic question is supervision by more than the artist's conscience, more than the public's willingness to listen to his conscience. This much is certain: Fellini did not selfishly, arbitrarily appeal to religious authority. I am sure he understood that his theme underwrites an essential creed of Catholicism. Man, says this creed, is born into sin; his sometime bestiality may exalt sin and bring both soul and body low. Well, *La Strada* is proof that, regardless of any concept of sin as *productive* of the Zampanos of Italy, these Zampanos statistically exist as ego-blind brutes of melancholy, unlettered and as sorrowful as figures from Dante's Purgatory.

Zampano's act (recognize Anthony Quinn?) has various antics for which Gelsomina, his new slave, is assistant and come-on; she proves a more winsome performer, he plainly sees, than *he* is or ever could be.

Zampano (played by Anthony Quinn with unexpected aptitude) is a lone wolf, travelling about Italy with a "strong man" act on a motorcycle trailer that itself is a symbol of defiant self-isolation. The surly, monosyllabic fellow, only partly human, has a social remnant of animal need, principally sexual. His habit is to buy a concubine-helper from indigent peasant families. Having lost the last one, he goes back to her family and finds available only the simple-minded Gelsomina, played by Giulietta Masina. They are soon off together after a morbid scene of separation from her family. Completely inexperienced, Gelsomina is at first fearful and puzzled, but introduced by Zampano to her duties, behaves submissively, and to his surprise, even becomes cheerful, performing so well as a clowning come-on for his act that it is obvious she is now the star of the show.

The moral is true and beautiful and perfectly lucid as presented. The innate sunniness of Gelsomina's nature, though she is virtually half-witted, has a humanity that communicates like that of several great comedians of our era. Masina's personality resembles both Chaplin's and that of the baby-faced, exquisitely textured (and departed) Harry Langdon of American films. Gelsomina is technically a slave and utterly defenceless, but like Christianity when it first opposed armed paganism, wins by happy, clear-souled surrender. The structure of events is plausible enough; it certainly is fatal and

final enough. The strange pair encounters a travelling circus, are induced to join it, but meet disaster when Zampano's ill nature clashes with some of the circus buffoons and he lands in jail.

Gelsomina, troubled by the irredeemable nature of her master and paramour, confides in a sympathetic circus performer called the Fool, being tempted to leave Zampano and join him. But the Fool, with the divinatory skill of clowns, perceives that she prefers staying with her brutal "lover" and explains to her that serving him may be her destiny in life. She seems to understand, especially because hers is really what may be called "the language of fools". Gelsomina passes from happiness to grief, grief to happiness, like the sun veiled and unveiled by clouds; this is her genius.

But a terrible act of blood takes place. She and Zampano again encounter the Fool, and Zampano, knowing the young man's bond of spirit with Gelsomina, ferociously attacks him, and meaning only to maul him, leaves him dead, and escapes. This is a mortal blow to his companion's equilibrium: the friendship of the world, Zampano's living alter ego, has been taken from her forever.

She can only mourn. Her grief takes the shape of

Actually she grows to love her heartless, taciturn master, and submitting in everything, tries to woo him into human companionship, but he won't succumb. As the girl, Giulietta Masina revealed a novel and authentic comic genius.

perpetual whimpering, which she cannot control and which works on Zampano as the bad conscience of the homicide he is. So, with the impulse that has made his character, he abandons her, asleep, in a ruined house where they have camped out. The heartbreak is universally contagious; one mourns with Gelsomina, who does not take long to die of grief. Zampano goes on with his act, duly breaking the chain with expansions of his ageing chest. But incoherently he misses Gelsomina. Learning by chance that she has died, he gets drunk, feels grief envelop him like a black cloud and goes to the seashore to sob out his bankrupt spirit. Is *this* the film that Fellini's professional colleagues thought "wrong"? It is, in some aspects of execution, a little imperfect. But I believe it will be with us long, long after the objections to it have become incomprehensible.

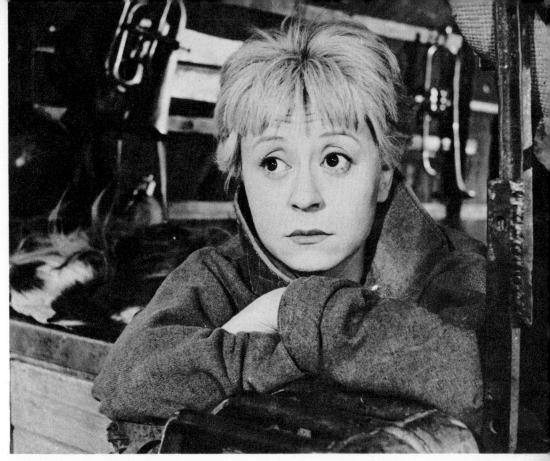

Great trouble comes for both when Zampano runs riot in a circus which they join; he lands in jail while Gelsomina finds the sympathy and counsel of a strange young clown, called the Fool, who tells her that serving this brute may be, after all, her destiny.

The Fool, however, has run into the pair once too often: Zampano has involuntarily killed him in a rage and escaped detection. Having witnessed the homicide, Gelsomina whimpers so much that Zampano decides to abandon her; after he does so, she dies of grief. Too late, he learns the agonizing truth that he has killed his own humanity.

In Kurosawa's adaptation of Shakespeare's *Macbeth*, the film screen seems a living picture on which feudal pageantry and passions are as if brushed there.

The encounter of "Macbeth" (right) with the powers of witchcraft is a magic deception: the pivotal incident is poetically rendered in this scrupulously fine version of a foreign masterpiece.

Throne of Blood   1957 · JAPAN

The influence of both Japan's elder classic drama, the Noh, and younger classic drama, the Kabuki, have contributed to the exquisite skill with which Akira Kurosawa has transferred Shakespeare's famous tragedy, *Macbeth*, to the film. The slow, highly precisioned pace of the former, hieratic and lyric, merges and contrasts with the impetuous, dramatically veering pulse of the latter; both, of course, hold elements of stylization. It seems a major artistic decision that Kurosawa refrained from using the colour medium to invoke the vivid life of the stage, though his black-and-white screen may have resulted from considerations of budget. However that may be, one can hardly imagine a better adaptation from stage to film or nation to nation: surely not a better one if plotted within the same scope and convention as chosen by Kurosawa.

The air of primitive history, joined with the eerie atmosphere of even more primitive magic, suffuses the screen from the instant we see, in the opening shots, the great fortress castle once held by Macbeth's Japanese counterpart, swathed in mist, desolate in space, and

rendered with the most exacting Japanese aestheticism which I, for one, have yet seen on film. From the purely *pictorial* viewpoint, *Throne of Blood* is more of a piece than any Japanese classic I have included here. Transition from event to event, emphasis to emphasis in the narrative action, long view to short view and close-up, take place with the even, certain, smooth rhythm that is true only of a highly controlled style.

The warrior as an image of force and terror, especially when on horseback, is of the utmost picturesqueness here. I cannot vouch for the historical accuracy of either costumes or general treatment, but an impression of savage fierceness and feudal might is uncannily conveyed by Kurosawa's imagery and never spoiled in its beauty. The dramatic arabesques of ceremonially grouped warriors, their alternate impassivity and emotional eruptions producing a gripping tension, are things that soon establish a remote, fatal and exotic mood for the tragedy.

That most-seen actor in Japanese films, and possibly their very best one, Toshiro Mifune, who played the

Japan's classic drama, the Noh, dominates the mood and style of "Lady Macbeth's" goading of her husband to kill his guest. The tragedy advances with remarkable fidelity to its source.

The hero in his mad fit when he sees "Banquo's" ghost: every turn of the plot is translated into an impeccable Japanese idiom.

Bandit in *Rashomon*, has the Macbeth rôle and seems to have been—as to all his rôles—born to it. We have here generally, in their most continuous and thus arresting form, certain style-traits of Far Eastern acting such as the guttural exclamations, the "face" making and the especially distinct hieroglyph of the medieval Japanese warrior; his postures derive from the dance itself, for we see it in the Gagaku, the Royal Court Ballet, as well as in the styled poses of the Japanese period films. The council of war lords sits in typical posture, knees spread wide and toes out, looking like so many "ideographs" of awesome military power.

Kurosawa makes a taut melodrama of the beginning, a Samurai war, then introduces us to the incident of the witches' prophecy, here that of one witch: magically, poetically rendered, indeed. The film then faithfully follows the plot of Shakespeare's tragedy, making ample use of all possibilities of headlong speed, open panorama and mysterious forest depths. An actress of classic face and style, Isuzu Yamada, is a perfect "Lady Macbeth". The reception of Banquo, his murder and that of the grooms, even the handwashing in Lady Macbeth's sleepwalking scene, all come in their turn, sustaining a most remarkable tragic tension. Macbeth's drunken vision of Banquo's ghost is beautifully, horrendously transposed to Oriental terms. We then actually see the wood in motion—and a lovely sight it is!—but Kurosawa reserves one radical innovation for the climax. His Macbeth has no mortal duel with Macduff but is shot to death inside his fortress by his own army, suddenly made aware that they, like him, have been

doomed by fulfilment of the witch's prophecy. Countless zooming arrows lodge in his chain armour as he staggers from corner to corner of a series of galleries opening on the courtyard. It is a stunning scene, as vividly catastrophic and final as any heroic death in films.

A magnificently designed climax offers no mortal combat with "Macduff": the frenzied warlord is riddled with arrows by his own soldiers when the prophecy of the moving wood is fulfilled.

In line with the screen's best melodramas, this one keeps the pulse alive with violent and unexpected action; here is the overture of fate for the politically involved young hero.

1958 · POLAND

Ashes and Diamonds

Poland's film industry seems to owe its post-war distinction wholly to one man, Andrzej Wajda. Only Wajda's work, at least, has attained a wide international recognition to date. It happens that *Ashes and Diamonds* has an extraordinary freedom of touch on a most touchy subject. The Polish Uprising against the Germans in 1944, in a country already split by two armies, brought the underground, loyal to the exiled Polish government in London, into a separate struggle with Polish Communists backed by the Soviet Union. When the film opens, Warsaw has been devastated, V-Day is at hand, and only a few "cells" of stubborn patriots hold out against the incoming Communist government. On a country road, one of the Communist Party leaders, returning from his sojourn in Russia to take an official position, is waylaid by gunmen.

It is astonishing enough that a film with so Olympian

a view of Polish history should have taken shape and received public honours on foreign soil, where it has been shown widely; all the more astonishing that it looks uncensored, self-sufficient, and so good as to invite inclusion in a book of this nature. Wajda stationed himself at the heart of the national and human situation in the crisis of V-Day: the Poles, just yesterday, had been torn between (no pun intended!) two poles of patriotism. Fighting the alien Germans had meant fighting the Poles, too. The point had become a world problem bound up with political interests. In step with one of the most bitter and gruelling moments in modern history, all the participants of this film were acting out the fatal plot of a people.

Again, Wajda and his collaborators have the rare virtue of being conscientiously moral and artistic. The portrayal of the opposed "sides" is tantalizingly impartial, bravely lucid, and comes through intact possibly because the true hero is all Polish youth incarnate and sacrificed to the implacable struggle within. Very fortunate, in this light, is the eloquent presence of Zbigniew Cybulski as the youth, Maciek, who, as a gunman sworn to uphold the exiled Polish government, must finish a bungled job; for the wrong car has been waylaid on the road: two ordinary workers have been machine-gunned instead of the Communist leader.

200

An acting personality at once young, vital and very original, Zbigniew Cybulski, dies one of the most eloquent deaths by violence ever staged in motion pictures; the film, *Ashes and Diamonds*, deserves a high place in its own right.

How Maciek completes the job, alone and in gory style, is the gist of the film. A refreshingly frank, tender romance with a barmaid, at the hotel where he and his quarry put up, intervenes; *he* has his distracting commission, *she* her willingness to enjoy sex provided she doesn't fall in love. Of course, inconveniently, they both fall in love, and we have a plausible, poetically graced portrait of young lives, pure in instinct, ruined by cruel circumstance. During a stroll in the rain, the couple enter a bombed chapel only to be confronted by the corpses of the men Maciek has killed, awaiting their burial. Maciek has thoughtlessly been searching for an instrument to repair Christina's shoe, whose heel has broken off. Ingenious touches such as this thread the film but never seem contrived. Even a subplot about a cowardly and silly member of the Uprising, manoeuvred as comic relief, is sure and controlled. The background characters of acquiescing local officials and some decadent gentility (who celebrate V-Day with a banquet and dance to Chopin's *Polonaise*) are woven skilfully into the well-rounded action.

The subplots mix pathetic irony with dry satire. But it is the stark mixture of realism and romanticism in Maciek's story (he gets his man at the end) that elevates the film, gives it beauty and high pathos. Beneath his chosen military duty, he nourishes a passion to live and learn and love. Only by an oddly timed fluke is he himself machine-gunned in the act of escaping unscathed after his job has been done. This praiseworthy film should be studied for its brilliantly reckoned rendering of what it means for youth and age to live in the shifting, dangerous and manifold political quarrels of our time. The Communist leader, shown as a serious and honest man, has just been apprised of a private tragedy before he runs into Maciek's bullets: his own son, who belongs to the anti-Communist underground, has been arrested by the police . . . Only a determined dedication to art could have resulted in *Ashes and Diamonds*.

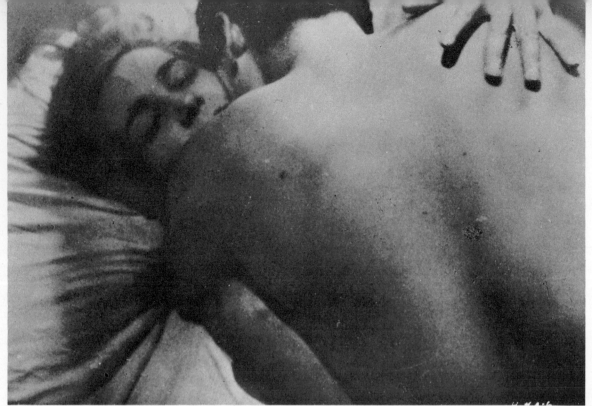

At once, we have one of the frankest, yet most beautifully presented, scenes of carnal love ever shown in a serious film; the woman is French, the man Japanese; she accompanies their love-making with a strange monologue.

1959 · FRANCE

Hiroshima, Mon Amour

Despite hundreds of films devoted in the past two decades to post-war problems —human bewilderment, pessimism, and the moral corruption of the individual— it remained for Alain Resnais' realization of Marguerite Duras' story, *Hiroshima, Mon Amour*, to put this drastic moral temper of humanity into its most eloquent international form. This film hit the spot in so many globally-echoing ways that it won a special Jury's Prize at the Cannes Film Festival in 1959, and shared with Truffaut's *Les Quatre Cent Coups*, in 1960, the Louis Méliès Prize (named after the pioneer French film-maker).

The importance of Mlle. Duras' original screen story must not be overlooked. The close collaboration in this case between author and director was repeated, with perhaps more emphasis, in Resnais' next film, *Last Year at Marienbad*, a story conceived for the screen by the novelist, Alain Robbe-Grillet, who has endorsed the result as ideal. Mlle. Duras must have been just as well pleased with the filming of her story; at the same time,

the two works show, in comparison, that Resnais has no personality of his own; he is not a filmic creator like Renoir or Carné among his own countrymen, like Fellini or Antonioni among the Italians.

Hiroshima, Mon Amour is tragically—one might say "existentially"—involved with the plight of love between men and women as a glorious sensual force brought perilously into question by the hostility of nations as bred from man's will to destroy his kind. Its Romeo-and-Juliet theme is transposed to a modern and global level. The scar left upon a young French woman by an erotic trauma, received during World War II when her town was occupied by the German Army, is such that, tempted much later into a serious affair with another man nationally (and now also racially) "alien" to her, the whole nightmare of her old affair appears like a nemesis that cripples her ethical consent to love.

Turning next to a theme which technically was realized just as well (though not acted, I think, so well)

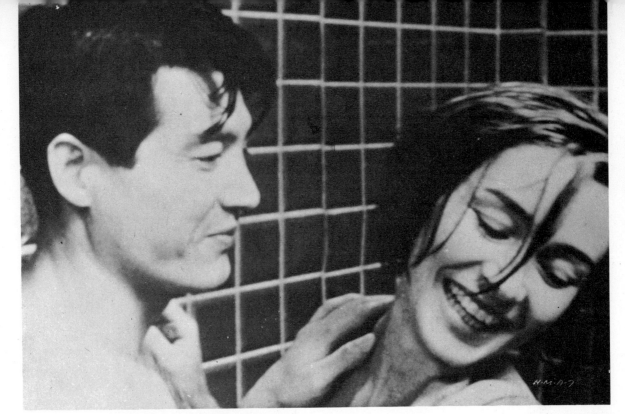

As played by Eiji Okada and Emmanuelle Riva, the man and woman are completely natural and convincing as a pair falling immediately and perfectly in love; next morning, however, she tells him of a taboo on their affair.

An actress scheduled to leave Hiroshima in two days, she insists she must make the plane while her lover (who confesses he is married) pursues her, insistent on knowing why she cannot stay and be his mistress.

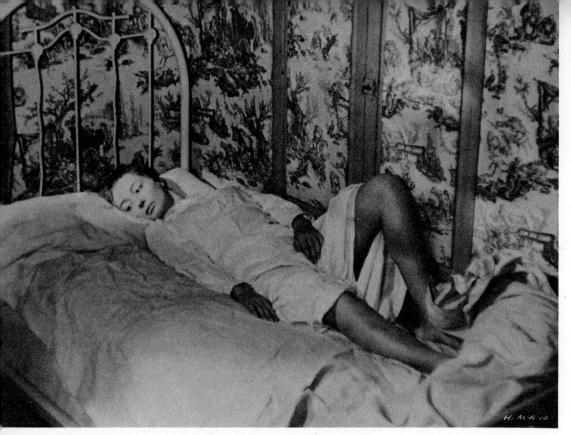

Finally, after a few drinks at a café, she tells him that her first love affair was in World War II with a German soldier, who was shot dead by a sniper; she was then publicly humiliated and imprisoned by her parents.

Resnais set forth in *Last Year at Marienbad* another frustrated love affair; far from being consciously serious and widely significant, this one seemed unconsciously frivolous and special, almost (saturated as it is with *avant-garde* "effects") a parody of what the French have held so sacred: *l'amour* itself. If personal love *is* slated for universal doom, surely it makes its formal exit with more honour and dignity, more genuine human concern, in the Hiroshima film. The subsequent work (made according to Robbe-Grillet's entirely mistaken notion of what the film medium is properly equipped to say) is a sort of psychological farce about traditional romantic love: helplessly hallucinated, irresponsible to reality.

Love in the Marienbad film becomes *absurdly ambiguous* through the imagination's illusive faculty, love in the Hiroshima film *cruelly clear* through the same faculty. The young French woman has had a clandestine affair with a young German soldier; the first affair of each and utterly overwhelming to both. At one rendezvous, he is shot by a sniper and she arrives only to have him die in her arms. She is then chastised in the terrible manner reserved for women who have consorted with the enemy, and even imprisoned in the basement of her home by her shamed parents. Her past is forced from her by her Japanese lover, whom she has met at a Hiroshima night club, only after he has persecuted her into explaining why their affair (he is married) cannot go on; actually, she is an actress who has come to Japan to make a propaganda film for peace, and is due to return to France in a couple of days. They seem so perfectly made for each other that her lover cannot understand her fatalistic sense of their affair's nullity: she insists she must make the scheduled flight. The story ends on a note similar to that ending Sartre's *No Exit*; the conflict between the lovers reaches an agonized stalemate: a dead end. We are forced to leave them and their problem in suspense. *Hiroshima, Mon Amour* is beautifully, sympathetically put. We know what the stakes are in this game of love—which is a great deal to know if *l'amour* be still a legitimate power.

Told in flashbacks, her story is very moving and explains why the horrors of Hiroshima's museum have affected her so drastically: love seems ruined for her by man's killing of man.

And yet . . . a tacit "but", a tacit question mark, rides the downward dip at the close of many French and Italian films of the New Wave *(Nouvelle Vague)*: human trust in love, human trust in the search for happiness, may not have been abandoned after all . . .

The boy Apu: this pure unvarnished close-up reveals in black eyes and hair, in swarthy skin, the universal depths of wondering childhood and its grave, placeless beauty.

1954—1959 · INDIA

Apu Trilogy

Pather Panchali

Aparajito

The World of Apu

Satyajit's Ray's trilogy came from India, whose teeming industry is still so little known to other countries because of its mediocre products. This work, however, shows India to us scenically, humanly and imaginatively. Even Ravi Shankar's musical accompaniment, its wizardry being better known to music listeners than movie-goers, joins the inviting, global familiarity of this film spectacle. Ray based his work on a two-volume novel by Bibhuti Bannerji, a best seller in India since 1934. Yet so intense an empathy is revealed by the film-maker for this story of one man's life that it might be his own autobiography. Made separately from 1954 to 1959, the films as a whole took more international honours than there is space to mention here. American reviewers tended to be ecstatic, and thus their superlatives—more fervent than usual—more convincing. Even considering that India is a country apt to awaken special sympathies among the liberal-minded, Ray's films, exceptional by any standard, won their fame honestly and (I should guess) lastingly.

Of the three parts, *Pather Panchali*, *Aparajito* and *The World of Apu*, those nay-sayers, who have ideals of what pure film should be, might complain of general staticness in Ray's screen imagery, too much restraint in his exploitation of the screen's possibilities. But Ray, a man of taste, and sincere as they come, had his special message and knew how it should be conveyed. The trilogy covers its hero's life from early childhood to manhood and fatherhood; it boasts, moreover, actors quite unaffected (so it seems to Western eyes) by either headlines or personal publicity; their very "anonymity" to foreigners helps their performances. To Western audiences, there seems nothing to stand in the way of their *being* their rôles. A series of small boys takes the rôle of Apu as he grows up and Apu's small son; the last of them, as played by Swapan Mukerji, has a personality half angelic and half demonic; in other words, that of a typical little boy with the added charm of being, to those unused to Indian actors, "exotic". And yet altogether, Apu himself, his mother, his sister, his friend

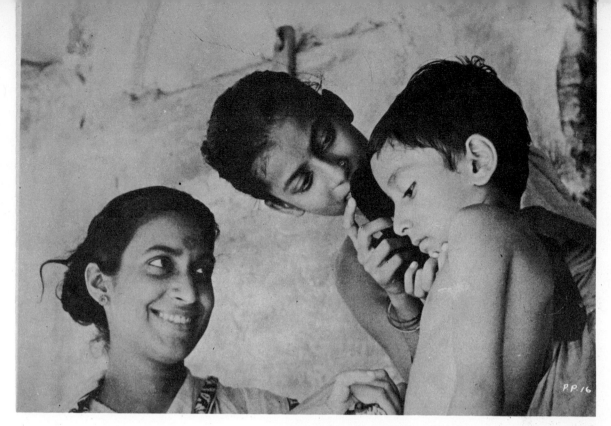

A little fugue in human personalities and their plastic attitudes: Apu, his mother and sister are played by ideal Indian types.

and then his wife, do not seem exotic. They have a quality of beauty and authenticity setting them apart from white-skinned players but marking them as types of native beauty and eloquent human beings. The grandmother in *Pather Panchali* is an old actress whom Ray brought out of retirement for the rôle. She is a model of the excessively aged, the excessively skinny, the ultra-pathetic: a sacred crone destined to wring our hearts with her unwantedness as she hovers on the edge of death.

Ray learned the film medium when still a very young man, going to Cinemas and taking notes about the films he saw. The rest was technique and his own experience and love of life. By the time he started converting Bannerji's novel to the screen, writing the film script himself, he knew both humanity and film, as it were, by heart. No cheapness mars his sure touch, his sense of what is visually needed to project his story, including the spare conversation among its characters. Noticeably, however, its action is quite wordless—and then are furnished the moments when the rectangle of the screen tells us most; for example, the sequence when Apu and his sister, outside their Bengal village, get caught in one of the dense Indian downpours, and the girl, with the proper medicine lacking, dies from the illness contracted. Here, as in the grandmother's redundant existence, economic considerations merge with individual human predicaments. The smallness and isolation of his village home, after his sister's death,

oppress the young Apu. He has received hints of a greater world, a domain of learning and more dynamic happenings where people do not simply wait around to die or sicken helplessly with some dangerous illness. His father's effort to break out of their narrow world into this other world completely fails, yet this does not daunt the younger Apu.

His father, Harihar, a lay priest who heals the sick, has been away on a mission at the time of his daughter's death. Despairing of his village's primitive decadence, Harihar decides to move his family to the great city of Benares. Too pious for its hustling pace, the kaleidoscope of its seething life, he dies from a neglected contagion, against which prayer is unavailing. Though having an impulse to turn away from his family tradition, Apu, now adolescent, starts training for the priesthood under the care of his mother, who works as a cook to support them both. Played by Karuna Banerji, she is a superb incarnation of mature Indian womanhood, solidly, realistically, tenderly drawn. Then death takes his mother, too; alone, Apu understands that he is really dominated by the desire for knowledge; he only wants to write and dream—and, of course, to love.

The manner in which he finally marries a young girl of beauty and refinement, taking her to live with him in poverty, is poetically and plausibly set forth. Their

Character comes across in incidental mature figures without evident make-up or any hint of rhetoric.

Apu's withered grandmother: an outright family burden, she is allowed to starve to death in a pitilessly gaunt sequence that puts the heart beyond pity.

The bridging years of Apu's growth: his father, lay priest and healer, moves his family desperately from their primitive village to the city, his death from illness then leaving his wife and son to their uprooted, now more precarious, existence.

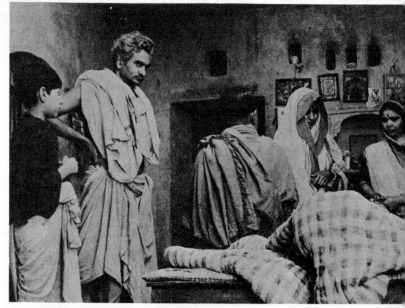

The black etching of poverty only enriches this scene where Apu, adolescent now, spends bleak domestic hours with his mother, shortly also to be taken from him by death.

Apu, as a young man, opens his heart to his friend. Grown up, he is played with magnificent authority and a wealth of virile beauty by Soumitra Chatterjee.

Apu's bride shyly contemplates the city through the ragged curtains of her new home. Hold this picture upside down to see with what abstract ingenuity of design it has been composed.

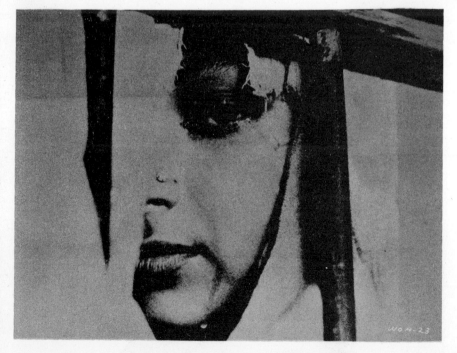

Apu returns for his son: the climactic action of the trilogy; hating the little boy for having "caused" his mother's death, Apu has at once abandoned him to the care of the grand-parents. This quietly tense sequence proceeds with a chore-ography hiding the calculation of its every move.

East and West are spanned in a twinkle by this close-up of Apu, junior, who might roam the city streets or the country-side, pitch stones into the Ganges or the East River.

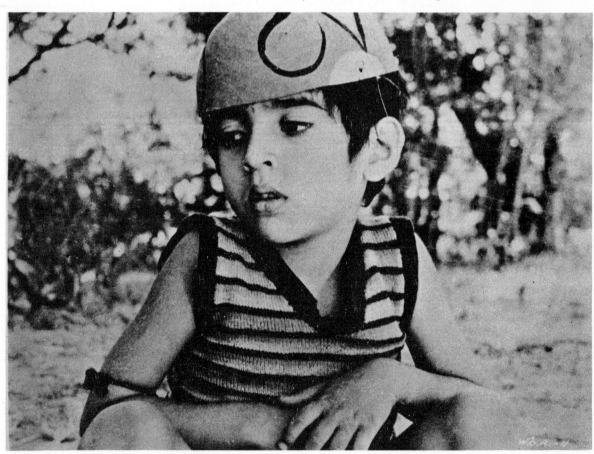

A study in black-and-white values, a happy family relationship and the tone of time: Apu, the man, is united with his son and with "the remembrance of things past".

brief happiness is cut short by her death in childbirth, which takes place at her parents' home. Apu, seized with grief, at once hates the surviving infant, whom he abandons to its grandparents' care, seeking isolation far away after destroying the manuscript of his precious novel. Only the loyalty of a man friend brings his life to a stage promising future happiness. The reunion of father and small son is the old-fashioned, even obvious, episode concluding the trilogy. Yet Ray manages this cliché of fact and fiction as though it were fresh to human experience. There is not a trace of self-consciousness in its forthright sentiment.

Those who, now and recently, wish to take the film world by storm with the dazzlement of means (while "selling" sex, corruption and crime) might well ponder Ray's remarkable courage and its almost flawless success. This man's camera reveals what may be called the unexpendable moral nudities of human nature; it demonstrates that two human heads may meet and blend in the same frame with ultimate plastic effect; that merely to "state" things as they exist may be better than finding an extraordinary way of "looking at" them; that beautiful chiaroscuro is created from the depths of a human action, magically rather than mechanically from artificial lighting. How costly the clothes of poverty seem here, how rich the texture of its flesh! Had Ray's trilogy not captured its special formal continuity and eloquence, no amount of human honesty could have earned the telling of it so much fame. The fact is that Satyajit Ray is one of the most unpretentious of film artists, a *leader* in the understated meaning of that term; a leader, in fact, such as was his countryman, Mahatma Gandhi.

After a dream of death introducing him to his own corpse, the eminent Dr. Borg (now on his way to be honoured for a lifetime of medical achievement) encounters at the roadside the phantom of his own cradle.

1959 · SWEDEN

Wild Strawberries

In this film I choose an earlier example of the work of a Swedish director who has risen to high acclaim recently from connoisseurs favouring the art film: Ingmar Bergman. Bergman has always been industrious, and is surely ingenious, bringing to the film medium a wide and lively cultural intelligence, a stage director's experience and a flair like Eisenstein's for showing Man as an historic quantity, bred from the past and the present, owing to his personal past, as well as his cultural and religious heritage, much that he is today. This Swede has that volatile quality of artists: true temperament. Yet strangely, though to him the film is theatre transported and transfigured by new expansions and possibilities, his effects are often too "theatrical", too art-conscious, facile of overstatement and stubbornly "literary".

I should say these demerits, making his virtues all the more striking, are because (1) he does not really think of the film space radically or plastically enough, but tends simply to photograph actors against backgrounds, and (2) he seems disdainful or simply negligent of stating an uncompromisingly personal version of anything;

His daughter-in-law (in the driver's seat) informs him he is just like his son, whose cold, selfish pride has brought about her decision to divorce him; then they pick up these hitch-hiking youngsters, who are much impressed with Dr. Borg.

The elderly Victor Sjöström, known as Seastrom when he came from Sweden to direct Hollywood films in the silent era, supplies for the doctor a face of epic human expressiveness. Moved by his daughter-in-law's indictment, Dr. Borg finds his subconscious invoking revivals of the past.

he would just as soon borrow as originate, even fake if so tempted; in any case, he relies solely on the ingenuity of idea generating idea, regardless of their ultimate function of conforming to one dominant conception. As a result, his work is uneven, not quite distinctly "felt" or thoroughly "thought out", and bears, in general, the look of brilliant opportunism of style and inspiration.

This is even rather true of what I consider his second best film up to the present: *Wild Strawberries*. What makes this steadier, truer, a better work of (incidentally filmic) art? Strangely enough, its chief actor, Victor Sjöström, himself a very distinguished foreign director who was invited to America to make films in the silent era and gave us two classics, *The Wind* and *The Scarlet Letter*, both with Lillian Gish and Lars Hanson. Bergman had the good fortune to obtain this former director, then quite advanced in age, for the rôle of the eminent Dr. Borg, about to be decorated for his life work by a University. On his way to the University of Lund, where his daughter-in-law is driving him, he is astonished to have the young woman accuse him of being a cold, selfish human being, basically unfair—however "ethically" just—even to those he loves.

At such a moment, this news provides a shocking anticlimax to the ceremony which is only a few hours ahead. His daughter-in-law is bitter and does not mince words; his son, she informs him for the first time, has been made in his father's mould, frigid in personal relations, and is about to ruin their marriage by inducing her to separate from him. As she explains, Dr. Borg grows the more perplexed and disturbed because it happens that the night before he has dreamed about death. The film has opened with this dream: the doctor has been walking along the street when suddenly a passing hearse has an accident, its coffin slides out to crash on the street and break open; rushing over to it, he peers in to see his own corpse reach out a hand and seek to drag him in with it.

This dream sets the key for daydreams aroused in the old man by his daughter-in-law's solemn reproach. He starts to examine the life that has led to his imminent moment of personal triumph: a life revealed in artfully introduced flashbacks full of charming Old-World atmosphere. The strange innocence of his youth, mostly forgotten, returns to him as he sits near a patch of wild strawberries during a rest along the highway; he has always been proud, calculating; he allowed his aggressive brother to win away from him the girl he originally wished to marry, eventually marrying a girl who would not give him "trouble". He is now self-arraigned in the depths of his soul. Arriving at his son's home, he dreams of the ceremony about to honour him and it seems one with the phantasmal past.

On the road, some teen-age hitchhikers have joined the old man and his daughter-in-law and they are tremendously impressed on casually learning his identity. The girl among them looks just like the girl he once lost to his brother. Soon, a married couple is also picked up as a result of an accident to their car; their vicious quarrel with each other becomes a horrible example of two disunited people permanently bound together. To Dr. Borg, all values are put in question as death throws its shadow, fame its light, across the path of his last days; all his achieved ambition dissolves in the twin impalpability of past and future, its tremor as of something about to expire. Dr. Borg's face—now phantasmally identified with the phantasmal nature of film itself—is the living mask of a perishing human consciousness.

The evocation is incarnate poetry; as much, I think, because of Sjöström as of Bergman. This old man has truly lived; good or evil, he shows it upon a quiet, impassive face having no need to distort its features to express profound feelings. Just an oblique message from the eyes, its animate controlled vibration, its stamp of having lived long and seriously, are sufficient. One wonders if this humanly complete mask can be achieved *without* "selfishness". It is true—a "family man" does have responsibilities to others; to his wife, his parents, his children. But he may not be strong enough to be himself and also give form and direction to even his closest of kin. It is the limitation of individual strength whose pathos appears so movingly in Victor Sjöström's face and figure. With thought-provoking paradox, it is not his daughter-in-law, already an adult with adult problems, who clearly sees this pathos married to dignity in Dr. Borg's face, but the inexperienced, adulative teenagers who see it. They have yet to make that most crucial of human choices (if there must be a choice): to honour oneself with selfishness or to honour others with charity.

He once permitted his brother to rob him of the girl he wished to marry and realizes, from the girl hitchhiker's resemblance to her, that obsessive ambition has made him cold, proud and calculating; he daydreams on.

A new sight of his son confirms everything. Has he cared for anyone, really, but himself? His dream fantasy about the approaching ceremony vividly dramatizes the poetry and irony of Ingmar Bergman's imaginative film.

An original director and his most original film boast a hero to remember: a pickpocket with a cause. The cause? The cleansing of a deep-laid guilt, exclusive, self-absorbing, that could belong to this man only.

1959 · FRANCE

Pickpocket

Undoubtedly France is the source of the most varied and inventive temperaments in film history. Robert Bresson, visually inspired creator of *A Man Escaped*, *Diary of a Country Priest*, the present work and the recent *Joan of Arc*, has made a distinct filmic contribution that is as singular far beyond French borders as it is in France. His most eloquent exhibit, I think, is here in this beautifully imprinted, intently pure memoir of a hero grand in no wise save in his straight-line simplicity: the starkness of his individual story. Not that he is un-akin to Bresson himself, to the type pattern of human experience which fascinates this director. On the contra-

ry, as vehicle of a submerged guilt and its obsessive practice in disguised form, the "I" of this subjectively told story seems the quintessence of the experience that Bresson has always tried to capture with his camera: a secret path of action, deceptively visible to others, one to which its enactor is a selfless sort of martyr, temperamentally obeying a law of compulsion as if it were the will of some remote deity.

Considering the atmosphere of inevitability in this story of a spiritually motivated criminal, the modernity of effect in *Pickpocket* is a considerable feat in itself. The flash, the extravagant show, of many talented directors is not here by so much as a flicker. True, to some it might appear that the skilled profession of a pickpocket is subtly lewd and sensational; surely, it is a feature of the "glamour" of crime and its manifold melodramas. Bresson has stated it as the melodrama of a soul, but ascetically sober, and exposing a beauty of sheer plastic values that hews to the simplest lines of reality without one camera trick, one camera rush or roll, and with no slightest lease to sensationalism of subject-matter. Oddly "sinister" for that reason? Why not oddly "sublime"?

That much disgraced *voyeur*, the film camera, seems to welcome Bresson's divinely impartial objectivity. How open and unassuming, so to speak, is the action beginning at the Longchamps race-track near Paris, where the hero, apparently with an impulse of kleptomania, successfully lifts a wallet. His voice tells us it was a moment of sheer elation, his success; immeasurably sweet as though the effect of a drug. Immediately arrested, however, and the money found on him, he cannot be convicted because he has disposed of the wallet. His sense of a new freedom of action is intoxicating. Secretively protecting it, he repulses the efforts of a close friend and a benevolent police officer (who feels he has a guilty man to watch) to wean him away from a spree of kleptomania by suggesting he take a job and behave like a normal citizen. Everyone guesses that a morbid self-absorption isolates him from ordinary feelings and behaviour. One such person is a very poor girl of cool, classic beauty whom he meets in the apartment building where his dying mother lives, and who becomes a kind of go-between for sorrowing mother and frigidly removed son.

Picking pockets is the only type of action that interests him. He lives in the same house with his mother, but in a different part in a small bedroom, where he hides his loot. He must force himself to visit the bedridden woman, occasionally bringing her some of his criminal "take". But he avoids the searching of all pleading, suspicious looks. Martin La Salle in the hero's part is ideal and magnificently cannily photographed. Handsome, without being in the least "pretty" like many male actors, the reverse of a dandy, he is a remarkably fixating figure, his shirt-collar always loose, his clothes worn as if invisible, his fine sympathetic features tranquillized by vision of the path on which his large haunted eyes are trained. The incident at Longchamps has all the earmarks of a stolen paradise, a guilty happiness which he is bent unconsciously on expiating.

As if magnetically, he draws to him a real professional of his hobby, and learning everything, makes up a small pickpocket team. Like disclosing new worlds of nature, rather than photographing a criminal technique, the camera offers dazzlingly clear-eyed examples of the team's operation; they are the figures of an utterly silent dance, mesmeric, fabulously true. They have the lyric surprise of pyrotechnic balletic feats, but muted, belonging to a guilt exquisitely precisioned from fear of detection. Minute by minute, one becomes certain that money, for this hero, is the token of a theoretic, incestuously motivated crime. The deft immaculacy of a pickpocket's movements wishes to hide their presence; so they take on the tone of constrained mimicry, they are inverted caresses; their value as personal contact is reduced to a minimum and wilfully effaced . . . Such is brought out by this pickpocket's career. Increasingly afraid of a "plant", the dummy victim that will catch him in the act, he seeks like a sleep-walker exactly this climax — and where but at Longchamps, where he strikes up an acquaintance with another horse-player? He cannot resist taking the supreme risk, and sure enough, as he slips out the cash-crammed wallet of the other player, manacles snap on his wrist! The form is perfect. Meanwhile his mother has died, and the girl (now much in love with him) has made her last voiceless appeal. Speaking to her as a prisoner, with an iron network between them, he realizes that she and everything else he has shunned has become lucid — and available! He has, he says, at last found his way to her. Perhaps the fabled world in which other men live stands open to him.

The beauty of the story's filming centres on flawlessly rendered performances of the well-known criminal art requiring a butterfly touch: a profusely repeated crime becomes a vehicle of the crystalline, clipped French manner: a model of rhythmically visual "dialogue".

Symbolism that need not speak its name: fleeting camera intimacies were never so charged with meaning; the pattern of objectified guilt unreels itself like music as this pickpocket moves surely toward his destiny: being nabbed.

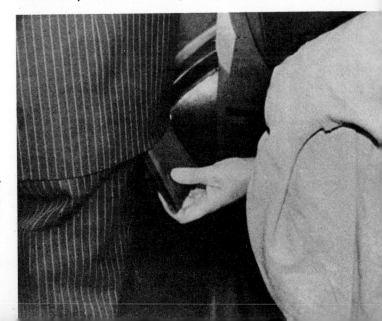

One is puzzled, intrigued, hypnotized by the ballet of constantly lifted cash until one realizes it is an immaculate stand-in for a crime which must be completely purged before the world of natural things (including love) can open at the hero's touch.

The fashionable, married Valmonts (far left and far right) carry their game as dedicated seducers to a Swiss ski lodge; between them, starting at left, a young virgin, Cécile, on whom Valmont presently has his eye, her rich American fiancé, and Mme Solange, her mother; gimmick: all is less than fair in love and war.

·1959 · FRANCE

Les Liaisons Dangereuses

Nothing daunts the French when tempted to revive— somehow, *anyhow!*—the chivalric emotion as it centres on woman, the sacred sex fetish. Roger Vadim's films made Brigitte Bardot the first *Nouvelle Vague* heroine, an important symbol of modern femininity, by bringing out her temperament as female, and by doing little besides. Parting from Miss Bardot (Mme Vadim) professionally and domestically, Vadim sought in this film version of a classic French novel a vehicle to accommodate his new mate, Annette Vadim, who is the Bardot type with incidental alterations. The alterations caused him to concentrate on the sex-idol theme and push further out of the picture any occasion for his ideal heroine to "act". An idol's indispensable basis is utter passivity: it must never seem to leave its pedestal. Mme Vadim surely has this faculty under better control than she has the virtue of the character she portrays, Marianne, from Laclos' novel of wanton eroticism. Supposedly, she is an untouchably chaste young matron with a child and a spotless reputation.

The trouble, undoubtedly, is that while Marianne is presumably the film's most covetable sex object (if one believes the story), narcissistic vanity, rather than a strict moral code, would seem the barrier to any man's despoiling her virtue. Mme Vadim is an "interesting" doll, a mask of the beauty parlour created by make-up man and hairdresser, thus wholly contrary to Laclos' original conception of a woman exceptionally beautiful but correspondingly, dishearteningly, chaste of spirit. Pitted against her (here the adaptation from the novel is happily inspired) is a dangerous team of professional seducers played by Jeanne Moreau and the late Gérard Philippe: M. and Mme Valmont in the film; Valmont and his mistress, the Marquise de Merteuil, in the novel. Perhaps being man and wife makes the predatory nature of the pair less offensive to the majority of the world film audience. The point is arguable. Anyway, the script effected the change, and the institution of marriage becomes the couple's headquarters for their inveterate war against social respectability regarding the softer passion,

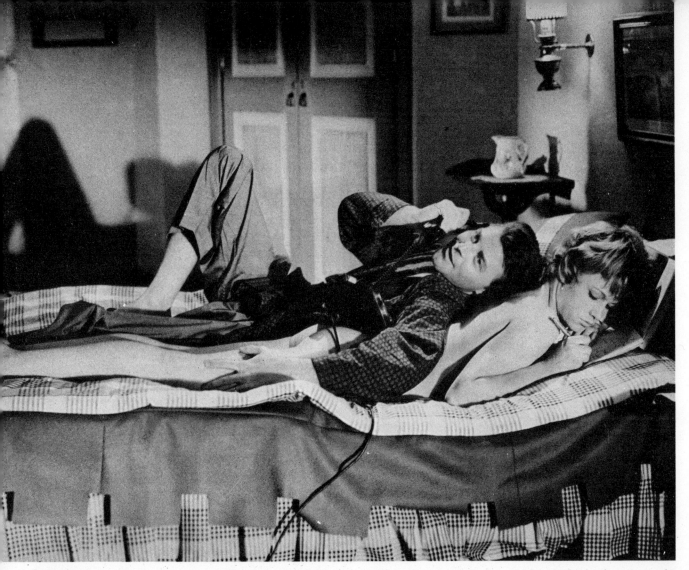

Seducing then spurning the victim is the game played by the married couple as if it were Contract Bridge. In Laclos' eighteenth-century novel, Valmont uses Cécile as a desk to apprise his partner-in-sin of his victory by letter; in this modern film, the speedier telephone takes over as Cécile finds a chance to do her lessons.

despised by them in the name of Free Love, or Eros, merciless and unbound.

The most praiseworthy element of this very well-built film, designed and edited with a French sharpness of economy and highlight, is its faithfulness to the essential spirit of the original: Choderos de Laclos' competently clear-eyed, unblinking view of his nation's ability to convert the exquisite sentiment of love, which it has made famous, into the most cruelly hard-hearted of sports. Love, says Laclos, can be a game decking itself with all the emotional display of frenzied eroticism and yet secretly be dedicated to slitting the throat of a love adventure with the precision and cool professionalism of an executioner at his appointed task. It is this morbid loyalty to Don Juanism (renouncing fidelity, legal or otherwise) that seems to hold the Valmonts together, making their successful marriage a matter of admiring comment in their fashionable circle.

Laclos disguised his canny commentary on French immorality of the eighteenth century by having one partner, ultimately outraged, manipulate the destruction of the other; war is declared at home when the pair breaks up over Valmont's sentimental compunction after his great triumph in seducing the untouchable Marianne. Valmont's victory has been a point of crucial honour, an actual wager with his wife, who vies with him in conquests whose code has it that the victim must be privately humiliated and, preferably, held up to public scorn.

In exacting the final surrender (as the eighteenth century used to say) from the hold-out, Marianne, Valmont has had to resort, a letter tells his wife, to his last weapon; an oath to take his life if the fair Marianne will not submit. His decisive victory declares him technically the winner; thus, a big point is scored against Juliette, his wife, who scents a weakness, however, in

A much worthier prize, however, becomes Valmont's aim: an irreproachably chaste young matron met around the lodge, Marianne; she offers a supreme resistance but gives way when Valmont tragically threatens suicide.

her husband's hesitation over promptly deserting and disillusioning his new mistress.

Meanwhile, following the flawless plot of the original (brilliantly related entirely in letters), Valmont has "ruined" a confiding young virgin, Cécile Solange, secretly in love with a young student named Danceny, although ostensibly she is engaged to a rich, rather plain, American playboy. Valmont has contrived the feat under cover of helping Cécile get together with her true love, Danceny. Under the same sort of cover, the competitive Mme Valmont has seduced the inexperienced Danceny (for the moment infatuated by this woman of the world) in order to give her score a boost in the perpetual game conducted with her husband. The unexpected happens: Marianne has proved such an exceptional charmer (her tears as the "fallen fortress", quite naked and ravished, provide a fleeting moment of pathos) that Valmont defies custom by intimating to Juliette that he might, at least for a while, keep Marianne on. This is too much for Mme Valmont, supreme in her sacred rage, and a telegram casting off poor Marianne is sent over the phone, by his wife, under Valmont's nose.

Learning that he is determined to be (at least experimentally) an apostate to their creed, wife declares war on husband, who accepts the challenge like every true soldier.

Juliette's trump card is to reveal to Danceny her husband's sneak seduction of Cécile, already the student's fiancée. Encountering the renegade Valmont at a wild night spot, Danceny assaults the notorious seducer, whose head, in a fall from Danceny's blow, hits an iron fender, the concussion killing him instantly. The lady would seem to have won the "war"—yet not without heavy penalty. Attempting to burn Valmont's letters while a police investigator waits in her parlour to question her in the homicide case, Juliette catches fire, so that when she arrives to testify in court, she shows a face horribly scarred by the accident. A few frames of her demolished beauty hold the screen as the voice of Cécile's mother exclaims: "Her soul is on her face!" Blackout: end of film.

Some reviewers greeted Vadim's ingenious modernization of the novel as inconsiderable; indeed, as so much trash, verging on the pornographic. I think time will dissipate their ill-advised strictures. True: official channels in France sought to ban the finished film after trying to prevent its going into production. The substance of the matter, on the other hand, must be an art work's relevance to life. Maybe, as Vadim himself was obliged to state in a two-minute, tongue-in-cheek preamble to his naughty film, no real French woman could be so immorally malign as a Juliette Valmont: Laclos said the same thing when his novel was first offered to an eager world. Mankind, in its reading rooms, knows best, and must be the final authority. This is why Roger Vadim,

The wife (Jeanne Moreau) cries, "Foul!", when the husband (Gérard Philippe) implies he intends to keep his fair fortress for a while; in this council of war she invokes their mutual oath: desertion of a victim must be clean, quick, decisive!

though not really a great director, wins a place for this filmic version as a classic. First in the sentiment of love, so gracious and tender, France has earned (in Laclos' novel and parallel works) the paradoxical right to turn this sentiment inside out, like a glove. Gérard Philippe's face, like Jeanne Moreau's, seems stamped with all the ins-and-outs of love: veritable mirrors for carnal memories. This is why they, and their every gesture, here and in the past, can show the deepest, warmest tenderness of love as well as the razor-edge of its coldness and cynicism.

The oath is executed and poor Marianne's mind gives way; repentant, Valmont denounces his wife and they declare "war" on each other: never has French eroticism been so starkly cynical; nevertheless both these connoisseurs of lust finally get their come-uppance.

From left to right: Claudia and Anna. The latter has Sandro, the former will inherit him; both seem to intuit this when Anna presents Claudia with a dress.

1960 · ITALY

L'Avventura

To the tourist of sex, these late days, open-air pleasure-seeking deserves as much alertness, preparation and ingenious craft as does space travel. So the brilliantly emergent director-creator Michelangelo Antonioni implies; so he implies, that is, if one takes seriously, in his present protagonists, the hothouse will-to-love and its sad, anticlimactic blossom, scattered as if by the winds of heaven. Antonioni, apprenticed to films as Fellini's script writer, announced that he had chosen here the rich and leisure-minded to illustrate modern erotic decadence because to have set this story of Cupid's wanderlust amid the working class or the poor would have suggested that circumstance alone drives people to escape life's ugliness by way of animal pleasure. Love blooms in this film, I repeat, in the wide-open spaces—and what spaces!—sought by those to whom sex seems primarily anarchic, not to say also avocational.

Does that include the heroine's love? If so, perforce, rather than by choice. The suite of stills issued to publicize L'Avventura indicates that its space-appeal, if not its sex appeal, was underrated by its handlers. Space, as such, implies for sex a wide choice and change-off. This change-off decidedly comes about, although not without hardy resistance from true love (or true love's facsimile). It all starts on an innocent enough pleasure trip by small yacht. Packed aboard are titles, an alluring negligée, a very bored married couple, taut sex motives and, of course, lurking infidelities. When a wonderful island rock, rising hugely out of the sea near Sicily, is met, and the party momentarily disembarks, the situation concentrates on a lost girl who wanders off alone. The all-out search for her spreads beyond the now-sinister island by land, sea and air.

The girl is Anna, who either accidentally falls to her death from a cliff, commits suicide somehow, or (as later seems possible) is assaulted and kidnapped by some prowling smugglers. Anyway, neither she nor her corpse is ever found. When the film opens, she and her lover, Sandro (to whom, for a concealed reason, she declines to be married) have been scheduled to go with her friend, Claudia, on the yachting trip. Monica Vitti, repeatedly glorified by Antonioni's films, plays Claudia, and Gabriele Ferzetti, a longtime matinée idol of Italian films, plays Sandro. Much that is unspoken eventually passes between Sandro and his female companions, including Anna's whimsical gift to Claudia of one of her dresses, an act which later seems prophetic, perhaps an unconscious ritual.

222

Minor guests of the yachting party: their "host" actually becomes the sinister, magnificent setting of rock, sea and air into which Anna disappears.

As, ultimately, all hope of finding Anna seems to vanish, Sandro, obviously attracted to Claudia, starts pursuing her while still searching for his lost mistress; he even induces Claudia to continue the search for her by his side. Actually, Sandro is looking for a "phantom" who exists in the flesh within reach of his hands.

When Anna is lost, Claudia and the other pleasure-seekers ransack the desolate island and get very wet as hope gets very dim.

At last, Claudia yields herself to him and the substitution for Anna is complete. Claudia's fears are fully justified when she begins to relax and accept the new situation. The lovers (their search an admitted failure) arrive exhausted at a picturesque luxury hotel on Sicily and encounter there their former hostess on the yacht: a placid, precious-proud, titled worldling. Claudia con-

Hope is still dimmer. But Sandro, dedicated to the search for his lost mistress, begins pursuing Claudia, though technically they form a searching twosome.

fesses to her that a great anxiety has taken possession of her heart.

Along the way, she has interpreted a very casual, very amusing, seduction of a silly, bored, married woman by a panting, teen-aged painter as a revolting impropriety, though everyone else, including the lady's husband, is geared to tolerate it as the natural order of the day. In this high-society milieu, open sex is about the same as open air: both are sheltered settings for pleasure-seeking unlimited. To such wealthy epicures, sex is the shameless, antique *luxure* of the senses. For our central triangle, however, the erotic life has not become the *No Exit* of Jean-Paul Sartre; not exactly. The bricked-up hotel window of Sartre's play is shown here as an ordinary door with a simple, workable handle: turn it and a new pair of arms is waiting for you. In her hotel room, Claudia awakens at dawn with a shudder of hysterical fear: Sandro has been away all night and she visualizes him with Anna! And the mercenary glamour girl, to whom she finds him making squalid love on a remote hotel lounge, might as well be Anna. . . . All women—now it stands exposed—are the same to Sandro; or, at least, *seem* the same to him. All that distinguishes between them is the rhythm of their availability. A mutual weeping scene between Claudia and Sandro, closing the film, touches us but leaves us perplexed. Antonioni hastens to break off his provocative tourist's view of sex: Mount Aetna in the background. Like *Hiroshima, Mon Amour*, his film may well be taken as a leading example of the new

erotic candour in the movies. It is lusciously photographed, meticulously rendered with a sure, even audacity. While it attained fame at once, *La Dolce Vita* nosed it out for the top prize at Cannes in 1960. In general, however, connoisseurs preferred it over Fellini's epic and in the international poll of 1961-62, it left *La Dolce Vita* far behind and joined the first ten.

Yielding to Sandro is hard, but his determination is harder. Love has a change-off in mid-career. Air becomes flesh again: Claudia takes Anna's place.

Exhausted by love and guilt, Claudia broods it out while Sandro saunters through the big luxury hotel where they have found breathing-space; she awakes to find dawn coming. Sandro has not returned to their room.

Where is he? He has found the welcoming embraces of a cruising, upcoming *luxure,* with whom Claudia finds him *in flagrante delicto* on a hotel lounge. Here the Whore of Babylon looks about for her victim: the image of tourist sex made glamorous.

The clear sky over Rome is visited, in our very first glimpse of *La Dolce Vita*, with the above ideograph straight from nature: religion aloft on the mechanical wings of publicity. Fellini's film seems to ask: "Is Christ more then another 'character' in modern society's sensational 'cast'?"

The lady has swallowed too many sleeping pills: this classic "accidental" near-tragedy takes place because her lover, a journalist-about-Rome, has stayed out all night with a nymphomaniac heiress, who used to be an old headline of his.

1960 · ITALY

La

Dolce Vita

For scores of newspaper readers, life is so dominantly that electrifying thread on which gossip-columnists string their product that Fellini's film is in the nature of a major inspiration. I think that *La Dolce Vita* (*The Sweet Life*) is destined to rank as a classic because of the eloquence and breadth of vision it evokes from what ethically is a trivial, disgusting occupation: the society-adulation and scandal-mongering of journalism. One key to Fellini's depth and relevance here is surely the fact that the film grew from his impulse to compose an

Keeping up with things, Marcello the journalist has switched from the hospital corridor to the airport: an American movie star has arrived in town and leads him, here, on a marathon to the top of St. Peter's.

autobiography; one, in all probability, with fictional elements, but one that he meant to be a sort of public confession and moral critique. A few commentators reacted against such egocentrism as indiscreetly exposed, open to suspicion as too personal. One divines the source of this reaction: Fellini, by imparting life's vibrancy and charm to what apparently are meant as images of social dissipation and moral decadence, seems to exploit as well as indict the objects of satire. But is this not normal—even inevitable? Let us suppose Fellini has yielded to the spell of youthful recollections; the film is an ideal instrument of evoking it even if some evil "magic" be attributed to it. The material is, indeed, not under perfect artistic control; this does not mean, on the other hand, that the case against *La Dolce Vita* is stronger than its claim on the permanence of our regard.

Fellini's position as both film artist and social critic is no weak-sister combination. It is a token of strength that he has rushed headlong into what I have defined on other pages here as the sphere of public relations. True, cinematic angels fear to tread there; he did not fear. To be realistic about this film, think of the bread and butter earned by an Art Buchwald from the gaudy fêtes, the celebrity-crushes, of the International Set (also Fellini's overt material); the cinema is surely more creative, here, than the printed page. Fellini has given us a mouth-watering, grandeur-screen portion of those same blow-outs as *tableaux-vivants*. "The sweet life" really seems to be—and not too mythologically—the paradise that innumerable newspaper-readers think it; granting, to be sure, that every paradise has *some* kind of serpent.

One concedes—one *must*, I think—a certain ambiguity to Fellini's film as satire. Is it not rather the irony attached to the permanent predilection of the human animal for the view that life is a sporting event to make one giddy with excitement, suspense and perhaps, at best, with that sublime thing: a sense of *gloire*? It is not news that this view often disappoints, that it reeks with frivolity and degrades all kinds of standards, both noble and vulgar. The old-fashionedness of Fellini's attitude is still one of social commitment: the dramatic verve, the competence of the angles on social revels, the curiously authentic vein of the autobiographical, are present for those who know. What has happened, in the fortunes of film style, may not be appetizing to Neo-Realists who wish to take a different

On a local film set, out of business hours, the lovely star is made to feel at home with help from champagne, jazz and Marcello, who slips away with her to guide her into the moonlit *campagna*; later, her husband, also a movie star, whacks them both.

But Marcello's line of work gets him to know people: different people – this lady, hemmed in by panting news cameras, has just been widowed by another friend of his, a cultured lover of the arts, who has first shot his two children and then himself.

direction, supposedly more "objective". But there is undeniable juice in Fellini's corniness, with just enough square judgment of it (as likewise in Antonioni's judgment of it), to make its vulgarity valid.

We have come, at the last shot, a significant way through the tangled public and private life of a professional scandalmonger; we have even been privileged to see how a fake religious miracle can be ingloriously rebuked by a downpour from Heaven that also routs those other fake miracles, the television trucks. Part of the film's scornful indulgence, warm with Fellini's past, is the impetuous presence of news cameras: those ambivalent Medusas wielded by Mercurys. These convene

at the feet of a most toothsomely fleshed American movie star alighting from a transoceanic plane. The photogenic flesh belongs to no other than Anita Ekberg and her romance with the sexy columnist (Marcello Mastroianni) is elegantly outfitted with some chicly condescending poetry—as bold and brassy in front as the episode with the columnist's father is gentle and golden at heart. Marcello's marathon with the movie star to the top of St. Peter's becomes a dead heat: she seems to want only the "view".

We never learn, of course, what she really wants aside from what any girl in her position inevitably wants and has: fame and glamour. The lavish party held on a local movie set focuses the life-centre of the film (and the mercurial fountain of its irony) on orgies—which proceed to take the forms considered by journalism to make spectacular "news" for all classes. The professional rivalry of the morally ambidextrous columnist

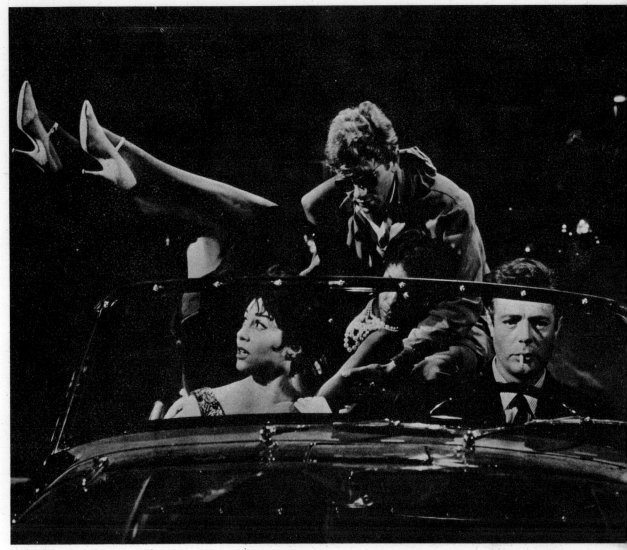

Variety is the soul of Marcello's gossip columns: he treats his visiting father to a nightclub spree and the old man likes it so much he almost has a heart attack. While Marcello and his companions drive home to his apartment, his father arrives there with one of the night club entertainers.

becomes sinister when, after his romantic but really innocent "night out" with the movie star, several news-cameras ambush the slap-in-the-face her husband gives her outside their hotel on the Via Veneto. The poor columnist is then himself messed up by the irate (and notably muscular) husband. Premonitions of mortality, as it were, begin to seep through the glittering, mass-manufactured glamour that supposedly envelops all "swell parties".

Started off by Marcello the columnist's grimly erotic fling with a nymphomaniac heiress, apparently one of his sidelines, we glide into the notorious sphere of "sleeping-pill accidents"; this time, it is news from home, where the columnist's despairing mistress, whom he declines to marry, has taken a dozen too many and has to have her stomach pumped. What keeps up Marcello's spirits? Partly, at least, the sound track, as it duly reports the mood music, jazzy or sentimental, which keeps his

ankles, head, and in fact his whole anatomy, on the wings of news-gathering. He has met a true friend on his travels, a cultivated highbrow, in whose house he can wistfully participate in the supposed advantages of intellectual conversation as well as (through the pathos of distance) his friend's loving wife and adorable children. Fellini has created a world where it hardly comes as a surprise, but only with the usual shock of headlines, that this same bland agnostic quietly kills, first, his two children, and then himself.

This shakes Marcello, and one is tempted to share his repulsion at the massed news cameras ambushing, outside the toney apartment house, the still unknowing,

Marcello worries, but not for long. Picked up by a blond mannequin (about to be made a Marquise), he is carried off to hobnob with the nobility; everyone decides to make the evening gala by spending the rest of it in a nearby haunted house.

newly-made widow. So that we can fully comprehend that Marcello is aware of the rottenness devouring his soul like a jungle, we have the pleasure of accompanying him on a jaunt among the real "swells", the aristocracy and its gilded playmates. The truth is, Fellini's film-reportage is pretty convincing: one might think one were there. This, too, is natural enough, because as Marcello courts very important people, being lured by the sweet life even while earning a living, Fellini has courted, in another sense, the same people; a couple of genuine nobles are in the cast. It's just that, Fellini hints, nobilities are decadent (what single datum of journalism could be more in public domain?) but that, too, they really have some style (something perhaps not appre-

ciated properly even by Foreign Editors or Fashion Editors) and that, in so many words, and as gossip-columns never cease pretending, *they really have some fun* . . .

Or maybe, and this is the sinister part, the VIPs of Rome's social world have been courting Fellini, and other Marcellos, who have come far, far up the starry paths of publicity. There, I think, we have the bitterest truth to be found in Fellini's satiric commentary, whether he has grasped it with groping intuition or acute deliberation. If Fellini be viewing his wicked youth from a certain high place, he still cannot really say it has been wasted: it gave him the meat and drink of this film, not the "feast" of frittering life away. Continually, life holds up such a patently admonitory finger that one feels Marcello is, in a sense, the "chosen" among all corrupt journalists of his ilk. At the end of a bang-up all-night bout for all comers, tending to fizzle out in the

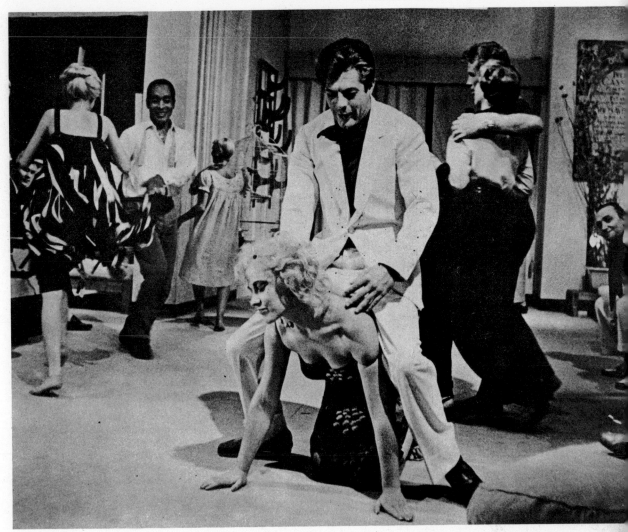

Still pursuing his profession, Marcello gives his friends and assorted guests the idea that he's taking it too seriously; it's true that, in the action above, he looks as though he's just "playing horsie", but he may be "playing for keeps".

damp purlieus of "existential" absurdity, the tired revellers (not one of whom seems even to have committed fornication) get a chilly, but seemingly a relaxing, stare from the immense eyes of some strange fish brought up on the beach at dawn. And Marcello sees, a little way down the beach, a chaste little waitress with whom he has had an innocent flirtation—yes, the incident has been exactly that conventional... One could say the international credit-rating of the Social Orgy has met a stunning reverse; if not in newspapers, at least in this supposedly autobiographic film. Yet, as I have more than insinuated, Fellini made *La Dolce Vita* with gustatory pride; he knows, and appreciates, that so long as there's someone we can call the Dutiful Party-goer, the gossip-columnist's image of the social whirl, or any other kind of whirl, will be solvent... and classical.

The International Style, via Milan, breeds a modern married couple: Jeanne Moreau and Marcello Mastroianni sense the great crisis of their marriage as it chances to show at the bedside of a dying friend of the family; Mastroianni plays a successful novelist.

His wife has disappeared from the cocktail party held in honour of his newest book and she is not at home when he arrives: she has told him on leaving their dying friend, however, that something like a cancer has been gnawing at their marriage.

La Notte

1961 · ITALY

The maker of *L'Avventura*, takes up the problem of sexual choice and fidelity more seriously in *La Notte* than in his previous film. With *La Notte*, *L'Avventura* and three works by Fellini (*La Strada*, *La Dolce Vita* and *Cabiria*—the last not represented here) Italy becomes foremost in world film as an intellectual *avant-garde*. Films of the fifties and the threshold of the sixties, including the Japanese works here, must still be tested as classics by time. I base my acceptance of them on the brilliant style of the Japanese films and on the brilliance of modern insight and fine workmanship in the Italian films. Perhaps very recent works by François Truffaut and Alain Resnais (to which I have various objections) may actually join the classic roster. But I may point out that even the classic has enough looseness of definition to make mere taste a deciding factor in a film's longevity.

This book, of course, does not contain all the films that have survived in the enlightened regard after ten years. In placing Italy's new products above France's— in a turnabout of the historic ratio observed here—I have been persuaded by the serious vigour of the moral sense which Italy's two leading film-makers have developed. De Sica's *Bicycle Thieves* still seems the best and last word on the image of the proletariat as a great myth, while *Potemkin* remains, I think, the supreme cinematic image of modern society in revolt. Antonioni's material is quite different. It concerns the dilemma of the professional and leisure classes in the toils of keeping intact the essences of their daily lives: the sweet life, love sweet or bittersweet, and basic moral equilibrium—that backbone of man whose collapse turns him into a sick animal.

The opening sequence of *La Notte*, set in a hospital in Milan, gives us modern man's confrontation with a death ambiguously "psychosomatic". An intellectual is dying of cancer. No solemn fate is present; no tragic grief; only a doleful depression. The surfaces of things

Anyhow, with the timeless human impulse to distract one-self from unpleasant truths, the couple goes to a gala party given by a wealthy industrialist: this social whirl, on the scale of Roman grandeur lately revived in films, has a stylish, almost Surrealist exuberance.

The novelist decides to chase the industrialist's comely, un-married daughter (Monica Vitti) after turning down her father's lucrative offer that he take charge of his industry's public relations; his wife, brooding, has been wandering around alone; she turns down an offer from an aggressive Don Juan.

seem drenched in sourness. At times the mature victim complains like a puzzled, irritable child (his mother is present) while the married couple to whom he is the "family friend" seem disturbed and powerless to console him. A sort of cancer is present in the couple's own relationship: a fact that soon becomes plain. The dying man, a glass of champagne like a cup of poison in his hand, symbolizes, one may guess, the death of a past and the death of a future. He has always been in love with his friend's wife (Jeanne Moreau); each of the three has long known this, and now that he is dying, everything difficult and frustrated in his position seems transplanted to the breasts of the married couple. Their mutual helplessness triply entwines them like an octopus. Yet the wife and the husband (Marcello Mastroianni) will supposedly go on living together, in good health, the remainder of their lives.

It is a profound mood Antonioni has seized on, a mood he pursues unflinchingly and ingeniously as the unusually long film progresses. The husband's encounter with a far-gone nymphomaniac has a truly weird air and is more sinister than any of the sexual encounters devised by Fellini (though no more interesting or brilliant than the more important episode, in *Cabiria*, between a bizarre little prostitute, Giulietta Masina, and a sportive film star). The husband here is a successful novelist. Now on the way to a cocktail party in honour

of his new book, his wife tells him that their marriage disgusts her, that he disgusts her, and she cannot go on living with him, so when they arrive, the chi-chi celebration seems, to them, a sort of wake. She leaves the party, undetected. When he comes home to their apartment, she is not there, having taken to wandering about the city. Jeanne Moreau acts the part with extraordinary feeling and authority. The sweet life turned acrid is written all over her face, which has little or no make-up and is always photographed to reveal mercilessly the pouches and wrinkles of a physical beauty gone bad.

Yet the lady has style, and so has the gentleman: they are the "clever" sort, slightly better than most of the devotees of high society they go to meet at an evening party given by a fabulously rich industrialist. Here we are in the exact stratum described in several varieties by Fellini in *La Dolce Vita*. As a party anatomist, Antonioni proves he can hold his own with anyone in the film world. The gaudy affair, with its calculatedly vulgar "good taste", becomes a sort of midway with sideshow booths: here a professional Don Juan after a new catch; there an idle, neurotic novel addict of the frailer sex; here an old school friend made of a worldly mask all the way to her bones; there and everywhere the Croesus and his wife doing their best to carry on tradition in the Roman style. The spacious scene bristles with authenticity; the invisible camera taking it seems

The novelist complies with the rules of eroticism played as an élite game: he and the industrialist's daughter draw a crowd as large as an Art Theatre audience; the fever and the fanfare of riot is momentarily quelled when a storm puts out the electric lights.

The storm, however, does not stay the surge of sex awakened by drink in starving libidos: these ladies demonstrate a truth that was antique, of course, when F. Scott Fitzgerald was in his prime; still, the swimming pool in this Antonioni film makes a more serious splash than did the Great Gatsby's.

no more out of place than the visible dance band, piano and all, transplanted to the open air and hired to play till dawn.

La Notte is indeed a blackboard displaying a chart of how seriously the rich, fast, toney set can take itself. Antonioni makes his society people more believable, and also more sympathetic, than those seen through the professional eyes of an Elsa Maxwell or an Art Buchwald. We see, as it were, the thing itself, rather than its society-column mirage. Thus it acquires a little shy pathos and (as in *L'Avventura*) a bit of serious romance. How bravely, too, the novelist (even after glimpsing his host's attractive, unmarried daughter, played by Monica Vitti) flatly turns down the industrialist's offer of a lucrative job directing his business' public relations! Antonioni won't give up the idea of a real hero and real heroine as freely as does Fellini in *La Dolce Vita*; after all, here Mastroianni plays not a common journalist but an intellectual novelist. And love, however morbidly, turns out to have its better "reasons".

While, as if obeying an orthodox "party" impulse, the novelist pursues his host's daughter, a rainstorm adds external melodrama and precipitates a sort of Dionysian outburst. The inebriated douse themselves further in the huge outdoor swimming pool, the soaked wife is spirited away by the Don Juan, and the guests, at last herding themselves in the house to escape the

storm, find themselves in semi-darkness as the electric power fails. Love-in-a-labyrinth is the quasi-mythological theme touched upon. The pair of shadowy pursuits, from which the wife turns back and where the husband meets a blind alley, end up as the action's dénouement. News of their friend's death phoned from the hospital is like some cryptic message received from another world in a film by Cocteau. Yet Antonioni's ingenuity keeps to the domain of realism: the wife and her strangely impersonal rival have a tête-à-tête when the former has to dry out her wet clothes; it appears the young virgin has no incentive to steal her, or anybody else's, husband but is one of those women self-stranded in the desert of an "existentialist" rejection of sex. Her encounter with the wife is clean, dry, veracious.

Then dawn, as it usually does, arrives with its magic change. Leaving together, husband and wife find themselves wandering into a field on their host's estate. Yes, this is their showdown. Antonioni, a truly creative filmmaker, imbues it with more than formality. *She* is a picture of marital woe, *he* a picture of marital languor and despair. Having sat down with him, she draws from her purse a paper (magic again!) and reads to him someone's poetic declaration of love; it is well written, it is moving. "Who wrote it?" he asks, quite blank. Her gaze and the sound of her answer are wonderfully wounded and reproachful: "You did." It may be a valuable hint to despondent wives on the edge of a preci-

The married woman and the virgin, about to succumb to the novelist's pursuit, meet informally after the general ducking and dry out the private situation in a dialogue remarkable for its conviction and psychological acuteness: the virgin declares herself as remote from sex as from romance.

Reunion between novelist and wife (at dawn on the industrialist's estate) does not came as easily as the above glimpse from the final scene makes it appear. Modern marriage, says this deeply concerned film, remains a firmly-rooted idea and destined to survive even the heel who grinds a woman into the dirt in broad daylight.

pice, for with the suddenness of a shot, she finds herself biting the dust, his lips on hers. It isn't squalid, either; it's nice because it's natural. It may not be such an edifying spectacle for us, the human race, in our present predicament. But it's definite! And it seems a step ahead of *L'Avventura*.

But it *is* a step into the night. We surely know, from this and other such "nightcaps" from Europe, that the night is symbolic: the quandary of mankind where the path is swamped with shadows as "the electric power fails". Insight-seeing souls, speaking freely of human experience in the arts and responsible to the latest heartbeat of the social body, sense danger and are paralyzed. Without reasoning about it, men are becoming like the world of Kafka, where the individual and his conscience

are crucified together, where men are commonly victimized by a conspiracy whose source, whose weapons, whose very signs are veiled or enigmatic. Even strong individuals hesitate, are puzzled, win Pyrrhic victories. A craftsman's grip is apt to shake and blur the supposed bright, efficient vision of art. Desperately gay at times, art mocks man the self-tormented. But the outer tour de force conceals an inner trembling. Under certain global attacks, spiritual or physical, the very notion of the *classic* may disintegrate. Is this in any way desirable? I think not. But to avoid it, film artists and all artists must have a stronger faith in human vision and human identity. The intense clarity of the camera eye must be screened from the cloud of passive doubt, passive despair.

Two young rustics, Simone and Rocco Parondi (the latter, Alain Delon), are dazzled by the night-lights of Milan, where their poverty-stricken family (including their mother and three younger brothers) hope to win prosperity.

Rocco and his Brothers

If Antonioni's outlook on modern life is to be called pessimistic, we can qualify it as also calm and civilized, "with a head on its shoulders". This "head" is virtually knocked off by the likewise very talented Luchino Visconti's most complete and powerful statement on film: *Rocco and his Brothers*. Less ruminative than Antonioni's works, *Rocco* combines the tender scrutiny of the common people displayed in Visconti's own *La Terra Trema* with the forthright richness of vision and "painterly" quality to which other of his films, such as the mutilated *Senso*, so strikingly testify. Yet this great film of Visconti's is baleful and throttles all hope of happy futures in the human heart. For this director, the theatrical medium (however used) is a thing of wayward fertility, a token of heedless emotional drives. He has an eye for casting character superior to that of any living competitor, I think, with the possible exception of Fellini. Antonioni and Bergman, possessed by their ideas, command their actors into obedience to them. Visconti simply picks a cast—and cherishes them as if they were plants, revitalizing their soil, framing them in the environment where they will grow, and show, at their best.

Rocco is the sort of film of which a summary account of its persons and events seems especially futile. Visconti, besides being an inspired caster, is a master editor. This film narrative flows with the variety and pulse of life as known in the most persuasive novels. The one thing to be said against either *Rocco* or its creator is the deliberate theatricalism of its design. The frieze of the peasant family, a mature widow and her five sons, uprooting itself from poverty in a Southern province to make its fortunes in Milan, is beautifully outlined and textured against a winter cityscape. The raw quarrel with their Milan relatives on the night of their arrival, the suffocating intimacy of their small basement flat, the emergent aim of the elder brothers, Rocco and Simone, to break into prizefighting—all display Visconti's fine eye for plot development and care for solidity of effect.

Rocco is Alain Delon, who might seem too slight and personable for a real walloper. Yet Visconti's control of camera and script transforms Delon into a lean, speedy, dead-earnest boxer while his huskier, more promising brother, heady with sudden success, is quickly ruined by drink and eroticism. The classic quarrel of Cain and Abel is built up into brute rivalry over the same girl: a pretty little prostitute who seems willing to reform for Rocco's sake. One of the most physically violent and hideous scenes, in our time of emancipated censorship, comes when Simone's gang waylay his brother and the girl, Nadia, at an outdoor rendezvous, and collectively rape her. Simone then mercilessly proceeds to maul Rocco, who is so filled with pity and loathing for his brother that he cannot take the offensive though he has once outboxed him with the gloves on.

This course of affairs corrodes the family spirit, heroically upheld by the mother, played by Katina Paxinou with strong and faultless simplicity. The abysmal evil into which Simone has fallen seems overborne by

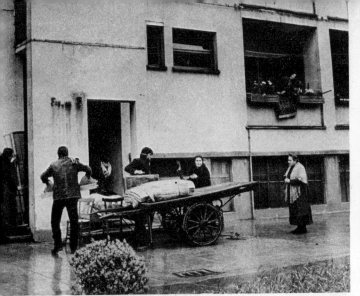

The Parondis unload their worldly possessions: the big boys, Rocco and Simone, eventually and literally punch their way to the top via the fight game. But soon the black-sheep Simone starts slipping.

Rivalry over a woman and their career bitterly, fatally divide the two prizefighters: screwball Simone (left) has reached Skid Row while gentle, sane, loyal Rocco (right) becomes boxing champion and the family staff.

the moment of triumph when Rocco, a loyal son and brother, wins a championship fight. A celebration, in which all their neighbours in the huge apartment building join, is under way when the knock of doom interrupts it . . . Simone has finally killed the paramour whom he has robbed from his brother and appears at their door in a state of shock. We have just witnessed Nadia's sickening murder and now, in all too logical succession, the domestic showdown explodes when Rocco, stunned, chastises the murderer of their family's peace. For horror and plain realism, I believe this scene of shrieking hysteria has never been equalled. An audience might fail to consider how hard it is to render such a scene without vulgar exaggeration or unintended funniness: Visconti and his three leads (the mother and her elder sons) carry it through in superb style. In its uncut version reaching almost three hours, *Rocco and his Brothers* enters film history as naturalism *par excellence*. No, it is not mere theatrical fancy, deftly melodramatized, but galling truth; the flaw that blackens the crystal of humanity is the unmanageable animal drive—lusty and more than life-sized in Visconti's cameras—that may bring reverence and sweetness, but also wild bitterness, deadly frustration and pain, to the hearts of the same family.

Renato Salvatori as Simone, Katina Paxinou as his mother: true, normal human tenderness at last fails to overcome insane bestiality; Rocco's love-affair has been ruined by his vindictive brother. A crisis approaches.

Luchino Visconti's epic of pathos and brutality is over-poweringly realistic: the maddened Simone finally murders his paramour (Annie Girardot) and touches off the tragic collapse of the family's ripening hope.

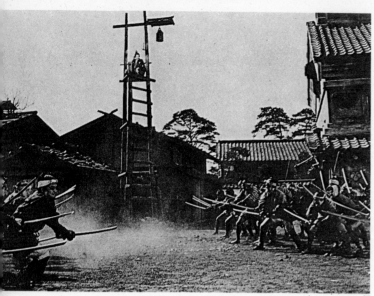

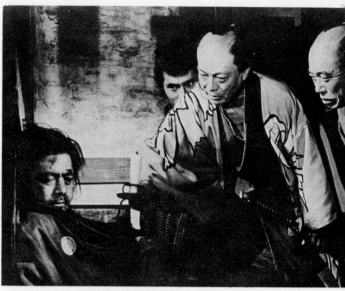

His profession wiped out, a wandering Samurai chances on a feud to the death between warring village parties, each of which bids for his trained services. Here he surveys the claimants from Olympian heights.

Following the impulse of necessity and his calling, he serves first one gang then the other, only to let his human sentiment tempt him into betraying his cruel employer; result: he is tortured with classic efficiency.

1961 · JAPAN

Yojimbo

or *The Knight's Bodyguard*

To Akira Kurosawa's other films here, add this one as decisive token of his mastery of an international idiom: the American-Japanese. His countrymen have a fierceness and tenderness of heart ignitable into hysterical displays of feeling. The style of all Japanese films of high emotional content secretes this trait and duly it emerges on the surface and in the depths of *Yojimbo*: a bang-up Period melodrama corresponding in the culture of Japan to the American film's lone-wolf saga and its destructive fireworks. The latter still finds its themes, its heroes and its diehard romantic morals in the nineteenth century; pathetically Grade C or expensively Grade A, this athletic myth is a "survival" by any fair standard of historic appraisal. As to just what the survival is, Kurosawa's slickly outfitted, closely crafted, beautifully modulated film has a "foreign" but suggestive answer.

If the Japanese have a curious, attraction-repulsion relation to the Americans, it may be located in the well-known brotherhood of polar opposites. In the four other Japanese classics reported here, we see how easily the Japanese heart is moved by various passions and how a traditional cultural form enfolds and expresses each

one. In the Japanese body, emotional drives blaze up as if very near a thin and vulnerable surface; not so with the less mercurial, better armoured American temperament, content to keep feelings under check or in the shade till the vital moment for action arrives. *American* inscrutability, *Oriental* inscrutability: what different things! And yet, on the face of Toshiro Mifune, as the tetherless Samurai whose profession has disappeared with the collapse of the feudal system in the last century, we see the honest, indubitable male strength visible in the salty seams and masklike caution of visages such as Gary Cooper's and John Wayne's, both archetypal of the old American West's heroic spirit.

So, not surprisingly, we find Mifune's Samurai —dusty but carrying his sacred sword —walking into the same sort of situation as would some noble-hearted but luckless ex-sheriff or lone-wolf adventurer in an American Western. The little mountain village seems ominously unpeopled, tight-shut and silent; at stray signs of human life, the Samurai learns why: a local reign of terror has been imposed by a feud between rival family camps, who live (equally barricaded) at either end of the main street. At intervals, the chiefs and their hooligan-retainers issue to defy each other and make gestures toward combat. Japanese fighting manners help the affair seem ludicrously grotesque to foreigners yet Kurosawa makes sure of the effect by acid accents of farce, so that when one party finally crushes the other in a manoeuvre of terrifying brutality, the hilarious achieves an awesome fusion with the sinister.

Escaping by the thinnest of margins, the Samurai witnesses the frightful slaughter of one camp by the other: the realism of bloodthirsty violence has seldom been so frighteningly exposed on the screen.

The solo comeback: like the familiar lone-wolf hero, the Samurai, recuperated, challenges the enemy crowd in the open field. Toshiro Mifune is magnificently authentic as a professional soldier in the rôle of champion.

Allegoric parallels are more than obvious: heartless modern war is being reflected in the microcosm of the antique blood feud. But Kurosawa has taken advantage of the chance to erect strangely moving tensions between burlesque of the heroic and its straight presentation. The compromised, beggared Samurai, essentially noble but wholly created from the ideal of force and soldierly skill, is the crucible of these tensions. At once he makes friends with the good-hearted "little people" of the town, the deathless but feeble peace-lovers, who have no active function save to assist a hero when he has been borne down, almost killed, by the mass of his enemies. Our déclassé professional, having condescendingly hired himself out as "bodyguard" (yojimbo) to one leader then the other, sees no "action" with either, but finds them equally vain, cowardly and cruel, low flattering cheats scheming only to exploit him. A sublime moment has come when, Olympianly disdainful, he has viewed a scrimmage between the rowdy combatants from the platform of the village's one street lamp. Yet he requires money and becomes fatally involved in this contemptible struggle for power.

According to type-pattern, he betrays the ascendant gang by saving a pair of lovers threatened with separation, à la Romeo and Juliet, by the feud. Trapped by the outraged gang, he is tortured half to death, then manages to escape at the chaotic moment that the losing side is mercilessly wiped out. While slowly recuperating in an abandoned temple, he logically plans his fearless revenge. It is an open dare, solo, to the choice warriors of his

enemies: he does not know a newly imported piece of firearms, the revolver, lies in the loop of a smart young bravo's kimono. The Samurai's split-second carnage of all his opponents has the effect of a prolonged thunderbolt. Gasping, one feels the suspicion that what survives in a hero's personal skill and courage may be great, and destined to last.

His vengeance on massed forces of the lust-for-power takes place like an explosion: the thrilling *montage* of this action has the impact of a whirlwind and the slice of a machine.

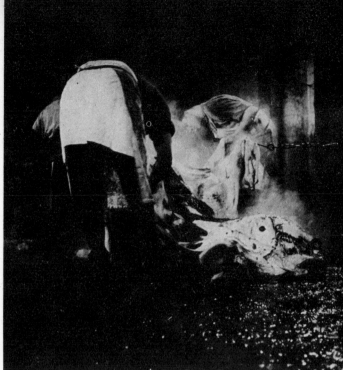

Poetry incredibly but cannily patterned from the unprintable: *Le Sang des Bêtes* centres on the daily, unconcealed routines of French stockyards.

1949 · FRANCE

Le Sang des Bêtes

1961 ITALY

Mondo Cane

In so far as a film endures past its service as transitory entertainment, it automatically adds itself to the classic roster. One of the present films anticipated the other by more than a decade: hence *Mondo Cane* (perhaps best translated as *World of Flesh*), though coming on the scene just recently as a barefaced shocker, fitted into the classic tradition of its less ambitious predecessor, *Le Sang des Bêtes*. Modest and fortified against the suspicion of mere sensationalism, the latter lends its prestige to the much gaudier film from Italy. Georges Franju's delicate determination to make his 20-minute film aesthetically superior as well as acceptable was well-rewarded; it casually picked up both the Prix Jean Vigo and the Grand Prix in France's International Film Festival of 1950. Using black-and-white film, without a large budget or expensive laboratory bills, *Le Sang des Bêtes* became a cleanly pointed, distinguished treatment of a subject held conventionally taboo: the daily routine of city *abattoirs*.

The intent to shock by deception, surprise being part of the shock, was realized by Franju with an easy Gallic finesse. Not for a moment did he consider showing anything but what actually takes place in the stockyards: from the animal on the hoof to its slung and dismembered carcass. Music, song and a poetic commentary gradually lead one to the brink of the blood and make the eyes drink . . . The song by Charles Trenet has the passionate, *triste* light-heartedness of a café ballad about love—that love of which Paris has had so many exponents, male and female. No nation is so rakishly disdainful of sorrow, so bittersweet in its embrace of brute facts, as the French. That Franju compassed the physical processes of the slaughter-house, step by step, and sustained his mood, is a positive feat. Though always surefooted, even when on tiptoe, the camera's realism does not fix upon the *audible abattoir*—that might have been too much! Franju designed the external scenes near his interiors as artificially as he could and even suggests a Surrealist type of decoration, as when a folding fan serves as an exquisite "wipe" and other *objets d'art* of a Flea Market prepare us for the devices of the butchers. Finally, the façade of the *abattoir* at Pantin, hardly more than a silhouette,

240

dissolves into the twilight and the train bringing a fresh load of animals arrives as a monstrous phantom.

The art of suggestion (at least, among the French) is so much a past-mastery that its simpler sort of practice is in danger of summoning up clichés. But the eloquence of the camera's unblinking eye overcomes a certain French smugness of taste: an electric gun is quietly placed against the forehead of a beautiful white horse (as old in wisdom as a philosopher!) and with a minimum of fuss the lovely animal drops dead, in perfect readiness, within a split second, for painless dissection. Very soon, we, too, exist painlessly in a world we dimly recognize as our own; soothingly, we are told that the apparent objections by lambs who have just had their throats slit are mere nervous reflexes: the delayed reaction of life. We are reassured! The butchers themselves (great craftsmen who earn titles as do actors, academicians and politicians) sing as they work—and naturally they sing

of the prospect of immortal bliss. Gathering pools of blood emit steam . . . become mirrors . . .

A little absurd in its arch sublimity, *Le Sang des Bêtes* was a "first" and is apt to remain unique as that rare species: the artful documentary. It would be superfluous for its praisers—the British Film Institute, Jean Cocteau, the New York *Times*—also to go on record in behalf of *Mondo Cane*. No film ever needed *less* the tactically reported approval of the expert. One just has to watch out that he isn't gobbled up by its huge, colourful maw. So plentiful are the innuendoes of this anthology of attitudes towards flesh-consumption that a very in-

Mondo Cane, an epic compilation, brings together from very far (although at times startlingly near) corners of our globe a diversity of customs to shock the inveterate local movie-goer: this one, from a sequence filmed at a Hamburg beerhall, is one of the commonest and ugliest.

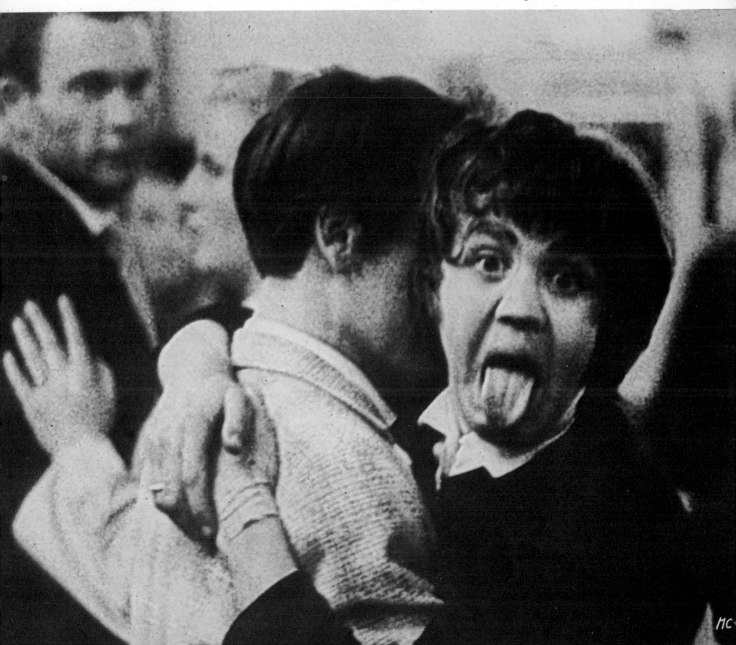

Mondo Cane has nothing if not variety: this action, seen over and over, shows toreador-dressed young Portuguese noblemen, weaponless, proving their manhood by playing nine-pins to a charging bull.

distinct line divides what we know as cuisine from what we know as cannibalism. Franju's angle was to de-anaesthetize our automatic mental blindness toward the normal processes that end up with steaks and chops. The makers of *Mondo Cane*—headed by its producer, Gualtiero Jacopetti, and numerous cameramen—decided not to recognize even the existence of polite masks. Do movie patrons want the *guts* of reality in their docu-

Death is a favourite subject of the far-out cameras of *Mondo Cane*: a very young member of a modern Roman sect religiously helps to preserve the skull of an unknown but revered ancestor.

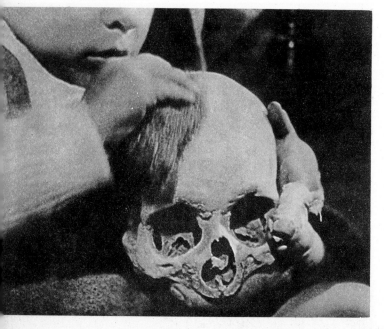

mentaries? Here they get them; literally, and with the trimmings, too.

Le Sang des Bêtes was a tasteful arrangement of a limited area of more or less brutal facts—as blithe as it was bloody. *Mondo Cane*, rushing at a grotesque galaxy of facts strung over the world, is also blithe and bloody. But its form of composition is far less simple, its tone and look being surrealistic mostly through juxtaposition; the exotic becomes (to make a phrase) a drug on the bull-market in *Mondo Cane*. The note sounded is insistently that of the holiday; the feasts are usually ritual: whether toasted pigs that have been clubbed to death in Africa or a banquet being consumed at a wake in China. A single commentator's voice tries to achieve a tour-de-force of truths, half mouth-watering and half stomach-turning, half blatant and half beautiful, half horrible and half sublime, half crazy and half reasonable, half normal and half fantastic; with the camera's revelations to help, of course. Considering the difficulties of any script bent on making such material coherent, *Mondo Cane*'s degree of accomplishment in that department is far from puny; in fact, it's immense.

Franju's film exploits the globe's addiction to flesh foods. *Mondo Cane* seizes on first one and then another local gustatory passion, always directly provoking a visceral response but sometimes scattering it from more than one polarity. In Spain, where bulls are victims of a surviving ritual contest before their flesh is eaten, the shock of the spectacle attacks several of the senses, including the moral sense; and in Portugal, not only, primarily, through the taut drama of the bullring, but also through the bravado (itself a ritual) of young noblemen who dress up like toreros and oppose themselves, weaponless, and like so many nine-pins in a vertical row, to the mad onrush of a bull; the gentlemen get considerably mussed up. On the other hand, outside the ring, in another phase of the festival, hysterical commoners (all men) run before a bull rampant in the streets, the animal goring some half-dozen of them to death. Plainly, the sense of this agglomeration of fleshly extremisms is the *ambivalence* of man's regard for the preservation of his own, and other animals', physical well-being.

The dining room is but *one* headquarters for the palate and for assorted touch-stones of etiquette. Gastronomic and anatomic standards of beauty have subtle ways of overlapping, subtle ways of provoking transgression of taboo in many spheres of taste.

The religion of the gourmet holds surprising secrets, even for local residents, and may be very close to the religion of the priest. *Mondo Cane*'s signal success is to have created a common denominator—violent though it be—among flesh as food, flesh as sex and flesh as the absolute receptacle of life. The film takes all the world's *gourmandise* in stride: force-fed savage brides and force-fed geese.

242

From the overall viewpoint, I should say, this film document's sensationalism is tasteless. Yet I could not mention another case where such boldly calculated tastelessness in a film is so significant, so finally *involving* to its audience, regardless of the spectator's nation, caste or moral persuasions. Flesh here is telescoped in a frighteningly fluid chameleonism. It is *patient* towards God's descent from the sky (the savage tribe that waits vigilantly for its ancestors to recapture the "divine" flying machine identified as the modern airplane) or *impatient* of the coming of death (the Chinese whose wake is a charivari to speed the burning out of life's last spark). Flesh, in the gangs of girls who gaily rape isolated males of their tribe, is primordially, exuberantly sexual; it is symbolically, ritually sexual in male officers of the British regiment of Indian soldiers who perform a sedate dance, dressed as women, after one of them has beheaded a sacred bull. *Mondo Cane* throws very much more than meat in our faces. It tangles our optical nerves within a continuous snarl of global boundary lines.

At times, something is to be said for the naïve school of film theory that plugs for the camera as the supreme eyewitness of objective reality. Yet *Mondo Cane* says it better than could the film theorist himself. In the end, of course, what visions are selected from objective reality, and how they are edited, make *all* the difference. Numb, bitter moments issue from these anecdotes, none of them being more unpleasant than the wily vengeance taken by natives on man-eating sharks. Several anecdotes of the most sordid humour are drawn from the innocent efforts of human beings to define with the flesh some ideal, some beautiful mould, the same efforts revealing how absurd and repulsive the misshaped, redundant flesh may be. Perhaps the most depressing example of such "humour" is the sight of elderly American tourists getting, en masse, their first lesson in dancing the Hula on arriving in Hawaii.

The common mood of *Mondo Cane*'s varied menu of fleshly customs is hysteria; it may appear as amoral alchoholism or long-practised religion: it is always hysteria, always induced from the self-shaping of some dominant instinct. Perhaps this heterogeneous infection of the nervous system, caught red-handed by the camera, is the basic cement holding this film together. These phenomena are so many *willed intensifications* of the world's good-evil consciousness of its flesh. Take the Italian episode where we find Rudolph Valentino being worshipped as a cult deity on an annual celebration in his home town. The cult has existed since his death and is composed of young men who model themselves on their idol in every physical (and presumably also "moral") respect. The full weight of the gruesome parody falls on the spectator at the climax, when a life-sized ceramic statue of Valentino is unveiled before his worshippers; it is not only atrocious sculpture, it bears the paltriest of resemblances to him. Who knows? In the distant future

An exotic diversion in a modern painter's studio: a Czechoslovakian artist induces virtually naked maidens to cover themselves in blue paint (*Mondo Cane* is in colour) and, inspired by music, roll themselves on large surfaces to make abstract "works of art".

(should our race endure), *Mondo Cane*'s strange travels may have reached the status of a morality play as archaic to people living centuries from now as *Everyman* to us today. Right now, all its data are literal and alive . . .

Gualtiero Jacopetti's film gains its status from the hardly speakable and the usually unappetizing: here a savage bride is being force-fed to qualify as mate for an elderly, scrawny tribal chief. *Mondo Cane* is an unparalleled guidebook to sacred and profane customs that still cling to humanity today.

Viridiana, a Roman Catholic novice, rashly stays with her uncle, a Spanish hidalgo, before taking her final vows: when she sleepwalks, Don Jaime (morbidly fixated on his bride who died on their wedding night) decides to seduce his attractive guest.

1962 · SPAIN

Viridiana

The name of Luis Buñuel's film is the name of its heroine, a novice in a Roman Catholic convent in Spain, and the name's root meaning is simply "green", as in the verdant stage of plant life. Surely, Buñuel's symbolist tendencies inform us that the pathetic fate of his beautiful, dignified and serious heroine may be taken to portend the coming disasters of a naïve world: the film is a collection of "viridiana", in the sense of being "annals", concerning the still immature delusions with which world civilization deceives itself, and which call down tragedy on classes and nations as on individuals. Frankly speaking, Buñuel is himself an immature philosopher, and however much

inspired, a "green" critic of our times; one who, since the two Surrealist films he made with Dali in 1929-30, has compromised himself by outright commercialism, making Grade B as well as Grade A films.

Yet here (we have Buñuel's word for it) he is at his most serious and ambitious. When asked recently in an interview which he considered his most "important" work, he replied laconically: "See *Viridiana*." The cue is bluntly sufficient. One sees and believes. However much this director may excel himself in the future, I doubt he will ever make a film with a more serious intonation or one more characteristic of his desperate

244

heart—a heart not of compassion, but of wrath. This personal wrath comes close, indeed, to what the Surrealists with whom he allied himself call *humeur noire* (black bile), a term denoting concentrated hate for the large and pitiable errors into which blundering human society is misled. For centuries now, social and economic institutions have been the target of all sorts of satire from the spheres of fiction and of facts. *Viridiana* presents satire of them with an individualistic difference and a national inflection.

The film's leading allegorical figures represent the Church (Viridiana herself), old-world aristocracy (Don Jaime, Viridiana's uncle), male youth as it inherits the modern tradition of forthright, cynical agnosticism (the Don's illegitimate son, Jorge) and last but not least, the pariahs that form a universal underground in our harassed world: the sheer have-nots devoid of all scruple and possessing a potential of combustion parallel with that of the atom bomb itself. One significant aspect of the background of *Viridiana* is that Buñuel was invited to make it in Spain, his own country, whose Fascist régime had made him an exile for many years; he accepted and there he made the film. But when finished, the satiric message and brutal quality of the work at once excited the antagonism of government headquarters, so that, with a more fatal emphasis, Buñuel is again a Spanish exile; and of course *Viridiana* was placed under ban.

The irony is typical for everybody and everything concerned. *Viridiana* is a much stronger work (so far as I know) than anything Buñuel has made in Mexico, and certainly stronger than the film of his to be most popularly received in other countries: *The Young and the Damned*. For various reasons, importation of his films, into English-speaking countries at least, has been neither easy nor wide. I regard *Viridiana* as his only film to rate with the artistic power and moral beauty of the savage Surrealist pieces on which Dali collaborated with him. Elsewhere in these pages, "sport" is my term for Buñuel's bold manipulation of human frailties: his *danse macabre* of unfettered human passion. Deep in this film-maker is a bitterness fed by a drive that is partly sexual, partly a zeal for social justice as prompted by the supposed failures of that justice. One thinks that at times Buñuel confuses these two passions of his, one erotic and the other vengeful. It is no surprise, therefore, that sadism and perversion should figure prominently in his films.

Are the Church and national politics, in the form of institutions, so entirely responsible for the distortion and sordid tenor of the human hungers unmasked by Buñuel? How precisely and exclusively can the blame for the

Luis Buñuel's twin obsessions, sex and social injustice, get their freest play as the Don almost carries out his plan, repents in time and offers Viridiana "honourable" marriage. Rejected by the shocked novice, he hangs himself, leaving his estate to be divided between her and his illegitimate son, Jorge.

Giving up conventual life, Viridiana snubs Jorge's attentions, lives humbly in a small bedroom in the mansion and turns to harbouring the village beggars: a sly, ungrateful, bestial lot. Jorge, attracted yet mystified by Viridiana, loafs in his new-found country ease.

Turning point: with both proprietors away on an evening's visit, their sinister guests break loose, take over the dining room for a stolen feast and stage an orgy.

At the riot's height, the sleazy crew automatically groups itself into a parody of Leonardo's masterpiece, *The Last Supper*: Buñuel's deepest dagger-thrust at religion. Jorge and Viridiana, returning, are ambushed by two of the male villains, who bind and assault Viridiana.

horrible, anarchic order of pariahs be placed on this or that element of the social structure? Many things in Buñuel's films suggest he himself is a titanic puppet moved by incoherent, imponderable obsessions! Any author, in any medium, bears a close family relation to his characters. Similar to other of his heroes, the hidalgo, Don Jaime, is a mature male childishly obsessed with female apparel as erotic fetishes. The gentleman lives in constant touch with the wardrobe of his dead bride, a girl who apparently died just before or just after the carnal consummation of their marriage. Some vagrant impulse had dictated to Don Jaime that he invite his niece to spend some time with him before she takes her final vows as a nun. Never having been close to him, Viridiana hesitates, then accepts when her Mother Superior gives consent.

A symbolic parallel suggests itself: Buñuel perhaps hesitated before accepting the Spanish government's invitation to make a film in Spain. Would he not, as a renowned film-maker, play cat's-paw in Spain's campaign for international prestige? After all, Spain has no national film industry to speak of. He could turn the tables—make *Viridiana* a true object-lesson: for Spain, for the world, perhaps (however unconscious his calculation) for himself. Yet the film speaks in its own behalf in a voice woeful and cruelly clear. A supernatural sort of atmosphere takes over, once Viridiana is installed in her bedroom in her uncle's country mansion. Observed by Don Jaime, she sleepwalks, performing, with ashes from the fireplace, an odd ceremony that invokes Freudian dream-symbolism. A world of fantasy opens up. To actualize it, Don Jaime (with the help of the housekeeper, also his mistress) drugs Viridiana, dresses her in the wedding clothes of his dead bride, and carries her to bed with an obvious intention. At the crucial moment, however, he draws up: he really loves and respects her. So he desists, and when the unknowing Viridiana wakes up next morning, he confesses his deceit and asks her outright to stay as his wife. The young woman's whole conscious character rebels with horror at the scandalous proposal and no plea can prevent her packing and departing at the earliest possible moment.

But she is not prompt enough to avoid the terrible news that catches up with her as she is about to board the bus taking her back to the convent: Don Jaime has hanged himself in his front yard. However, he has left her half his estate, which she is to share with Jorge, the hidalgo's son. It is as if the turns of the plot ambushed us like cut-throats. Jorge appears; he is a virile, good-looking, materialistic young man, quite mystified by the former novice, whom he quickly classifies as a hopeless prude. Viridiana elects to live in a small, remote room, leaving the comforts of the sumptuous mansion, as a favour, to Jorge. The latter is so obviously attracted by her that his fiancée, who has arrived with him, quarrels with him and breaks their engagement. She disappears and the two are alone with the housekeeper. Without notice, Viridiana returns one day from devotions at the village church, bringing with her all the male and female riff-raff that collect to beg before its portals. They are to live in quarters on the estate, fed and even served at table, their only obligation in return being a little routine work and daily religious observances with their bene-factress, who has decided to give up conventual life.

Observed as keenly by Jorge as she was by his father, Viridiana now blindly, blandly becomes the "dupe" of a social stratum which—unlike the beggars of *The Three-penny Opera* or the criminal world in *M*—are too de-praved to have a semblance of group consciousness or organization. In comparison with this set of antic "uglies", deformed and bestial, traditional gypsies are lovely, noble and romantic creatures: thus the grimness of Buñuel's impassioned eyesight. A chance soon comes for the graceless, sinister crew to display its mettle as Viridiana, Jorge and the housekeeper make a trip to town one evening. Scenting a feast for vultures, they take over the splendid dining room like a marauding army and its camp-followers. The transformation is awesomely con-vincing. One is hardly surprised that it should inspire Buñuel's most audacious thrust—the deadliest yet—at a sacred, world-renowned image of beauty. When the hideous orgy seems almost exhausted, the mongrel "Venus" of the lot exclaims she wishes to photograph the happy company. Almost automatically the drunken celebrants fall into conscious poses behind the long table. *Stop camera*: the image is a parody, figure for figure, of Leonardo's group in *The Last Supper*. Now the "photographer", instead of producing a camera, throws her skirt above her waist . . .

Whatever one's exact response to this contrived blas-phemy, it is tops of its kind. Only a few moments now intervene before the return of the mansion's proprietors. Unflinchingly, Buñuel proceeds with what is known, justly, as piling it on. Two of the male villains arrogantly hold their ground as the others flee. Jorge is ambushed, tied up and a knife held to his throat while Viridiana is dragged to the bed to be raped. It is the familiar shock of the incredible happening before the eyes and here, with a curiously cold, blood-curdling realism. What remains of Viridiana's chastity is rescued as the frantic Jorge finally bribes the man watching him to plant his knife in the rapist's back. The remaining brute is about to replace his confederate when the police, called in by the housekeeper, end the matter. The upheaval produces its upside-down domestic result. With tantalizing brevity, we see Viridiana humbled into being Jorge's erotic minion, impatient of her pleasure as Jorge insists (to the tune of a blaring jazz record) on playing cards with her before they retire. Along with a strange austerity, even approaching sublimity, what brutality lies in Buñuel's fuming Spanish blood! Yes, it is Spanish, rearing a kind of white hot apparition in the depths of a cathedral-like darkness. It is a violence, a pride and a realism akin to Goya's images of revolutionary carnage and the grand, inhumane sport of the bullring. *Viridiana* can leave a bad taste in the mouth, literally; yet it can also open the floodgates of moral outrage.

Though police at last intervene, the ex-novice's virtue is destroyed. Viridiana (played by Sylvia Pinal) settles down to a profane life with her triumphant lover (Francisco Rabal). Despite the bad taste it leaves in one's mouth, this most malignant of modern satires seems destined for the hall of fame.

Piero (Alain Delon), brisk young member of a going stock-broker's firm in Rome, wishes to make love into an equally going concern with Vittoria (Monica Vitti), free of an affair she recently broke off and yet oddly shy at the prospect of a new one.

Long, plangent scenes at the Roman Stock Exchange suggest money-lust as the arch enemy of love in contemporary times; money frenzies insidiously replace, in this third instalment of its maker's trilogy, the celebrated frenzies of love.

L'Eclisse

1962 · ITALY

This book is surely the place to note—is case it go unguessed—that the career of a distinguished commercial film-maker is one where great obstacles must be overcome if he is to say anything personal in his medium, and say it well. Michelangelo Antonioni, author of the trilogy of which *L'Eclisse* is the concluding part, has himself told, in an introduction to a volume of four of his film scripts (including *Il Grido*, 1957, a sort of prologue to the trilogy) how much painful labour he endured while rising to the place in his profession where he could make his very own films—"empty words, cleverness, business sense, patience, stratagems" are some of the ambiguous devices by which he climbed the ladder toward directorial autonomy. By 1950 (having begun work in the studios in 1940) he persuaded someone to finance one of his stories and also to let him direct its realization. That film, *Cronaca di un Amore* (Story of a Love), was begun, he says, "with fifty million non-existent lire". The expression he chose casts a penetrating beam into the heart of the present film.

Much has been written about the "romantic" adventures of film-making behind the scenes, though not much of it stirs the imagination. However, this third part of Antonioni's trilogy (*L'Avventura* and *La Notte* being the first and second parts) reveals the insidious rôle of money in the special human situation so patiently and deeply illuminated by this director. The result is distinguished in the superlative sense, the trilogy ranking with parallel efforts by Pagnol, Satyajit Ray and Eisenstein—the last compelled by circumstance to finish his *Ivan the Terrible* in two parts. Antonioni, exclusively and seriously preoccupied with contemporary relations between the sexes, has had to show (like some modern novelists) traditional attitudes toward love as dying vestiges. The erotic instinct remains: its values are transformed. Yet Vittoria and Piero, the young adult lovers here, are conceived by their manipulator as *the* modern lovers: the Adam and Eve of a mysteriously spoiled paradise of the senses.

Not exactly a *new* theme, perhaps even one obvious in its features. Yet, in delineating it for the camera, Antonioni has exercised shrewd judgment and original observation. These positive movements of erotic attraction, quite recognizable, have the tension of that oddly rapid, oddly prolonged, natural event named in the film's title: the Sun's eclipse by the Moon. Only along

248

The war between love and money is dramatized through a stock-market "crash", nearly ruining Piero's firm and one of its clients: Vittoria's mother; the abstract design of the bulletin board (note its resemblance to the blinds in another illustration) defines that mechanization of life charged here by Antonioni with the "eclipse" of natural love.

a very narrow path was the eclipse, in the most recent phenomenon, total—one might say, accordingly, that Vittoria's and Piero's frustrated affair is set by Antonioni exactly in that narrow path of love's total eclipse. But eclipse by *what*? That is a question for moralists, psychologists and philosophers. Antonioni presents, as it were, the evidence of the camera, although not, we see, without a strong hint of at least the *general* nature of the villain at large in human love-affairs today.

Clearly, since this film is part of a trilogy, we have to note that heroines in all three are essentially the same woman: a woman with the same love-defeating destiny. She is Claudia of *L'Avventura*, Valentina of *La Notte* (so uninterested in love that she declines to take away another woman's husband), and here Vittoria, who drops a current affair as if bored with its satiety and becomes slowly, rather listlessly, involved with another. This composite heroine (played in each case by Monica Vitti) is of a sceptical and anxious nature, puzzled, as it were, by the very compulsion that brings the two sexes together. Through long, carefully managed love scenes, Vittoria's new affair shows much promise, only to peter out, leaving us with several minutes of the suburban background of the rendezvous that was to have decided everything. Antonioni has "painted in" with his camera a series of life's most commonplace incidents that could be interpreted to spell out the paradise of the sexes deprived of its last oasis of joy. Love has gone: only its environment, quivering with lost expectation, remains . . .

Where is the villain, the despoiling Serpent? Antonioni has made it a vital function of our modern economic world: the Stock Exchange, here located in Rome. What may seem only a sensational "setting" is actually, I believe, part of the plot-structure of this "eclipse". Vittoria has found her next suitor in a brisk, bright, good-looking young member of a stockbroker's firm, with whom her mother, a devoted speculator, has dealings. But just because her mother thinks of nothing but the stock-market and its profits, she bores and alienates Vittoria. Piero, the young stockbroker, then lays siege to the languishing young woman. Before very long, there is a stock-market "crash" that wipes out many, is a blow to Piero's firm, and almost, if not quite, ruins Vittoria's mother. The atmosphere created by this financial calamity seems to spread like a poison in the air, strangling the new and wonderful affair that seems ready for the two lovers. Carnally, and seemingly with their hearts, both are at the very point . . . Yet the crucial rendezvous is kept by neither: the camera is here a terrible witness not of what *does* happen but of what *does not*. In this story, the passion of sex seems not just to have changed its mind, or to hang suspended, but literally to have expired. In tune with Existentialist emotions, we have in *L'Eclisse* not the culmination of a tragic event but that of a tragic impasse: a *no-event* of heavy and disturbing presence. If, in this distinctively wrought film, we do not have a truly prophetic sign of a general doom for human love, we have an eloquent version of its peril—and an art of the film remarkably freed from stage and literal conventions.

Favourite scene of the lovers' rendezvous: a suburban corner where a new building is going up: a date is made here for Vittoria's final answer to Piero's suit but neither appears for it. Its foreground still void of the lovers, the suburb's background-routines speak volumes of futility into the camera's waiting, apprehensive eye.

Two sisters, and the little son of the younger, have to inter-
rupt a journey through a foreign country because the elder
(Ingrid Thulin, foreground) falls ill. Some force, hardly seen
or heard, is bent on separating them.

1962 · SWEDEN

The Silence

It seems strange to end this volume, so filled with the advances of film as a talking medium, with a talking film named—with perfect inevitability—*The Silence*. But among works of the past three years, there are few indeed seeming to me to have a claim on the future so commanding, so self-assured, as this film: Ingmar Bergman's masterpiece to date. I can imagine enthusiasts removing it from its case many decades from now, when world society may be much changed, and experiencing once more, with intent pleasure, its eye of surgical scruple, its purity of conception, the enlightenment of its portrayal of man. Despite an unflinching picture of human frailty and waywardness, dispensing altogether with eloquence—of words or cinematic spectacle—it bids fair to be, indefinitely, a film for the cherishers of wisdom to live with.

The austere message, realistic and allegorical at once, has a surface and point that hurt, yet not without implying some power to cure the wound. The film's variety of silences all shed doom, even in words, and yet sympathy as such is not mute. Voices of kindness appear, mirage-like, as the legendary desert oasis that is a haven from drought, aridity and death. The dialogue, when not dry, commonplace, bitter, suffers from rage and asphyxia. But we sense the heart springing forward, pathetically determined, upon paths of least resistance. Such is the structure of Bergman's profound moral rhythm. Ministering angels of good-will are much needed in the contemporary theatre, where a self-indulgent "existential" cant has largely taken over. Yet *The Silence* is clean of garrulous self-pity and a clarion force is the result.

This film, properly speaking, is full not of silence but of reticence: the instructor of silence. What a world of meaning Bergman has discovered on grounds choked with so much muttering! His first step was to understand the aesthetic uses of abstention, a "void" packed with significant restraints, with urgent lapses of things unsaid, undone. We are vividly reminded that *silence* is far from

250

Symbol of morbid fixation: this shot suggests the fatal struggle in which the two women are joined. Even ordinary conversation is exiled in the nervous silence of their combat.

being, except rarely, really desolate and empty. Aside from religious silence (meditation and inner prayer), the interval and pause are essential factors in the structure of time as used in the arts; not only in music, but on the stage and even among the figures of painting as "unoccupied" space. Empty screen space—as a new American critic, Charles Boultenhouse, has said in writing of *The Silence*—is what led Bergman to the positive elements of his screen composition. Silence as a "buttressing" appears in this film as an agonized, orthodox-seeming doldrums. Not that we are deceived:

any more so than sailors once could fail to take the doldrums for anything but a presage of isolation, suffering and perhaps death.

Poets have always known and exploited the hypnotic, immobilizing calm, restive, unnerving, as a *dramatic pause* behind which terrible things are being prepared: outbursts from unexpected directions, climaxes that finish off. Three people in *The Silence*, two adult sisters and the younger's little son, have to leave their train while travelling through a strange (presumably European) country on account of a sudden symptom of illness in the

A gesture of freedom amid the boredom of waiting for her sister to be well enough to travel makes the younger woman (Gunnel Lindblom) a target for the sexual advances of a café waiter; meanwhile her neglected little boy roams their hotel in search of amusement.

elder. It is soon evident that the symptom, automatic strangulation, is psychosomatic in portent: there is a gnawing inner threat to the family's unity and equilibrium. Conversation notably fails between the two women, or appears only, on the part of the younger, as grudging, the necessary evil of a household unhappy from the withering of the mere urge to communicate with each other.

The action has begun, as it were, with a sustained, oppressive interval. One is aware of tension provided by the submerged dynamics of nature, foiled, fuming, hardly able to plot anything at this point of suspense. On the periphery, in the street outside the antique luxury hotel where the three are stopping, there are signs of gloom — and military activity. Alarm centres and ripens in the condition of the elder woman, as she tries to keep up

daily routine with her translating work till she feels well enough to renew their journey. She is obviously, however, in deep despair and we detect that she has a morbid—partly physical, partly moral—fixation on her sister, who is brutally indifferent. The unspeakable spars with the unspoken. In this ominous situation, the little boy is estranged and somewhat neglected, being allowed to wander the unfrequented, ornate hotel corridors alone.

Actually, his aunt is more fond of him than is his own mother, but she is too ill to devote much time to him. It is only a matter of waiting for the silence, heavy with the unheard, to be heard. Desperately bored, the younger woman dresses to go to a café unaccompanied; there a waiter serving her makes sly but unmistakable sexual advances. He is personable; her resistance is momentary. He finds himself with her in a room she has engaged

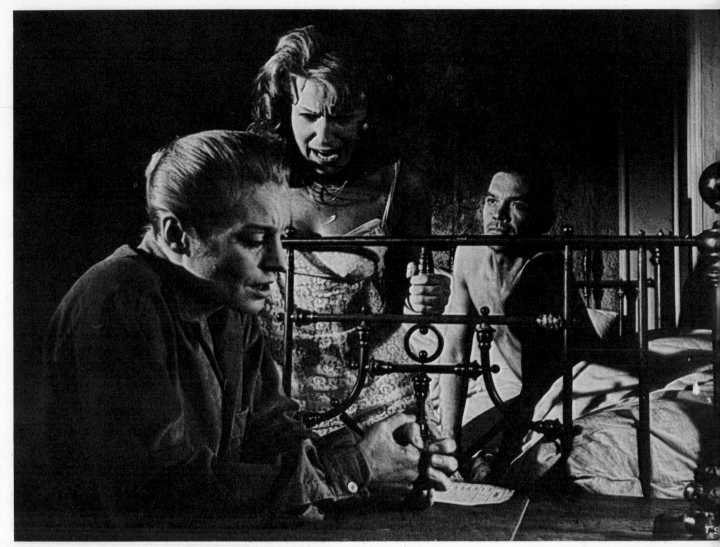

The elder sister discovers the affair and a raucous quarrel ensues, placing the women in even more hopeless and open estrangement. Bergman's film is a great study in the exercise of the unspeakable.

on the same floor as the family's suite. The cries of civilized lust are shed in withdrawn silence, like the sheltered frictions of flesh. But magnetically this "disturbance" attracts, at different moments, both the woman's sister and her son. The former is moved beyond control and steps into the room where the lovers have reached a half-naked interval in bed. Voice and word exact a long withheld toll as the sisters have it out while the man crouches, mute and still, amid the bedclothes.

The language barrier imposed by the foreign country has been but one stream in this counterpoint of rebellious silences. Their canker, their centre, has shown up.

Meanwhile, the boy's interval, speechless from the deprivation of playmates, has been occupied with travels through the spacious corridors. He chances on a troupe of acrobatic dwarfs, who good-naturedly enter into a game with him, but from these he is quickly wrested by his mother. And a kindly old butler, very "European", has made a quaint effort to amuse the forlorn, questing boy, who is deep in the silence of childhood's ignorance. Now his aunt's repeated choking fits—great spasmodic yawnings in which inarticulate words seem swallowed— bring her, she thinks, to the verge of death. She longs for the absolute voicelessness death carries behind it.

Only a cold contract of decency joins her to her obstinate sister, blandly content with animal voices. The younger one insists on resuming the journey although now her sister is confined to bed. The sick woman makes her choice: she will stay behind. At the leavetaking, she hands the boy a sheet of paper on which are written three or four words of the unknown language amid which they have been living.

Bergman's rigorously told story is not just one of tight economy, self-contained, "stripped". Underneath, it is not lean but rich, filling out moulds of strong invention. His "silences" magnify rather than reduce. And if voice and its intervals cannot be reduced here, neither can they be amplified. Whatever is fully stated is irreducible in bulk. Within the total physique of communication he has simply shown the visible action of silence. In the distance of planetary time, we may pause to think, silence was an overwhelming condition binding the very first forms of human life. In the beginning man spoke only in concert with the lower animals. Words, "speech", rose from later complications of his development: when some force made him find expression for emotions, for intentions, for promises, for giving information. Finally, chant, invocation and prayer brought invisible things into visibility and wrought "silence" into the shapes of sound.

Bergman has given us this majestic film in knowledge of the fact that the late age of our civilization is afflicted with moral silences meaning doubt, delay, confusion, fear and lack of hope. With suggestiveness, it is the mellow, sweet-tempered old butler who has supplied the doomed woman with the words she hands to her little nephew as a legacy. As he and his mother stare at them, on the train, wonderingly, they are tragic symbols of the incommunicable in the form of the untranslatable—for, while supposedly they have ordinary meanings, Bergman knowingly *invented* them. They are locked in the golden silence of past and future. *L'Eclisse*, Antonioni's film, dealt with a world producing too little for deeds; *The Silence* deals with a world producing too much for words.

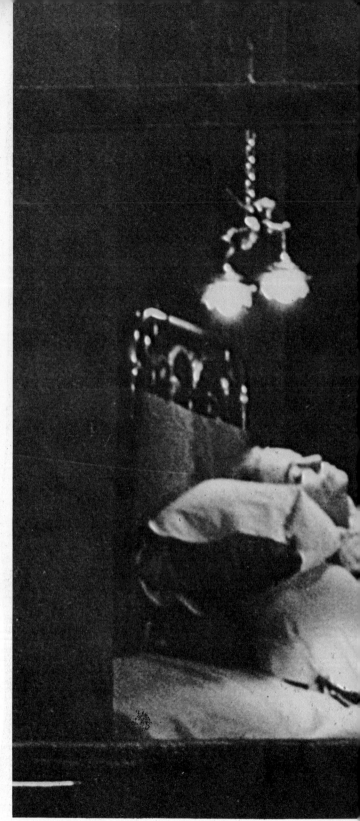

The sick woman's choking fits prostrate her: certain things cannot be said in any language she knows. As the mother and son leave her to her self-chosen death in this foreign place, she hands her nephew a sheet containing a few words of its native tongue. This "gold" may mean the rebirth of civilized communication.